Complete MathSmart

Grade 4

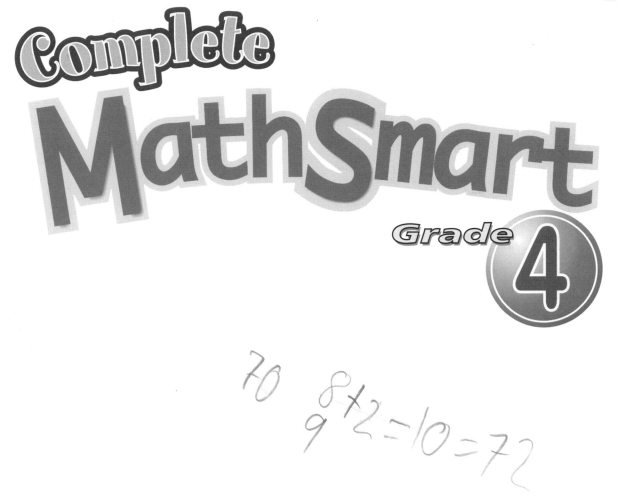

Contents

Overview

In Grade 3, students practised the four basic arithmetic operations and were introduced to mixed operations and using brackets with whole numbers. In Grade 4, these skills are further developed and practised.

In Section I, the emphasis is placed on Multiplication and Division. Students are given ample opportunity to learn the multiplication and division facts to 81, and to see the relationship between multiplication and division operations. They learn to multiply 2- and 3-digit numbers by 1-dight numbers, to multiply 2-digit numbers by 2-digit numbers, and to understand the concept of a multiple.

They practise multiplying by 10, 100 and 1000.

They also learn to divide 2-, 3- and 4-digit numbers by 1-digit numbers with or without a remainder.

Multiplication and Division Fact Families

EXAMPLES

1.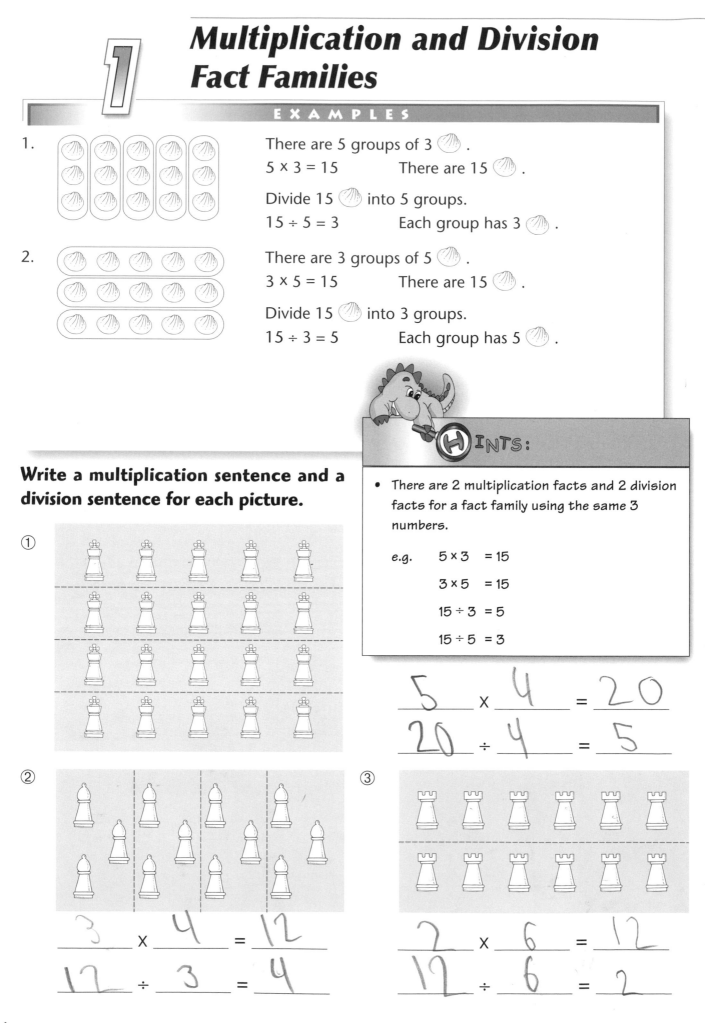

   There are 5 groups of 3 🥟 .

   5 × 3 = 15   There are 15 🥟 .

   Divide 15 🥟 into 5 groups.

   15 ÷ 5 = 3   Each group has 3 🥟 .

2. There are 3 groups of 5 🥟 .

   3 × 5 = 15   There are 15 🥟 .

   Divide 15 🥟 into 3 groups.

   15 ÷ 3 = 5   Each group has 5 🥟 .

Write a multiplication sentence and a division sentence for each picture.

HINTS:

- There are 2 multiplication facts and 2 division facts for a fact family using the same 3 numbers.

  e.g.   5 × 3   = 15

          3 × 5   = 15

          15 ÷ 3   = 5

          15 ÷ 5   = 3

①

    _5_ × _4_ = _20_

    _20_ ÷ _4_ = _5_

②

    _3_ × _4_ = _12_

    _12_ ÷ _3_ = _4_

③

    _2_ × _6_ = _12_

    _12_ ÷ _6_ = _2_

Find the products. Then write the related multiplication and division sentences.

④ 7 x 6 = __42__

⑤ 9 x 8 = __72__

⑥ 4 x 9 = __36__

⑦ 5 x 8 = __40__

⑧ 6 x 9 = __54__

⑨ 7 x 8 = __56__

⑩ 9 x 7 = __63__

⑪ 8 x 6 = __48__

⑫ 9 x 5 = __45__

Write the fact families for each group of numbers.

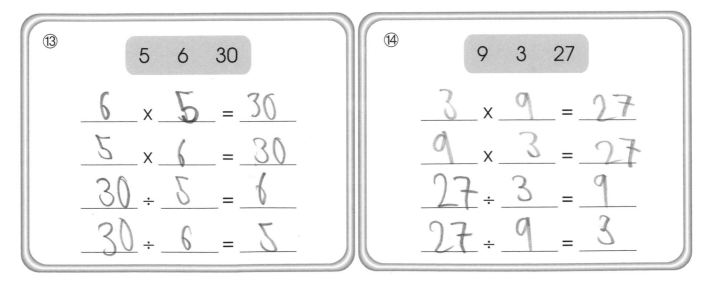

⑬

| 5 | 6 | 30 |

__6__ x __5__ = __30__

__5__ x __6__ = __30__

__30__ ÷ __5__ = __6__

__30__ ÷ __6__ = __5__

⑭

| 9 | 3 | 27 |

__3__ x __9__ = __27__

__9__ x __3__ = __27__

__27__ ÷ __3__ = __9__

__27__ ÷ __9__ = __3__

Find the quotients using multiplication facts.

⑮ 2 × 8 = 16

16 ÷ 2 = _8_

16 ÷ 8 = _2_

⑯ 3 × 7 = 21

21 ÷ 3 = _7_

21 ÷ 7 = _3_

⑰ 4 × 5 = 20

20 ÷ 4 = _5_

20 ÷ 5 = _4_

⑱ 8 × 3 = 24

24 ÷ 3 = _8_

24 ÷ 8 = _3_

⑲ 5 × 6 = 30

30 ÷ 5 = _6_

30 ÷ 6 = _5_

⑳ 4 × 3 = 12

12 ÷ 4 = _4_

12 ÷ 3 = _3_

Complete the multiplication and division sentences.

㉑ 7 × 8 = _56_

56 ÷ 8 = _7_

㉒ 9 × 2 = _18_

18 ÷ 9 = _2_

㉓ 5 × 8 = _40_

40 ÷ 8 = _5_

㉔ 6 × 3 = _18_

18 ÷ 3 = _6_

㉕ 5 × 7 = _35_

35 ÷ 7 = _5_

㉖ 7 × 4 = _28_

28 ÷ 7 = _4_

Fill in the missing numbers.

㉗ _9_ × 5 = 45

45 ÷ 5 = _9_

㉘ 6 × _4_ = 24

24 ÷ _4_ = 6

㉙ _8_ × 4 = 32

32 ÷ _8_ = 4

㉚ 7 × _5_ = 35

35 ÷ _5_ = 7

㉛ _9_ × 4 = 36

36 ÷ 4 = _9_

㉜ _9_ × 3 = 27

27 ÷ 3 = _9_

㉝ _7_ × 9 = 63

63 ÷ 9 = _7_

㉞ 2 × _7_ = 14

14 ÷ _7_ = 2

㉟ 6 × _2_ = 18

18 ÷ _2_ = 6

㊱ 5 × _3_ = 15

15 ÷ _3_ = 5

㊲ _7_ × 6 = 42

42 ÷ 6 = _7_

㊳ 7 × _8_ = 56

56 ÷ _8_ = 7

Write a multiplication sentence and a division sentence for each story.

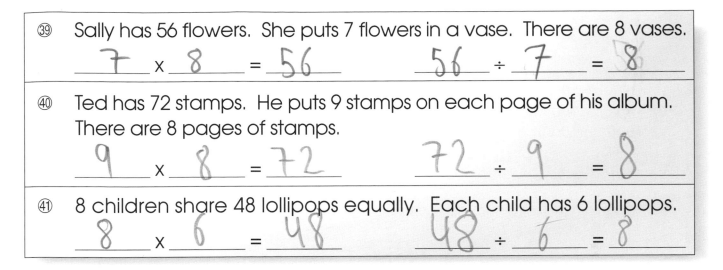

㊴ Sally has 56 flowers. She puts 7 flowers in a vase. There are 8 vases.

___7___ x ___8___ = __56__   __56__ ÷ __7__ = __8__

㊵ Ted has 72 stamps. He puts 9 stamps on each page of his album. There are 8 pages of stamps.

___9___ x ___8___ = _72_   _72_ ÷ _9_ = _8_

㊶ 8 children share 48 lollipops equally. Each child has 6 lollipops.

___8___ x ___6___ = _48_   _48_ ÷ _6_ = _8_

Solve the problems.

㊷ A bag of marbles is shared equally among 9 children. Each child has 6 marbles. If it is shared among 6 children, each child will have __9__ marbles.

㊸ Jonathan puts his baseball cards equally in 5 boxes. Each box contains 9 cards. If he puts the cards in 9 boxes, each box will contain __5__ cards.

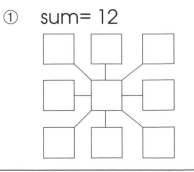

Complete the puzzles.

Put 1, 2, 3, 4, 5, 6, 7, 8 or 9 in each of the nine boxes in each diagram, so that adding the numbers horizontally, vertically or diagonally will give the sum indicated for each diagram.

① sum= 12

② sum= 15

③ sum= 18

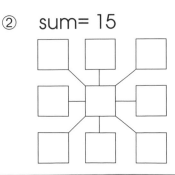

Multiplying by 10, 100 or 1000

E X A M P L E S

1. $3 \times 10 \quad = 10 \times 3 \quad = 30$ ← the number of zeros in the product equals the number of zeros in the factors
   $3 \times 100 \quad = 100 \times 3 \quad = 300$
   $3 \times 1000 \quad = 1000 \times 3 \quad = 3000$

2. $3 \times 3 \times 10 = 9 \times 10 \quad = 90$

3. $3 \times 30 \quad = 3 \times 3 \times 10 = 9 \times 10 = 90$

Find the products mentally.

① $10 \times 5 \quad = \underline{50}$

② $6 \times 100 \quad = \underline{600}$

③ $7 \times 100 \quad = \underline{700}$

④ $100 \times 9 \quad = \underline{900}$

⑤ $8 \times 10 \quad = \underline{80}$

⑥ $0 \times 1000 \quad = \underline{0}$

⑦ $10 \times 14 \quad = \underline{140}$

⑧ $13 \times 100 \quad = \underline{1300}$

⑨ $7 \times 1000 \quad = \underline{7000}$

⑩ $100 \times 32 \quad = \underline{3200}$

⑪ $25 \times 100 \quad = \underline{2500}$

⑫ $6 \times 100 \quad = \underline{600}$

⑬ $100 \times 8 \quad = \underline{800}$

⑭ $10 \times 0 \quad = \underline{0}$

⑮ $1000 \times 6 \quad = \underline{6000}$

HINTS:

- The product of multiplying a number by 10, 100 or 1000 can be found by writing 1, 2 or 3 zeros to the right of that number.

  e.g. $3 \times 10 \quad = 10 \times 3 \quad = 30$
  $= 3 \text{ tens}$

  $3 \times 100 \quad = 100 \times 3 \quad = 300$
  $= 3 \text{ hundreds}$

  $3 \times 1000 \quad = 1000 \times 3 \quad = 3000$
  $= 3 \text{ thousands}$

  $13 \times 10 \quad = 10 \times 13 \quad = 130$
  $= 13 \text{ tens}$

  $23 \times 100 \quad = 100 \times 23 \quad = 2300$
  $= 23 \text{ hundreds}$

  $33 \times 1000 = 1000 \times 33 = 33000$
  $= 33 \text{ thousands}$

- To calculate the product of a number and multiples of 10, 100 or 1000 :

  First multiply the digits in front of the zeros. Then write the same number of zeros as in the factors at the end of the product.

  e.g. 3×30 3 times 3 tens
  $= 3 \times 3 \times 10$ $= 9 \text{ tens}$
  $= 9 \times 10$ $= 90$
  $= 90$

- Estimate the products by rounding the numbers to the nearest ten, hundred or thousand.

  e.g $56 \times 7 \quad = ?$ **estimate** $60 \times 7 \quad = 420$

  $325 \times 4 = ?$ **estimate** $300 \times 4 = 1200$

Find the products.

⑯ 2 × 20
= __40__

⑰ 4 × 30
= __120__

⑱ 3 × 20
= __60__

⑲ 4 × 20
= __80__

⑳ 2 × 30
= __60__

㉑ 3 × 30
= __90__

㉒ 2 × 40
= __80__

㉓ 3 × 60
= __180__

㉔ 5 × 20
= __100__

㉕ 4 × 40
= __160__

㉖ 5 × 30
= __150__

㉗ 6 × 30
= __180__

㉘ 2 × 70
= __140__

㉙ 3 × 80
= __240__

㉚ 4 × 60
= __240__

㉛
```
   60
×   2
─────
  120
```

㉜
```
   70
×   3
─────
  210
```

㉝
```
   50
×   4
─────
  200
```

㉞
```
   30
×   6
─────
  180
```

㉟
```
   80
×   4
─────
  320
```

㊱
```
   50
×   5
─────
  250
```

㊲
```
   40
×   7
─────
  280
```

㊳
```
   90
×   2
─────
  180
```

㊴
```
   50
×   8
─────
  400
```

㊵
```
   90
×   4
─────
  360
```

㊶
```
   60
×   6
─────
  360
```

㊷
```
   30
×   9
─────
  270
```

㊸
```
   20
×   8
─────
  160
```

㊹
```
   30
×   8
─────
  240
```

㊺
```
   80
×   6
─────
  480
```

㊻
```
   60
×   9
─────
  540
```

Find the answers.

(47) 3 x 200 = 600	(48) 2 x 3000 = 6000	(49) 4 x 300 = 1200
(50) 5 x 300 = 1500	(51) 3 x 2000 = 6000	(52) 2 x 400 = 800
(53) 4 x 200 = 800	(54) 4 x 1000 = 4000	(55) 5 x 200 = 1000
(56) 6 x 300 = 1800	(57) 5 x 700 = 3500	(58) 3 x 3000 = 9000
(59) 5 x 2000 = 10000	(60) 6 x 400 = 2400	(61) 8 x 300 = 2400
(62) 200 x 8 = 1600	(63) 1000 x 5 = 5000	(64) 500 x 8 = 4000
(65) 400 x 6 = 2400	(66) 900 x 2 = 1800	(67) 700 x 4 = 2800
(68) 800 x 3 = 2400	(69) 5000 x 2 = 10,000	(70) 900 x 4 = 3600
(71) 700 x 2 = 1400	(72) 600 x 9 = 5400	(73) 2000 x 3 = 6000

Estimate each product by rounding the 2-digit number to the nearest ten.

74   53 × 6   estimate   ___50___ × 6 = 300

75   69 × 4   estimate   ___70___ × 4 = 280

76   72 × 3   estimate   ___70___ × 3 = 210

77   47 × 7   estimate   ___50___ × 7 = 350

78   34 × 5   estimate   ___30___ × 5 = 150

Estimate each product by rounding the 3-digit number to the nearest hundred or rounding the 4-digit number to the nearest thousand.

79   420 × 5   estimate   ___400___ × 5 = 2000

80   297 × 3   estimate   ___300___ × 3 = 900

81   2875 × 2   estimate   ___3000___ × 2 = 6000

82   1365 × 5   estimate   ___1000___ × 5 = 5000

83   673 × 4   estimate   ___700___ × 4 = 2800

84   816 × 7   estimate   ___800___ × 7 = 5600

85   367 × 5   estimate   ___400___ × 5 = 2000

86   1792 × 3   estimate   ___2000___ × 3 = 6000

87   3278 × 2   estimate   ___3000___ × 2 = 6000

88   571 × 8   estimate   ___600___ × 8 = 4800

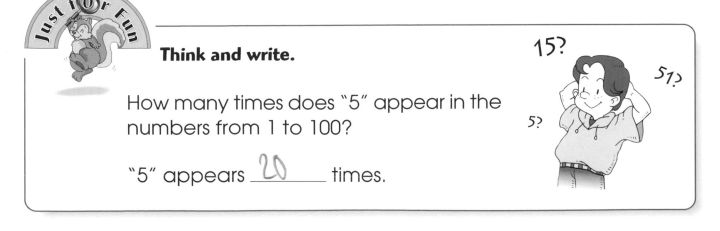

Think and write.

How many times does "5" appear in the numbers from 1 to 100?

"5" appears ___20___ times.

15?
51?
5?

3 Multiplication Facts to 81

1. 5 groups of 2 = 5 twos = 5 times 2 = 5 × 2 = 2 + 2 + 2 + 2 + 2 = 10

2. 2 groups of 5 = 2 fives = 2 times 5 = 2 × 5 = 5 + 5 = 10

Multiply.

①
$$\begin{array}{r} 4 \\ \times\ 3 \\ \hline 12 \end{array}$$

②
$$\begin{array}{r} 5 \\ \times\ 6 \\ \hline 30 \end{array}$$

③
$$\begin{array}{r} 9 \\ \times\ 7 \\ \hline 63 \end{array}$$

④
$$\begin{array}{r} 3 \\ \times\ 8 \\ \hline 24 \end{array}$$

⑤
$$\begin{array}{r} 2 \\ \times\ 6 \\ \hline 12 \end{array}$$

⑥
$$\begin{array}{r} 7 \\ \times\ 4 \\ \hline 28 \end{array}$$

⑦
$$\begin{array}{r} 0 \\ \times\ 4 \\ \hline 0 \end{array}$$

⑧
$$\begin{array}{r} 1 \\ \times\ 5 \\ \hline 5 \end{array}$$

⑨
$$\begin{array}{r} 6 \\ \times\ 6 \\ \hline 36 \end{array}$$

⑩
$$\begin{array}{r} 7 \\ \times\ 7 \\ \hline 49 \end{array}$$

⑪
$$\begin{array}{r} 6 \\ \times\ 3 \\ \hline 18 \end{array}$$

⑫
$$\begin{array}{r} 7 \\ \times\ 2 \\ \hline 14 \end{array}$$

⑬
$$\begin{array}{r} 8 \\ \times\ 5 \\ \hline 40 \end{array}$$

⑭
$$\begin{array}{r} 3 \\ \times\ 9 \\ \hline \end{array}$$

⑮
$$\begin{array}{r} 5 \\ \times\ 9 \\ \hline 48 \end{array}$$

⑯
$$\begin{array}{r} 7 \\ \times\ 0 \\ \hline 0 \end{array}$$

⑰
$$\begin{array}{r} 4 \\ \times\ 8 \\ \hline 32 \end{array}$$

⑱
$$\begin{array}{r} 9 \\ \times\ 9 \\ \hline 81 \end{array}$$

HINTS:

- Multiplication is a short way to add groups of the same size.

- "x" means "MULTIPLY".

- Multiplication facts can be written in 2 different ways.

  e.g. $2 \times 5 = 10$ or $\begin{array}{r} 5 \\ \times\ 2 \\ \hline 10 \end{array}$

  factors product

- Changing the order of multiplication does not affect the product.

  e.g. $2 \times 5 = 5 \times 2 = 10$

Write 2 multiplication sentences for each picture.

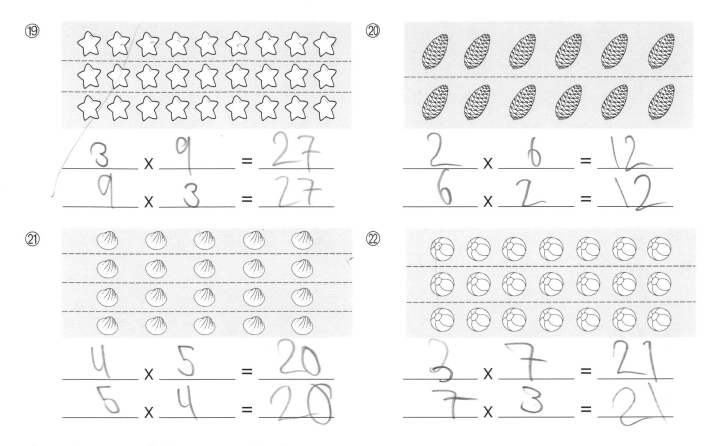

⑲ $\underline{3} \times \underline{9} = \underline{27}$
$\underline{9} \times \underline{3} = \underline{27}$

⑳ $\underline{2} \times \underline{6} = \underline{12}$
$\underline{6} \times \underline{2} = \underline{12}$

㉑ $\underline{4} \times \underline{5} = \underline{20}$
$\underline{5} \times \underline{4} = \underline{20}$

㉒ $\underline{3} \times \underline{7} = \underline{21}$
$\underline{7} \times \underline{3} = \underline{21}$

Complete the following multiplication sentences.

㉓ $7 \times 9 = \underline{63}$

㉔ $5 \times 2 = \underline{10}$

㉕ $1 \times 3 = \underline{3}$

㉖ $6 \times 0 = \underline{0}$

㉗ $8 \times 4 = \underline{32}$

㉘ $5 \times 7 = \underline{35}$

㉙ $2 \times 4 = \underline{8}$

㉚ $6 \times 6 = \underline{36}$

㉛ $6 \times 8 = \underline{48}$

㉜ $3 \times 7 = \underline{21}$

㉝ $4 \times 5 = \underline{20}$

㉞ $9 \times 2 = \underline{18}$

㉟ $0 \times 3 \times 6 = \underline{0}$

㊱ $8 \times 1 \times 6 = \underline{48}$

㊲ $1 \times 7 \times 8 = \underline{56}$

㊳ $5 \times 4 \times 0 = \underline{0}$

㊴ $4 \times 7 = 7 \times \underline{4}$
$7 \times 2 = \underline{14}$

㊵ $5 \times \underline{8} = \underline{8} \times 5$
$5 \times 8 = 40$

㊶ $3 \times 3 = \underline{1} \times 9$
$6 \times 6 = \underline{36}$

㊷ $8 \times \underline{0} = 0 \times 4$
$8 \times 3 = \underline{24}$

In each group, put a X in the ◯ beside the number sentence that is different.

㊸ A. 7 × 6 ◯

 B. 7 + 6 ⊗

 C. 6 sevens ◯

 D. 7 groups of 6 ◯

㊹ A. 5 threes ◯

 B. 3 × 5 ◯

 C. 5 + 5 + 5 + 5 + 5 ⊗

 D. 3 times 5 ◯

㊺ A. 4 + 4 + 4 + 4 ⊗

 B. 4 ones ◯

 C. 1 × 4 ◯

 D. 1 group of 4 ◯

㊻ A. 5 times 6 ◯

 B. 5 + 5 + 5 + 5 + 5 ⊗

 C. 6 groups of 5 ◯

 D. 6 × 5 ◯

Fill in the missing numbers.

㊼ 10 15 20 25 30 35 40 45

㊽ 9 18 27 36 45 54 63 72

㊾ 7 14 28 35 42 49 56 73

Circle the correct answers.

㊿ When a number is multiplied by these numbers, the products are always even numbers.

0 1 2 3 4 5 6 7 8 9

51 When a number is multiplied by 5, these numbers are at the ones place of the product.

0 1 2 3 4 5 6 7 8 9

52 When a number is multiplied by this number, the product is always zero.

0 1 2 3 4 5 6 7 8 9

Solve the problems. Show your work.

53. A dragonfly has 4 wings. How many wings do 7 dragonflies have?

7 dragonflies have __28__ wings.

54. May plants 8 rows of tulips in the garden. There are 9 tulips in a row. How many tulips does May plant?

May plants _____ tulips.

55. There are 3 hands on a clock. How many hands are there on 6 clocks?

There are __18__ hands on 6 clocks.

56. The teacher has 7 boxes of crayons. Each box contains 8 crayons. How many crayons does the teacher have?

The teacher has __64__ crayons.

57. A bag of cookies contains 4 different shapes. There are 6 cookies for each shape. How many cookies are there in the bag?

There are __24__ cookies in the bag.

Just for Fun

Complete the puzzles.

Put 1, 2, 3, 4 or 5 in each of the five boxes in each diagram, so that adding the numbers either vertically or horizontally will give the sum indicated for each diagram.

① sum = 8

② sum = 9

③ sum = 10

Division Facts to 81

Sally has 15 stickers.

1. Divide the stickers in groups of 5. How many groups are there?

    15 ÷ 5 = 3

    There are 3 groups.

2. Divide the stickers into 3 groups. How many stickers are there in each group?

    15 ÷ 3 = 5

    There are 5 stickers in each group.

HINTS:

- To divide is to share things equally into groups of the same size.

- "÷" means DIVIDE.

- Division facts can be written in 2 different ways.

    e.g.   15 ÷ 5 = 3   or   align the numbers on the right-hand side

    quotient → 3

    $5\overline{)15}$

    15

    dividend   divisor

- Do the division by recalling the multiplication facts.

    e.g.   15 ÷ 5 = ?

    recall   5 × 3 = 15

    so   15 ÷ 5 = 3

Do the division.

① $9\overline{)63}$ **8**

② $6\overline{)48}$ **8**

③ $7\overline{)42}$ **6**

④ $5\overline{)35}$ **7**

⑤ $3\overline{)24}$ **8**

⑥ $6\overline{)36}$ **6**

⑦ $2\overline{)18}$ **9**

⑧ $4\overline{)32}$ **8**

⑨ $1\overline{)5}$ **5**

⑩ $8\overline{)56}$

⑪ $6\overline{)42}$ **7**

⑫ $9\overline{)0}$ **0**

⑬ $7\overline{)63}$

⑭ $5\overline{)30}$ **6**

⑮ $3\overline{)21}$ **7**

⑯ $5\overline{)25}$ **5**

⑰ $9\overline{)45}$

⑱ $4\overline{)28}$

Write 2 division sentences for each picture.

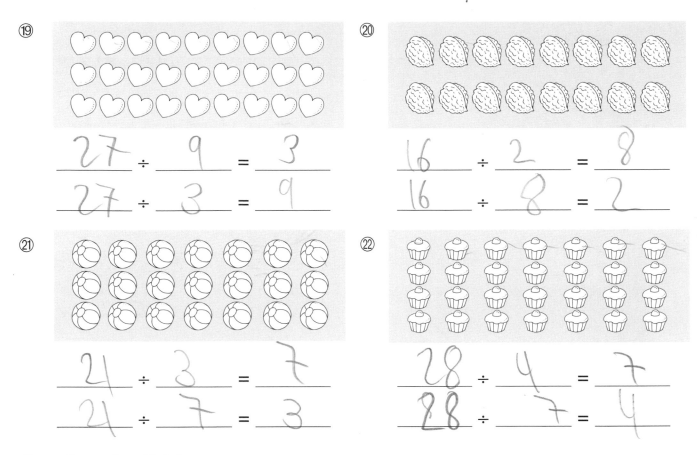

⑲ 27 ÷ 9 = 3
27 ÷ 3 = 9

⑳ 16 ÷ 2 = 8
16 ÷ 8 = 2

㉑ 21 ÷ 3 = 7
21 ÷ 7 = 3

㉒ 28 ÷ 4 = 7
28 ÷ 7 = 4

Complete the division sentences.

㉓ 63 ÷ 7 = _____

63 ÷ _____ = 7

㉖ 40 ÷ 5 = 8

40 ÷ 8 = 5

㉙ 72 ÷ 9 = _____

72 ÷ _____ = 9

㉜ 5 ÷ 1 = 5

5 ÷ 5 = 1

㉟ 3 ÷ 3 = 1

3 ÷ 1 = 3

㉔ 32 ÷ 8 = _____

32 ÷ _____ = 8

㉗ 20 ÷ 4 = 5

20 ÷ 5 = 4

㉚ 12 ÷ 2 = 6

12 ÷ 6 = 2

㉝ 35 ÷ 7 = 5

35 ÷ 5 = 7

㊱ 25 ÷ 5 = 5

25 ÷ 5 = 5

㉕ 6 ÷ 6 = 1

6 ÷ 1 = 6

㉘ 18 ÷ 3 = 6

18 ÷ 6 = 3

㉛ 64 ÷ 8 = _____

64 ÷ _____ = 8

㉞ 16 ÷ 4 = _____

16 ÷ _____ = 4

㊲ 30 ÷ 6 = 5

30 ÷ 5 = 6

Match the quotient with the division sentences in each group. Circle the correct letters.

38 — 9

A. $54 \div 6$ B. $56 \div 7$ C. $18 \div 2$

39 — 8

A. $48 \div 8$ B. $40 \div 5$ C. $72 \div 9$

40 — 7

A. $63 \div 9$ B. $21 \div 3$ C. $35 \div 7$

41 — 6

A. $14 \div 2$ B. $48 \div 8$ C. $24 \div 4$

42 — 5

A. $45 \div 9$ B. $10 \div 2$ C. $24 \div 6$

43 — 4

A. $32 \div 8$ B. $15 \div 3$ C. $20 \div 5$

44 — 3

A. $20 \div 5$ B. $27 \div 9$ C. $24 \div 8$

45 — 2

A. $18 \div 9$ B. $18 \div 6$ C. $14 \div 7$

Solve the problems. Show your work.

㊻ The gardener planted 72 pine trees in 9 rows. How many pine trees were planted in each row?

$9 \times 8 = 72$
$72 \div 9 = 8$

_____8_____ pine trees were planted in each row.

㊼ May puts 32 books equally on 4 shelves. How many books are there on each shelf?

$32 \div 4 = 8$

8    $8 \times 4 = 32$

㊽ Ted has 18 socks. How many pairs of socks does he have?

9    $18 \div 2 = 9$

㊾ Mom divides 54 chocolates among Sally and her 5 friends. How many chocolates does each child get?

$54 \div 6 = 9$

㊿ Tom buys 5 boxes of coloured pencils for $40. What is the price of 1 box of coloured pencils?

$40 \div 5 = 8$

Just for Fun

Solve the puzzle.

A, B, C, D, E and F participated in a badminton competition. A ⟶ B means A won the match. Find out from the diagram who did not win a single match.

A ⟶ B
F ⟶ D ⟵ C
E ⟶ (to D)

_____D_____ did not win a single match.

Multiplying 2-digit Numbers by 1-digit Numbers

4 x 23 = ?   Long way:

```
        2 3   ← align the numbers on the right-hand side
    x     4
        1 2   ← 4 x 3  = 12
        8 0   ← 4 x 20 = 80
        9 2   ← 12 + 80 = 92
```

Short way:

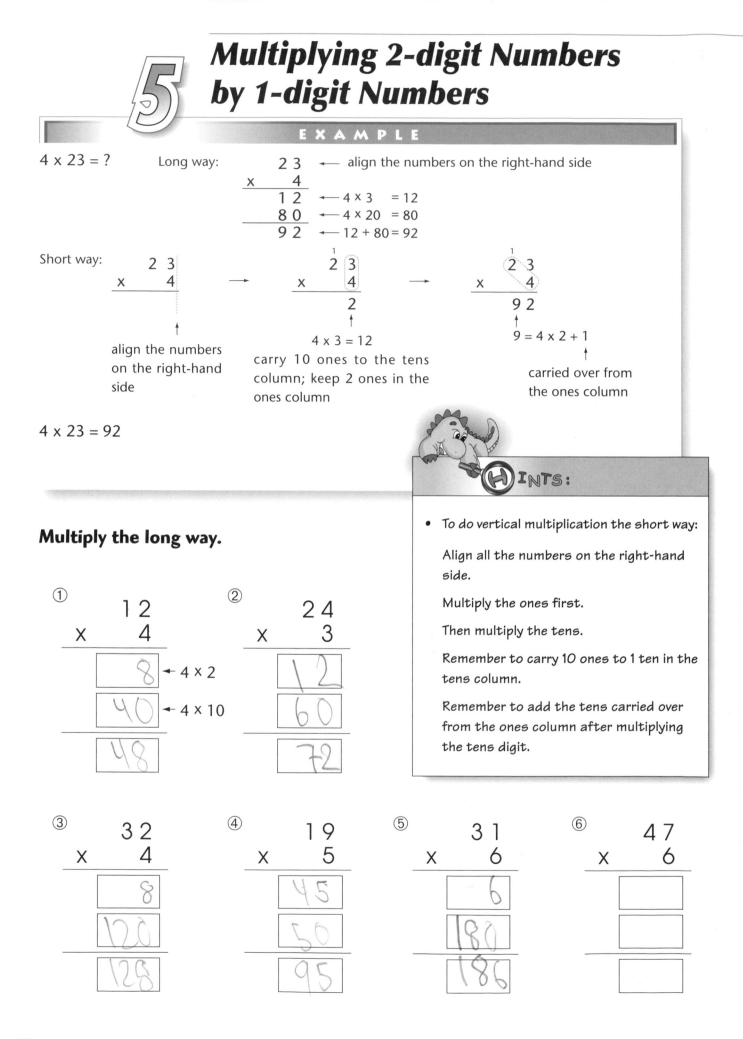

```
    2 3              2 3              2 3
  x   4            x   4            x   4
                      2              9 2
```

align the numbers on the right-hand side

4 x 3 = 12
carry 10 ones to the tens column; keep 2 ones in the ones column

9 = 4 x 2 + 1
carried over from the ones column

4 x 23 = 92

HINTS:

- To do vertical multiplication the short way:

  Align all the numbers on the right-hand side.

  Multiply the ones first.

  Then multiply the tens.

  Remember to carry 10 ones to 1 ten in the tens column.

  Remember to add the tens carried over from the ones column after multiplying the tens digit.

Multiply the long way.

①
```
      1 2
  x     4
      8   ← 4 x 2
    4 0   ← 4 x 10
    4 8
```

②
```
      2 4
  x     3
    1 2
    6 0
    7 2
```

③
```
      3 2
  x     4
      8
    1 2 0
    1 2 8
```

④
```
      1 9
  x     5
    4 5
    5 0
    9 5
```

⑤
```
      3 1
  x     6
      6
    1 8 0
    1 8 6
```

⑥
```
      4 7
  x     6
```

Do the multiplication the short way.

⑦
```
    ¹
    3 4
  ×   4
  1 3 6
```

⑧
```
    2 3
  ×   3
    6 9
```

⑨
```
    ²
    3 7
  ×   4
  1 4 8
```

⑩
```
    ³
    2 5
  ×   6
  1 5 0
```

⑪
```
    ¹
    3 2
  ×   9
  2 8 8
```

⑫
```
    ¹
    2 8
  ×   2
    5 6
```

⑬
```
    ⁴
    5 7
  ×   7
  3 9 9
```

⑭
```
  (7)⁻⁵³⁺⁴          36
    4 8
  ×   9
  4 3 2
```

⑮
```
    3
    6 5
  ×   6
  3 9 0
```

⑯
```
    4
    3 9
  ×   5
  1 9 5
```

⑰
```
    2
    5 3
  ×   8
  4 2 4
```

⑱
```
    2
    6 7
  ×   3
  2 0 1
```

⑲
```
    4
    4 6
  ×   8
  3 6 8
```

⑳
```
    2
    2 7
  ×   4
  1 0 8
```

㉑
```
    3
    7 7
  ×   5
  3 8 5
```

㉒
```
    6
    3 9
  ×   7
  2 7 3
```

㉓
```
    7
    1 8
  ×   9
      2
```

㉔
```
    1
    2 2
  ×   6
  1 3 2
```

㉕
```
    8 1
  ×   9
```

㉖
```
    5 2
  ×   4
  2 0 8
```

㉗
```
    3
    3 5
  ×   6
  2 1 0
```

㉘
```
    1
    4 2
  ×   8
  3 3 6
```

㉙
```
    6 3
  ×   9
```

㉚
```
    2
    9 5
  ×   4
  3 8 0
```

㉛
```
    1
    7 2
  ×   7
  5 0 4
```

㉜
```
    9 2
  ×   3
  2 7 6
```

㉝
```
    4
    2 5
  ×   8
  2 0 0
```

㉞
```
    5 8
  ×   6
```

㉟ 88 × 6 = _____

㊱ 74 × 9 = _____

㊲ 43 × 8 = _____

㊳ 15 × 7 = _____

㊴ 21 × 5 = _____

㊵ 98 × 2 = _____

Find the products. Then write the letters in the boxes in ㊿ to see what birthday gift May wants to receive.

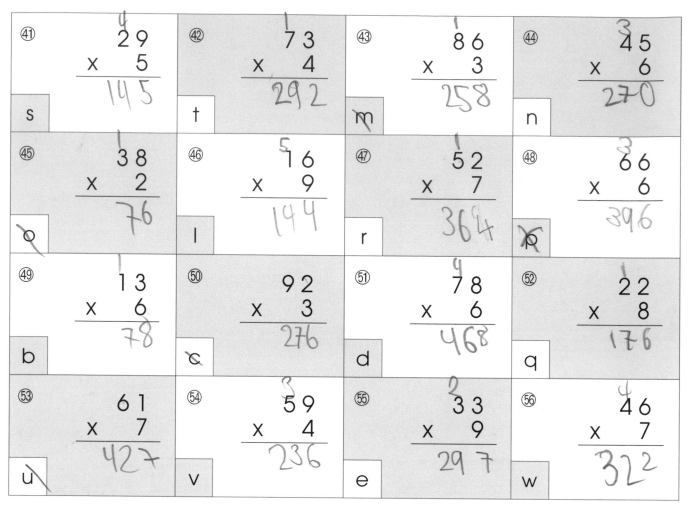

㊶
$$\overset{4}{2}9 \times 5 = 145$$
s

㊷
$$\overset{1}{7}3 \times 4 = 292$$
t

㊸
$$\overset{1}{8}6 \times 3 = 258$$
m

㊹
$$\overset{3}{4}5 \times 6 = 270$$
n

㊺
$$38 \times 2 = 76$$
o

㊻
$$\overset{5}{1}6 \times 9 = 144$$
l

㊼
$$\overset{1}{5}2 \times 7 = 364$$
r

㊽
$$\overset{3}{6}6 \times 6 = 396$$
p

㊾
$$13 \times 6 = 78$$
b

㊿
$$92 \times 3 = 276$$
c

(51)
$$\overset{4}{7}8 \times 6 = 468$$
d

(52)
$$22 \times 8 = 176$$
q

(53)
$$61 \times 7 = 427$$
u

(54)
$$\overset{3}{5}9 \times 4 = 236$$
v

(55)
$$\overset{2}{3}3 \times 9 = 297$$
e

(56)
$$\overset{4}{4}6 \times 7 = 322$$
w

(57)

276	76	258	396	427	292	297	364
A c	o	m	p	u	t	e	r .

Estimate first. Then find the products.

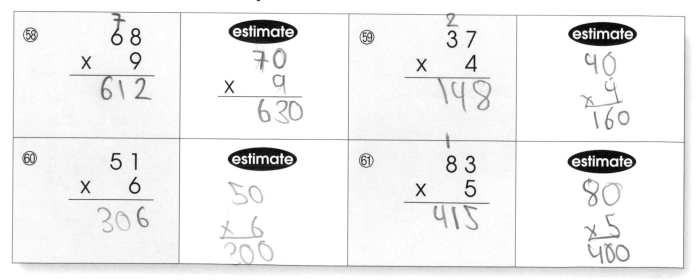

(58)
$$\overset{7}{6}8 \times 9 = 612$$

estimate
$$70 \times 9 = 630$$

(59)
$$\overset{2}{3}7 \times 4 = 148$$

estimate
$$90 \times 4 = 160$$

(60)
$$51 \times 6 = 306$$

estimate
$$50 \times 6 = 300$$

(61)
$$\overset{1}{8}3 \times 5 = 415$$

estimate
$$80 \times 5 = 400$$

Solve the problems. Show your work.

62. Mom bought 4 boxes of chocolate for May's birthday party. There were 36 chocolates in each box. How many chocolates did Mom buy?

    4 × 36 =

    Mom bought ___144___ chocolates.

    $$\begin{array}{r} \overset{2}{3}6 \\ \times\quad 4 \\ \hline 144 \end{array}$$

63. There were 24 party hats in a bag. How many party hats were there in 3 bags?

    72

    $$\begin{array}{r} \overset{1}{2}4 \\ \times\quad 3 \\ \hline 72 \end{array}$$

64. Mom bought 2 bags of straws with 98 straws in each bag. How many straws did Mom buy?

    196

    $$\begin{array}{r} \overset{1}{9}8 \\ \times\quad 2 \\ \hline 196 \end{array}$$

65. Ted and 4 friends each contributed $18 to buy a birthday gift for May. What was the cost of the birthday gift?

    72

    $$\begin{array}{r} \overset{3}{1}8 \\ \times\quad 4 \\ \hline 72 \end{array}$$

66. May put 42 cookies on a plate. How many cookies were there on 4 plates?

    $$\begin{array}{r} 42 \\ \times\quad 4 \\ \hline 168 \end{array}$$

Just for Fun

Solve the problem.

Show how you can move the least number of beads to change the shape of the triangle on the left-hand side to that on the right-hand side.

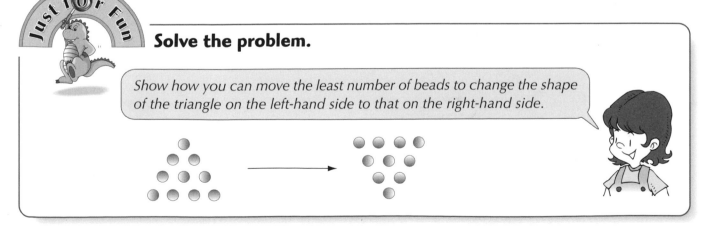

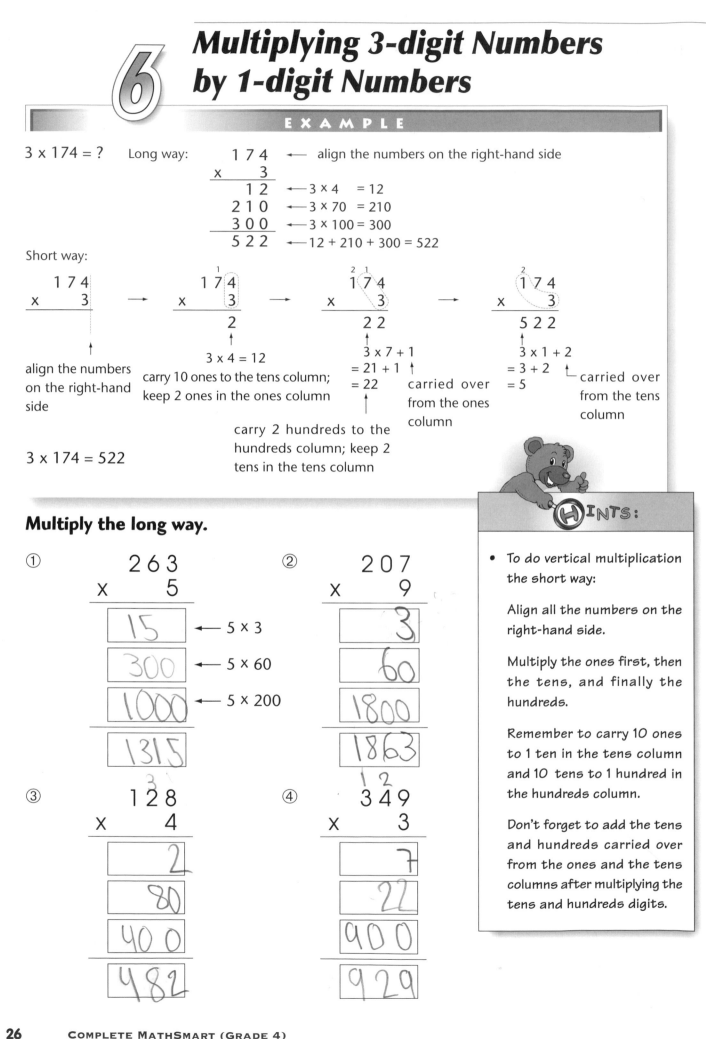

Multiplying 3-digit Numbers by 1-digit Numbers

3 x 174 = ?   Long way:

```
        1 7 4   ← align the numbers on the right-hand side
      x   3
        1 2     ← 3 × 4   = 12
      2 1 0     ← 3 × 70  = 210
      3 0 0     ← 3 × 100 = 300
      5 2 2     ← 12 + 210 + 300 = 522
```

Short way:

```
    1 7 4            1 7⁴4          ²  ¹          ²
  x   3      →     x   3    →     1⁷4    →      1 7 4
                                 x   3         x   3
                      2            2 2           5 2 2
```

align the numbers
on the right-hand
side

3 x 4 = 12
carry 10 ones to the tens column;
keep 2 ones in the ones column

3 x 7 + 1
= 21 + 1
= 22
carried over
from the ones
column
carry 2 hundreds to the
hundreds column; keep 2
tens in the tens column

3 x 1 + 2
= 3 + 2
= 5
carried over
from the tens
column

3 x 174 = 522

Multiply the long way.

①
```
      2 6 3
    x     5
    ┌─────┐
    │ 15  │ ← 5 × 3
    ├─────┤
    │ 300 │ ← 5 × 60
    ├─────┤
    │1000 │ ← 5 × 200
    ├─────┤
    │1315 │
    └─────┘
```

②
```
      2 0 7
    x     9
    ┌─────┐
    │  3  │
    ├─────┤
    │ 60  │
    ├─────┤
    │1800 │
    ├─────┤
    │1863 │
    └─────┘
      1 2
```

③
```
        3
      1 2 8
    x     4
    ┌─────┐
    │  2  │
    ├─────┤
    │ 80  │
    ├─────┤
    │400  │
    ├─────┤
    │482  │
    └─────┘
```

④
```
      3 4 9
    x     3
    ┌─────┐
    │  7  │
    ├─────┤
    │ 22  │
    ├─────┤
    │900  │
    ├─────┤
    │929  │
    └─────┘
```

HINTS:

- To do vertical multiplication the short way:

  Align all the numbers on the right-hand side.

  Multiply the ones first, then the tens, and finally the hundreds.

  Remember to carry 10 ones to 1 ten in the tens column and 10 tens to 1 hundred in the hundreds column.

  Don't forget to add the tens and hundreds carried over from the ones and the tens columns after multiplying the tens and hundreds digits.

Do the multiplication the short way.

⑤ $\begin{array}{r} {}^3{}^1\,\,\,\\ 463 \\ \times\quad 5 \\ \hline 2315 \end{array}$	⑥ $\begin{array}{r} 612 \\ \times\quad 4 \\ \hline 2948 \end{array}$	⑦ $\begin{array}{r} 575 \\ \times\quad 2 \\ \hline 1150 \end{array}$
⑧ $\begin{array}{r} {}^2{}^4\,\,\,\\ 348 \\ \times\quad 6 \\ \hline 2088 \end{array}$	⑨ $\begin{array}{r} {}^2\,\,\,\\ 405 \\ \times\quad 4 \\ \hline 1620 \end{array}$	⑩ $\begin{array}{r} 701 \\ \times\quad 5 \\ \hline 3505 \end{array}$
⑪ $\begin{array}{r} {}^1\,\,\,\\ 315 \\ \times\quad 3 \\ \hline 945 \end{array}$	⑫ $\begin{array}{r} {}^5{}^3\,\,\,\\ 374 \\ \times\quad 8 \\ \hline 2692 \end{array}$	⑬ $\begin{array}{r} {}^4{}^5\,\,\,\\ 169 \\ \times\quad 6 \\ \hline 1014 \end{array}$
⑭ $\begin{array}{r} {}^3{}^2\,\,\,\\ 476 \\ \times\quad 4 \\ \hline 1904 \end{array}$	⑮ $\begin{array}{r} {}^1\,\,\,\\ 502 \\ \times\quad 9 \\ \hline 4518 \end{array}$	⑯ $\begin{array}{r} {}^5\,\,\,\\ 781 \\ \times\quad 7 \\ \hline 5467 \end{array}$
⑰ $\begin{array}{r} {}^1{}^2\,\,\,\\ 236 \\ \times\quad 4 \\ \hline 944 \end{array}$	⑱ $\begin{array}{r} {}^6{}^5\,\,\,\\ 677 \\ \times\quad 8 \\ \hline 5416 \end{array}$	⑲ $\begin{array}{r} {}^4{}^2\,\,\,\\ 564 \\ \times\quad 7 \\ \hline 3948 \end{array}$
⑳ $\begin{array}{r} {}^2\,\,\,\\ 804 \\ \times\quad 5 \\ \hline 4020 \end{array}$	㉑ $\begin{array}{r} {}^2{}^2\,\,\,\\ 369 \\ \times\quad 3 \\ \hline 1107 \end{array}$	㉒ $\begin{array}{r} 911 \\ \times\quad 6 \\ \hline 5466 \end{array}$
㉓ $\begin{array}{r} {}^1\,\,\,\\ 749 \\ \times\quad 2 \\ \hline 1498 \end{array}$	㉔ $\begin{array}{r} {}^3{}^1\,\,\,\\ 183 \\ \times\quad 4 \\ \hline 722 \end{array}$	㉕ $\begin{array}{r} {}^4\,\,\,\\ 480 \\ \times\quad 5 \\ \hline 2400 \end{array}$

㉖ 7 x 142 = __994__

㉗ 9 x 313 = __2817__

㉘ 3 x 569 = __1698__

㉙ 428 x 8 = __3424__

Find the products. Write the letters in ㊷ to solve the riddle.

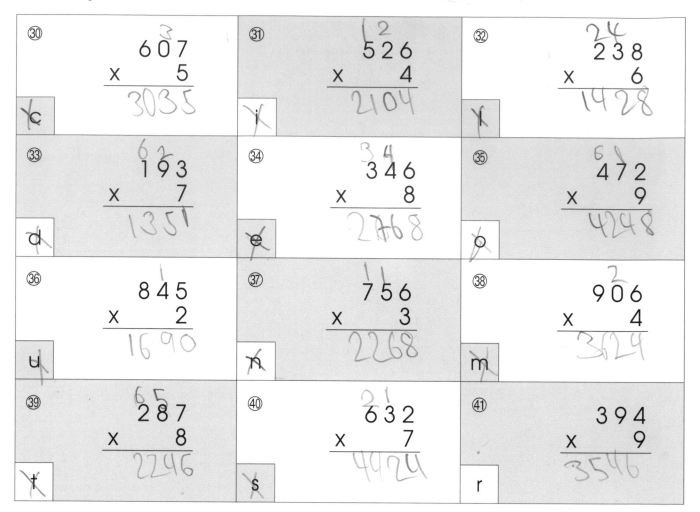

㉚
```
    3
  607
x   5
 3035
```
c

㉛
```
 12
 526
x   4
2104
```
i

㉜
```
  24
 238
x   6
1428
```
x

㉝
```
 62
 193
x   7
1351
```
d

㉞
```
 34
 346
x   8
2768
```
e

㉟
```
 61
 472
x   9
4248
```
o

㊱
```
   1
 845
x   2
1690
```
u

㊲
```
 11
 756
x   3
2268
```
n

㊳
```
   2
 906
x   4
3624
```
m

㊴
```
 65
 287
x   8
2246
```
t

㊵
```
 21
 632
x   7
4424
```
s

㊶
```
 394
x   9
3546
```
r

Riddle: A large reptile that lives in the rainforest.

㊷

3035	3546	4248	3035	4248	1351	2104	1428	2768
C	r	O	C	O	d	i	L	e

A _____ .

Estimate first. Then calculate the products.

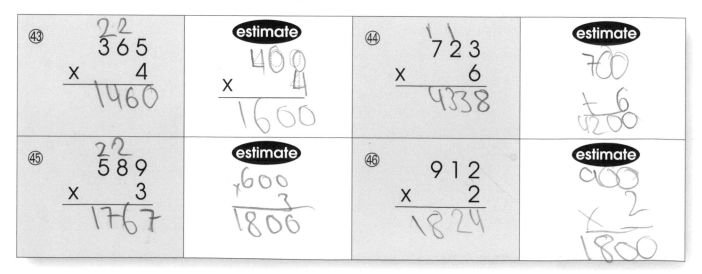

㊸
```
 22
 365
x   4
1460
```
estimate
```
  400
x   4
 1600
```

㊹
```
 11
 723
x   6
4338
```
estimate
```
 700
x  6
4200
```

㊺
```
 22
 589
x   3
1767
```
estimate
```
 600
x  3
1800
```

㊻
```
 912
x   2
1824
```
estimate
```
 900
x   2
1800
```

Solve the problems. Show your work.

㊼	A bag of potato chips weighs 225 g. What is the total weight of 4 bags of potato chips? The total weight of 4 bags of potato chips is ___900 g___ .	$\begin{array}{r}^{1}{}^{2}\\225\\ \times\quad 4\\\hline 900\end{array}$
㊽	A box of sugar contains 125 packets. How many packets are there in 6 boxes?	$\begin{array}{r}^{1}{}^{3}\\125\\ \times\quad 6\\\hline 750\end{array}$
㊾	The capacity of one can of pop is 355 mL. How many mL of pop are there in 6 cans?	$\begin{array}{r}^{3}{}^{3}\\355\\ \times\quad 6\\\hline 2130\end{array}$
㊿	Ted drinks 1 box of juice each day. If the capacity of a box of juice is 250 mL, how many mL of juice does Ted drink in one week?	$\begin{array}{r}^{3}\\250\\ \times\quad 7\\\hline 1750\end{array}$

Solve the problem.

Write 2 to 11 in the circles so that the sum of the numbers at the centre and the 4 corners of each rectangle is 27.

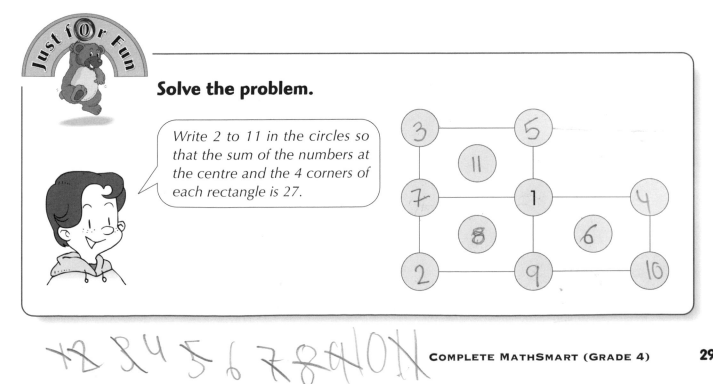

Multiplying 2-digit Numbers by 2-digit Numbers

EXAMPLES

1. $20 \times 40 = 20 \times 4 \times 10 = 80 \times 10 = 800$
2. $23 \times 40 = 23 \times 4 \times 10 = 92 \times 10 = 920$
3. $23 \times 46 = 1058$

$$
\begin{array}{r}
4\,6 \\
\times \quad 2\,3 \\
\hline
1\,3\,8 \\
9\,2\,0 \\
\hline
1\,0\,5\,8
\end{array}
$$

align the numbers on the right-hand side

← $3 \times 46 = 138$
← $20 \times 46 = 920$
← $138 + 920 = 1058$

HINTS:

- To multiply a 2-digit number by another 2-digit number:

  Align the numbers on the right-hand side.

  Multiply the first 2-digit number by the ones digit and then by the tens digit of the second 2-digit number.

  Add the products to get the final answer.

- Don't forget to put a zero under the ones column when multiplying by the tens digit.

- To multiply 2 multiples of 10, multiply the digits at the tens column and write 2 zeros to the right of that product.

  e.g. $20 \times 40 = 800$

  $2 \times 4 = 8$ — 2 zeros to the right of 8

Complete the multiplication.

①
$$
\begin{array}{r}
3\,5 \\
\times \quad 1\,7 \\
\hline
245 \\
350 \\
\hline
505
\end{array}
$$
← 7×35
← 10×35

②
$$
\begin{array}{r}
2\,6 \\
\times \quad 4\,3 \\
\hline
78 \\
80 \\
\hline
158
\end{array}
$$
← 3×26
← 40×26

③
$$
\begin{array}{r}
3\,7 \\
\times \quad 5\,4 \\
\hline
128 \\
150 \\
\hline
278
\end{array}
$$

④
$$
\begin{array}{r}
8\,1 \\
\times \quad 4\,2 \\
\hline
162 \\
320 \\
\hline
482
\end{array}
$$
81
40

⑤
$$
\begin{array}{r}
3\,6 \\
\times \quad 7\,3 \\
\hline
108 \\
210 \\
\hline
318
\end{array}
$$

⑥
$$
\begin{array}{r}
1\,3 \\
\times \quad 4\,1 \\
\hline
13 \\
40 \\
\hline
53
\end{array}
$$

Find the products.

⑦ 30 × 50 = 1500   ⑧ 60 × 20 = 1200   ⑨ 10 × 80 = 800

⑩ 40 × 70 = 2800   ⑪ 20 × 30 = 600   ⑫ 50 × 20 = 1000

⑬ 50 × 80 = 4000   ⑭ 40 × 90 = 3600   ⑮ 30 × 40 = 1200

⑯ 20 × 90 = 1800   ⑰ 70 × 30 = 2100   ⑱ 60 × 70 = 4200

⑲ 60 × 30 = 1800   ⑳ 80 × 20 = 1600   ㉑ 50 × 60 = 3000

Do the multiplication. Show your work.

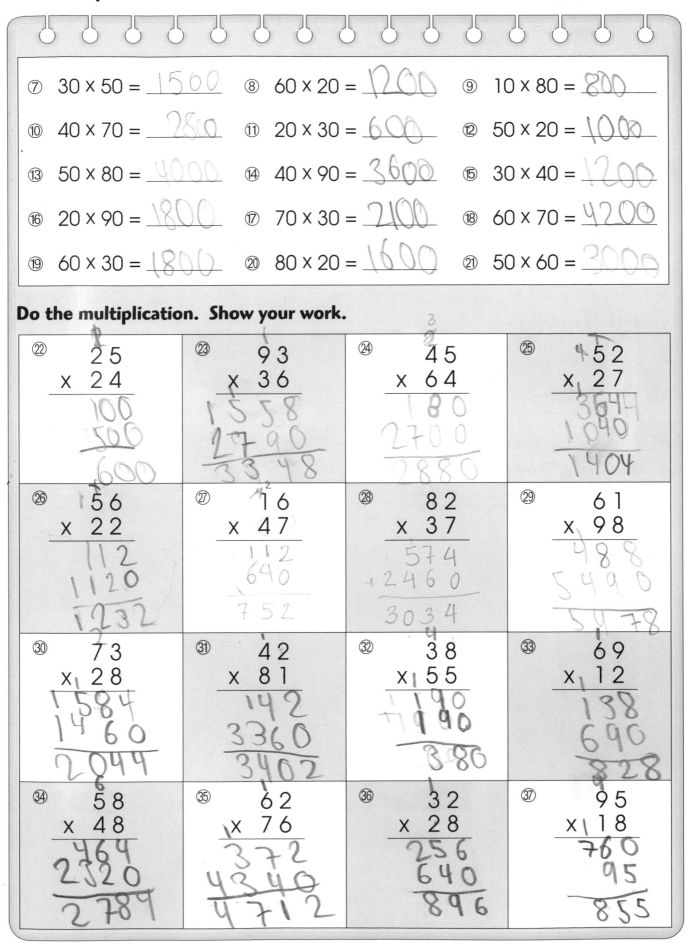

㉒
$$\begin{array}{r} 25 \\ \times\ 24 \\ \hline 100 \\ 500 \\ \hline 600 \end{array}$$

㉓
$$\begin{array}{r} 93 \\ \times\ 36 \\ \hline 1558 \\ 2790 \\ \hline 3348 \end{array}$$

㉔
$$\begin{array}{r} 45 \\ \times\ 64 \\ \hline 180 \\ 2700 \\ \hline 2880 \end{array}$$

㉕
$$\begin{array}{r} 52 \\ \times\ 27 \\ \hline 364 \\ 1040 \\ \hline 1404 \end{array}$$

㉖
$$\begin{array}{r} 56 \\ \times\ 22 \\ \hline 112 \\ 1120 \\ \hline 1232 \end{array}$$

㉗
$$\begin{array}{r} 16 \\ \times\ 47 \\ \hline 112 \\ 640 \\ \hline 752 \end{array}$$

㉘
$$\begin{array}{r} 82 \\ \times\ 37 \\ \hline 574 \\ +2460 \\ \hline 3034 \end{array}$$

㉙
$$\begin{array}{r} 61 \\ \times\ 98 \\ \hline 488 \\ 5490 \\ \hline 5978 \end{array}$$

㉚
$$\begin{array}{r} 73 \\ \times\ 28 \\ \hline 584 \\ 1460 \\ \hline 2044 \end{array}$$

㉛
$$\begin{array}{r} 42 \\ \times\ 81 \\ \hline 42 \\ 3360 \\ \hline 3402 \end{array}$$

㉜
$$\begin{array}{r} 38 \\ \times\ 55 \\ \hline 190 \\ +190 \\ \hline 880 \end{array}$$

㉝
$$\begin{array}{r} 69 \\ \times\ 12 \\ \hline 138 \\ 690 \\ \hline 828 \end{array}$$

㉞
$$\begin{array}{r} 58 \\ \times\ 48 \\ \hline 464 \\ 2320 \\ \hline 2784 \end{array}$$

㉟
$$\begin{array}{r} 62 \\ \times\ 76 \\ \hline 372 \\ 4340 \\ \hline 4712 \end{array}$$

㊱
$$\begin{array}{r} 32 \\ \times\ 28 \\ \hline 256 \\ 640 \\ \hline 896 \end{array}$$

㊲
$$\begin{array}{r} 95 \\ \times\ 18 \\ \hline 760 \\ 95 \\ \hline 855 \end{array}$$

Write your answers in the puzzle below.

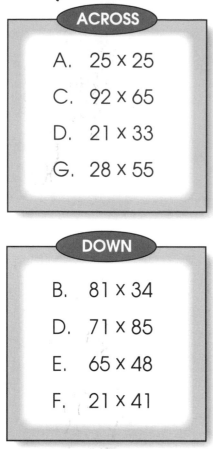

ACROSS

A. 25 × 25

C. 92 × 65

D. 21 × 33

G. 28 × 55

DOWN

B. 81 × 34

D. 71 × 85

E. 65 × 48

F. 21 × 41

㊳

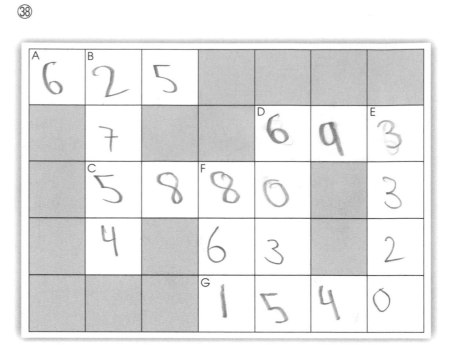

A 6	B 2	5				
	7			D 6	9	E 3
	C 5	8	F 8	0		3
	4		6	3		2
			G 1	5	4	0

Estimate first. Then find the products.

㊴
```
    3
    3 8
  ×  4 2
  ───────
  1 5 7 6
  1 5 2 0
  ───────
  1 5 9 6
```
estimate
```
    4 0
  ×  4 0
  ───────
  1 6 0 0
```

㊵
```
    1
    9 2
  ×  6 6
  ───────
  2 5 5 2
  5 5 2 0
  ───────
  7 5 7 2
```
estimate
```
    9 0
  ×  7 0
  ───────
  6 3 0 0
```

㊶
```
    6
    4 7
  ×  5 9
  ───────
  4 2 3
  2 3 5 0
  ───────
  2 7 7 3
```
estimate
```
    5 0
    6 0
  ───────
  3 0 0 0
```

㊷
```
    7 3
  ×  2 1
  ───────
    7 3
  1 4 6 0
  ───────
  1 5 3 3
```
estimate
```
    7 0
    2 0
  ───────
  1 4 0 0
```

㊸
```
    3
    8 9
  ×  1 4
  ───────
  3 6 6
  8 9 0
  ───────
  1 2 5 6
```
estimate
```
    9 0
    1 0
  ───────
  9 0 0
```

㊹
```
    1
    6 3
  ×  3 5
  ───────
  1 3 1 5
  1 8 9 0
  ───────
  2 2 0 5
```
estimate
```
    6 0
    4 0
  ───────
  2 4 0 0
```

Solve the problems. Show your work.

㊺ There are 32 classes in May's school. Each class has 26 students. How many students are there in May's school?

There are ___732___ students in May's school.

$$\begin{array}{r} \overset{1}{3}2 \\ 26 \\ \hline 192 \\ 64 \\ \hline 732 \end{array}$$

㊻ May receives $35 pocket money each month. How much pocket money does she receive in one year?

420

$$\begin{array}{r} \overset{1}{3}5 \\ 12 \\ \hline 170 \\ 350 \\ \hline 420 \end{array}$$

㊼ There are 28 rows of 42 seats in the school theatre. How many seats are there in the school theatre?

8376

$$\begin{array}{r} 28 \\ 42 \\ \hline 56 \\ 8320 \\ \hline 8376 \end{array}$$

㊽ Ted's school is organizing a fundraising campaign. Each of the 48 classes raises $90. What will be the total amount raised in the campaign?

4320

$$\begin{array}{r} \overset{7}{4}8 \\ 90 \\ \hline 00 \\ 4320 \end{array}$$

Just for Fun

How many possible routes are there for Little Squirrel to get the walnut? (Little Squirrel cannot move backward.)

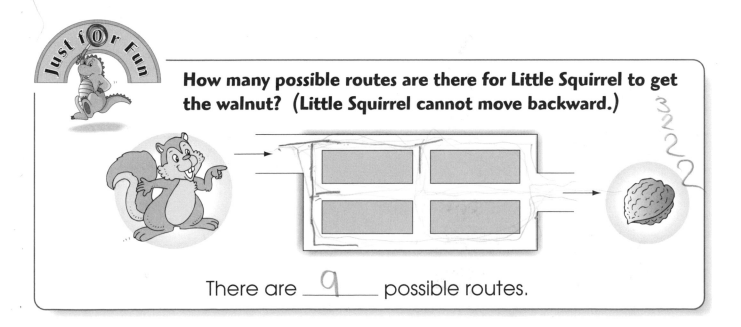

There are ___9___ possible routes.

8 More Multiplying and Multiples

1. How many stickers are there in all?

   $5 \times 4 \times 3 = 20 \times 3 = 60$

   There are 60 stickers in all.

2. $5 \times 4 \times 3 = 5 \times 12 = 60$

3. Show all the multiples of 3 up to 20.

   3 , 6 , 9 , 12 , 15 , 18

   3×1 3×2 3×3 3×4 3×5 3×6 3×7

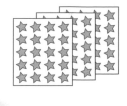

HINTS:

- The product of 3 factors remains the same if the order of multiplication is changed.

  e.g. $5 \times 4 \times 3 = 3 \times 4 \times 5 = 3 \times 5 \times 4$
  $= 4 \times 5 \times 3 = 4 \times 3 \times 5$
  $= 5 \times 3 \times 4$
  $= 60$

- If possible, multiply the numbers with a product of 10, 20, 30 ... etc. first, and then multiply the 3rd number.

- Multiples of a number can be obtained by multiplying the number by 1, 2, 3 ... and so on.

Find the products.

① $2 \times 3 \times 6$ = _6 x 6 = 3__

② $5 \times 6 \times 7$ = _30 x 7 = 210_

③ $6 \times 7 \times 8$ = _56 x 6_

④ $7 \times 8 \times 9$ = _63 x 8_

⑤ $7 \times 2 \times 9$ = _18 x 7_

⑥ $6 \times 3 \times 4$ = _12 x 6_

⑦ $5 \times 2 \times 3$ = _6 x 5_

⑧ $9 \times 3 \times 5$ = _27 x 5_

⑨ $6 \times 4 \times 8$ = _24 x 8_

⑩ $7 \times 2 \times 8$ = _14 x 8_

⑪ $9 \times 5 \times 6$ = _30 x 9_

⑫ $4 \times 6 \times 7$ = _24 x 7_

⑬ $3 \times 8 \times 5$ = _40 x 3_

⑭ $6 \times 2 \times 9$ = _18 x 6_

⑮ $14 \times 2 \times 8$ = _16 x 14_

⑯ $13 \times 7 \times 9$ = _63 x 13_

⑰ $8 \times 6 \times 15$ = _48 x 15_

⑱ $11 \times 3 \times 7$ = _33 x 7_

⑲ $7 \times 9 \times 27$ = _63 x 27_

⑳ $5 \times 16 \times 4$ = _20 x 16_

㉑ $23 \times 2 \times 5$ = _10 x 23_

㉒ $6 \times 8 \times 31$ = _48 x 31_

㉓ $6 \times 37 \times 5$ = _30 x 37_

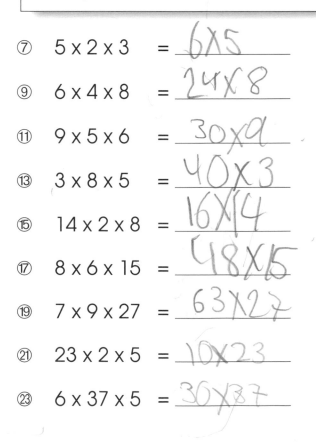

Help the students pick the balls they are going to colour. Write the numbers in the ⃝.

㉔ Ted is going to colour the balls which are multiples of 3 between 25 and 50.

(27) (30) (33) (36) (39) (42) (45) (48)

㉕ May is going to colour the balls which are multiples of 4 up to 24.

(4) (8) (12) (16) (20) (24)

㉖ Sally is going to colour the balls which are multiples of 5 and not yet coloured.

(5) (10) (15) (25) (35) (40) (50)

㉗ Tim is going to draw a red star on each of the balls which are multiples of 2 up to 25.

(2) (4) (6) (8) (10) (12) (14) (16) (18) (20) (22) (24)

㉘ Ben is going to mark a black dot on each of the balls which are multiples of 2 between 25 and 50.

(26) (28) (30) (32) (34) (36) (38) (40) (42) (44) (46) (48) (50)

㉙ Bob is going to draw a brown dot on each of the balls which are multiples of 6.

(6) (12) (18) (24) (30) (36) (42) (48)

㉚ Tom is asked to pick the balls which are multiples of 7.

(7) (14) (21) (28) (35) (42) (49)

Look at the 100-chart and complete the following questions.

③① The shaded numbers are multiples of ___8___ .

③② Circle the multiples of 9.

③③ Put a **X** on each multiple of 10.

③④ The multiples of 8 up to 60 are:

8, 16, 24, 32, 40, 48, 56

1, 2, 3, 4, 5, 6, 7 .

1	2	3	4	5	6	7	8	9	10
11	12	13	14	15	16	17	18	19	20
21	22	23	24	25	26	27	28	29	30
31	32	33	34	35	36	37	38	39	40
41	42	43	44	45	46	47	48	49	50
51	52	53	54	55	56	57	58	59	60
61	62	63	64	65	66	67	68	69	70
71	72	73	74	75	76	77	78	79	80
81	82	83	84	85	86	87	88	89	90
91	92	93	94	95	96	97	98	99	100

③⑤ What is the largest multiple of 8 up to 100?   96 or 12

③⑥ What is the largest multiple of 9 up to 100?   81 or 11

③⑦ What is the largest multiple of 5 up to 80?   80 or 160

③⑧ What is the largest multiple of 7 up to 80?   77 or 11

③⑨ How many multiples of 8 are there in 100?   8 N 12

④⓪ How many multiples of 9 are there in 100?   11

④① How many 3s are there in 30?   10

④② How many 6s are there in 84?   14

④③ How many 2s are there in 30?   15

④④ How many 4s are there in 60?   15

④⑤ How many 5s are there in 75?   15

List the first 5 multiples of the following numbers.

46. 6 _12_ _18_ _24_ _30_ _36_   47. 11 _22_ _33_ _44_ _55_ _66_
48. 9 _18_ _27_ _36_ _45_ _54_   49. 12 _24_ _36_ _48_ _50_ _62_
50. 13 _26_ _39_ _52_ _65_ _78_   51. 15 _____ _____ _____ _____ _____

Solve the problems. Show your work.

52. The children shared 2 boxes of chocolate among them. There were 5 rows of 6 chocolates in each box. How many chocolates were shared among the children?

$96 = 30$
$5 \times 6 = 30$ $2 \times 5 \times 6 = 60$

_60_ chocolates were shared among the children.

53. There are 3 rows of 4 tables in the school cafeteria. Each table can seat 8 students. How many students can the cafeteria hold?

$3 \times 4 \times 8 =$ 96

54. Mom plants 3 kinds of roses in the backyard. There are 2 rows of 6 rose bushes of each kind. How many rose bushes does Mom plant in the backyard?

$3 \times (2 \times 6)$

55. May drinks 2 full glasses of milk each day. The capacity of a glass is 70 mL. How many mL of milk does May drink in one week?

$70 + 70 = 140$ mL   440

each day
$2 \times 70 \times 7 = 140 \times 7 = 980$ mL

$\begin{array}{r} 140 \\ \times\ 7 \\ \hline 980 \end{array}$

Count the number of triangles in the diagram.

There are _9_ triangles.

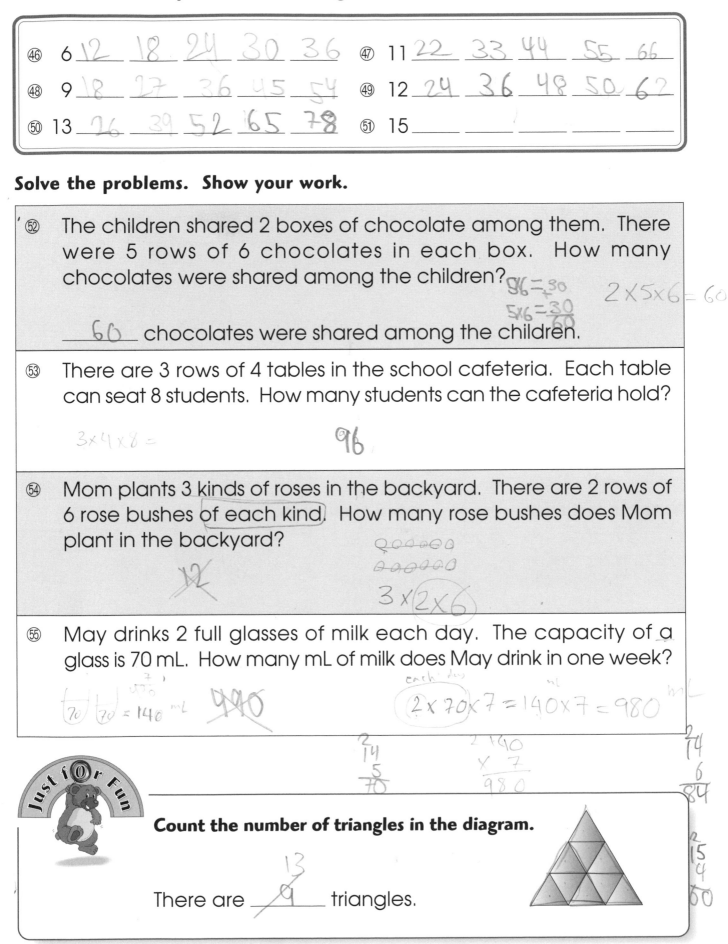

Find the answers mentally.

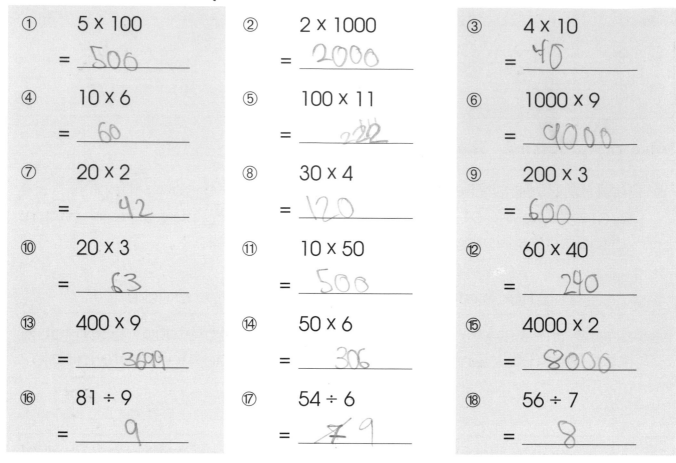

① 5 × 100

= 500

② 2 × 1000

= 2000

③ 4 × 10

= 40

④ 10 × 6

= 60

⑤ 100 × 11

= 222

⑥ 1000 × 9

= 9000

⑦ 20 × 2

= 42

⑧ 30 × 4

= 120

⑨ 200 × 3

= 600

⑩ 20 × 3

= 63

⑪ 10 × 50

= 500

⑫ 60 × 40

= 240

⑬ 400 × 9

= 3600

⑭ 50 × 6

= 306

⑮ 4000 × 2

= 8000

⑯ 81 ÷ 9

= 9

⑰ 54 ÷ 6

= 79

⑱ 56 ÷ 7

= 8

Write the fact families for each group of numbers.

⑲ 9 7 63

9 x 7 = 63
7 x 9 = 63
63 ÷ 7 = 9
63 ÷ 9 = 7

⑳ 5 8 40

5 x 8 = 40
8 x 5 = 40
40 ÷ 5 = 8
40 ÷ 8 = 5

Write the following.

㉑ The largest multiple of 6 up to 50   48

㉒ The number of multiples of 5 in ⑳40   8

㉓ The number of multiples of 8 in 60   7x8=56   7

㉔ The largest multiple of 7 up to 55   49

Do the multiplication. Show your work.

㉕ $\begin{array}{r} {}^{4}209 \\ \times\ \ 5 \\ \hline 1095 \end{array}$	㉖ $\begin{array}{r} {}^{1\ 3}314 \\ \times\ \ 8 \\ \hline 2512 \end{array}$	㉗ $\begin{array}{r} {}^{1\ 1}659 \\ \times\ \ 2 \\ \hline 1318 \end{array}$
㉘ $\begin{array}{r} {}^{1}562 \\ \times\ \ 3 \\ \hline 1686 \end{array}$	㉙ $\begin{array}{r} {}^{4\ 1}483 \\ \times\ \ 5 \\ \hline 2415 \end{array}$	㉚ $\begin{array}{r} {}^{1\ 3}748 \\ \times\ \ 4 \\ \hline 2992 \end{array}$
㉛ $\begin{array}{r} {}^{3}25 \\ \times\ 6 \\ \hline 150 \end{array}$	㉜ $\begin{array}{r} {}^{5}37 \\ \times\ 8 \\ \hline 296 \end{array}$	㉝ $\begin{array}{r} {}^{5}58 \\ \times\ 7 \\ \hline 406 \end{array}$	㉞ $\begin{array}{r} {}^{8}49 \\ \times\ 9 \\ \hline 941 \end{array}$
㉟ $\begin{array}{r} 73 \\ \times\ 4 \\ \hline 292 \end{array}$	㊱ $\begin{array}{r} 45 \\ \times\ 3 \\ \hline 135 \end{array}$	㊲ $\begin{array}{r} 62 \\ \times\ 5 \\ \hline 310 \end{array}$	㊳ $\begin{array}{r} 96 \\ \times\ 2 \\ \hline 192 \end{array}$
㊴ $\begin{array}{r} {}^{2}37 \\ \times\ 14 \\ \hline 148 \\ +370 \\ \hline 518 \end{array}$	㊵ $\begin{array}{r} {}^{2}53 \\ \times\ 28 \\ \hline 424 \\ 1060 \\ \hline 1484 \end{array}$	㊶ $\begin{array}{r} {}^{1}66 \\ \times\ 33 \\ \hline 198 \\ 2080 \\ \hline 2378 \end{array}$	㊷ $\begin{array}{r} 82 \\ \times\ 49 \\ \hline 1738 \\ +3280 \\ \hline 4018 \end{array}$
㊸ $\begin{array}{r} 43 \\ \times\ 22 \\ \hline 186 \\ 860 \\ \hline 946 \end{array}$	㊹ $\begin{array}{r} 75 \\ \times\ 52 \\ \hline 150 \\ 3550 \\ \hline 3700 \end{array}$	㊺ $\begin{array}{r} {}^{1}32 \\ \times\ 88 \\ \hline 256 \\ 2560 \\ \hline 2816 \end{array}$	㊻ $\begin{array}{r} {}^{5}97 \\ \times\ 18 \\ \hline 776 \\ 970 \\ \hline 1746 \end{array}$

Put the numbers in the right boxes.

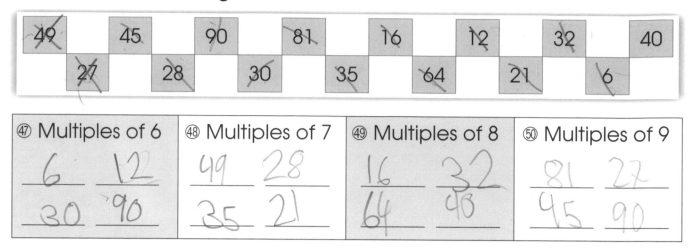

| 49 | | 45 | | 90 | | 81 | | 16 | | 12 | | 32 | | 40 |
| | 27 | | 28 | | 30 | | 35 | | 64 | | 21 | | 6 | |

㊼ Multiples of 6	㊽ Multiples of 7	㊾ Multiples of 8	㊿ Multiples of 9
6 12	49 28	16 32	81 27
30 90	35 21	64 40	45 90

Find the products. Then estimate the products to see if they are reasonable.

㊿1
$$\begin{array}{r} 36 \\ \times\ 23 \\ \hline 108 \\ 720 \\ \hline 828 \end{array}$$

estimate
$$\begin{array}{r} 40 \\ \times\ 20 \\ \hline 800 \end{array}$$

52
$$\begin{array}{r} 58 \\ \times\ 19 \\ \hline 522 \\ 580 \\ \hline 1102 \end{array}$$

estimate
$$\begin{array}{r} 60 \\ \times\ 20 \\ \hline 1200 \end{array}$$

53
$$\begin{array}{r} 673 \\ \times\ 4 \\ \hline 2692 \end{array}$$

estimate
$$\begin{array}{r} 675 \\ \times\ 5 \\ \hline 3375 \end{array}$$

54
$$\begin{array}{r} 286 \\ \times\ 6 \\ \hline 1716 \end{array}$$

estimate
$$\begin{array}{r} 290 \\ \times\ 6 \\ \hline 1740 \end{array}$$

55
$$\begin{array}{r} 718 \\ \times\ 6 \\ \hline 4358 \end{array}$$

estimate
$$\begin{array}{r} 720 \\ \times\ 6 \\ \hline 4320 \end{array}$$

56
$$\begin{array}{r} 329 \\ \times\ 8 \\ \hline 2632 \end{array}$$

estimate
$$\begin{array}{r} 330 \\ \times\ 8 \\ \hline 2640 \end{array}$$

Find the answers.

㊄7   3 x 5 x 9 = __135__

㊄8   2 x 4 x 5 = __40__

㊄9   4 x 8 x 6 = __192__

㊅0   6 x 7 x 5 = __210__

㊅1   7 x 3 x 2 = __42__

㊅2   3 x 4 x 9 = __108__

Solve the problems. Show your work.

63. On Games Day 18 students from each of the 32 classes participated in the competitions. How many students participated in the competitions?

   _576_ students participated in the competitions.

64. There were 26 events on Games Day. 3 prizes were awarded for each event. How many prizes were awarded to the students?

65. The Parents' Association made 15 trays of hot dogs. There were 24 hot dogs in each tray. How many hot dogs were prepared ?

66. Each bag contains 12 buns. The parents bought 36 bags for making hamburgers. How many buns were bought in all?

67. The student helpers put 48 cups of soft drinks into each box. There were 16 boxes. How many cups of soft drinks were in the boxes?

68. May baked 2 trays of 118 cookies each for the bake sale to raise funds for Games Day. How many cookies did May bake?

69. The cookies were sold for 10¢ each in the bake sale. If all the cookies were sold out, how much did May raise in dollars?

   23,60 $

Dividing Multiples of 10, 100 or 1000

EXAMPLE

3 children share 600 stickers. How many stickers does each child get?

600 ÷ 3 = 6 hundreds ÷ 3
         = 2 hundreds
         = 200

Each child gets 200 stickers.

divisor → 3) 600 ← dividend
             200 ← quotient
             600

HINTS:

- Dividing the multiples of 10, 100 or 1000 is similar to dividing other dividends, but don't forget to write the zero(s) in the quotient.

  e.g.   420 ÷ 7 =

  $$7\overline{)420} \rightarrow 7\overline{)\underset{42}{420}}^{6} \rightarrow 7\overline{)\underset{\underset{0}{420}}{420}}^{60}$$

- Estimate the quotient by rounding the numbers to the nearest ten, hundred or thousand.

  e.g.   621 ÷ 2 = ?

  estimate   600 ÷ 2 = 300   the answer should be close to 300

  There are about 300 twos in 621.

Fill in the missing numbers.

①   800 ÷ 2 = __8__ hundreds ÷ 2

              = __4__ hundreds

              = __400__

②   550 ÷ 5 = __55__ tens ÷ 5

              = __11__ tens

              = __110__

$$5\overline{)550}^{110}$$
$$\underline{-5}$$
$$05$$
$$5$$

③   360 ÷ 9 = __36__ tens ÷ 9

              = __4__ tens

              = __40__

④   480 ÷ 8 = __48__ tens ÷ 8

              = __6__ tens

              = __60__

⑤   600 ÷ 6 = __6__ hundreds ÷ 6

              = __1__ hundred

              = __100__

⑥   240 ÷ 4 = __24__ tens ÷ 4

              = __6__ tens

              = __60__

Do the division. Then write the letters representing the answers to find what Ted says.

⑦
$$\frac{50}{9 \overline{)450}}$$
b

⑧
$$\frac{300}{4 \overline{)1200}}$$
m

⑨
$$\frac{10}{5 \overline{)50}}$$
s

⑩
$$\frac{700}{8 \overline{)5600}}$$
i

⑪
$$\frac{30}{9 \overline{)270}}$$
c

⑫
$$\frac{60}{2 \overline{)120}}$$
d

⑬
$$\frac{200}{8 \overline{)1600}}$$
p

⑭
$$\frac{70}{9 \overline{)630}}$$
f

⑮
$$\frac{20}{2 \overline{)40}}$$
e

⑯
$$\frac{600}{6 \overline{)3600}}$$
h

⑰
$$\frac{20}{7 \overline{)140}}$$
a

⑱
$$\frac{3000}{2 \overline{)6000}}$$
n

⑲ $2100 \div 7 = 300$ q

⑳ $400 \div 5 = 80$ w

㉑ $90 \div 3 = 30$ t

㉒ $80 \div 4 = 20$ j

㉓ $5600 \div 7 = 800$ g

㉔ $180 \div 6 = 30$ l

㉕ $240 \div 6 = 40$ y

㉖ $5400 \div 6 = 900$ i

㉗ $400 \div 8 = 50$ z

㉘ $60 \div 3 = 20$ k

㉙ $300 \div 3 = 100$ u

㉚ $200 \div 4 = 50$ r

㉛

I like f i s h i n g .
   70 900 10 600 700 3000 800

Solve the problems. Show your work.

③② May puts 60 cookies equally into 2 jars. How many cookies are there in each jar?

There are __30__ cookies in each jar. $\frac{\div \ 60}{\div \ 30}$

③③ Each box can hold 4 muffins. How many boxes does Mrs White need to hold 320 muffins?

$4\overline{)320}$ 80

③④ 180 boy scouts are divided into groups. Each group has 6 boy scouts. How many groups are there?

$6\overline{)180}$ 36

③⑤ Ted puts 900 grams of candies equally into 3 bags. How many grams of candies are there in each bag?

$3\overline{)900}$ 300

③⑥ How many weeks are there in 2100 days?

$7\overline{)2100}$ 300

③⑦ Mr Stanley divides 4500 stamps equally for 5 albums. How many stamps are there in each album?

$5\overline{)4500}$ 900

③⑧ A bag of apples costs $6. How many bags of apples can Mrs Smith buy with $60?

$6\overline{)60}$ 10

44   COMPLETE MATHSMART (GRADE 4)

Round the dividend to the nearest ten, hundred or thousand. Then estimate.

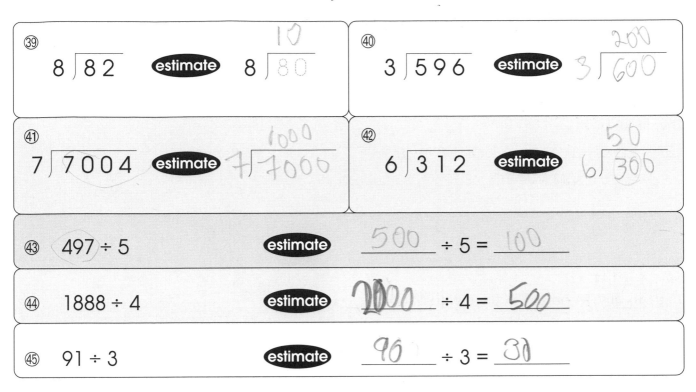

㊴ 8⟌82   estimate 8⟌80 — 10

㊵ 3⟌596   estimate 3⟌600 — 200

㊶ 7⟌7004 estimate 7⟌7000 — 1000

㊷ 6⟌312   estimate 6⟌300 — 50

㊸ 497 ÷ 5   estimate 500 ÷ 5 = 100

㊹ 1888 ÷ 4   estimate 2000 ÷ 4 = 500

㊺ 91 ÷ 3   estimate 90 ÷ 3 = 30

Solve the problems. Show your work.

㊻ May divides 81 flowers among 4 vases. About how many flowers are there in each vase?

81 ÷ 4   estimate 80 ÷ 4 = 20

There are about __20__ flowers in each vase.

㊼ 8 children share 796 blocks. About how many blocks does each child get?

796 ÷ 8   estimate 800 ÷ 8 = 100

Each child gets about __100__ blocks.

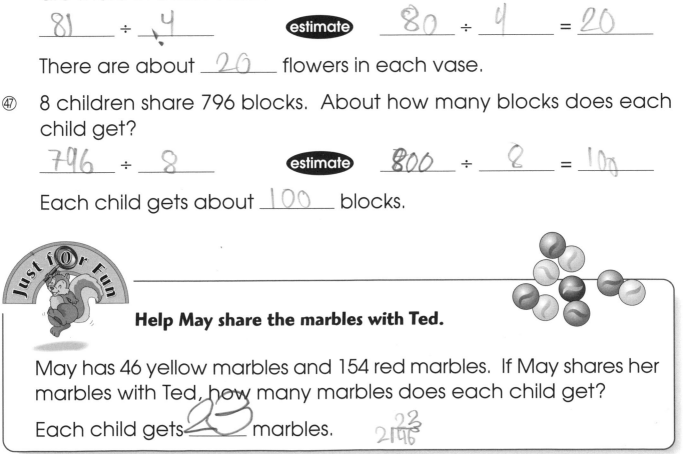

Just for Fun

Help May share the marbles with Ted.

May has 46 yellow marbles and 154 red marbles. If May shares her marbles with Ted, how many marbles does each child get?

Each child gets __23__ marbles.

23
2⟌46

10 Dividing 2-digit Numbers with No Remainders

EXAMPLE

A bottle of juice costs $4. How many bottles of juice can Ted buy with $56?
Divide 56 by 4.

$$4\overline{)56} \xrightarrow{\text{Divide the tens}}$$

Tens	Ones
1	
4)5	6
-4	
1	

$$\xrightarrow{\text{Divide the ones}}$$

Tens	Ones
1	4
4)5	6
4	
1	6
-1	6
	0

56 ÷ 4 = 14
Ted can buy 14 bottles of juice with $56.

HINTS:

- Dividing a 2-digit number by a 1-digit number:

  Divide the tens and then subtract.

  Bring down the ones.

  Combine the difference from the tens and the ones and then divide.

  e.g.
  $$5\overline{)65}\;,\;5 \quad\to\quad 5\overline{)65}\;,\;5\;,\;15 \quad\to\quad 5\overline{)65}\;,\;13\;,\;5\;,\;15\;,\;15$$

  65 ÷ 5 = 13

Do the division.

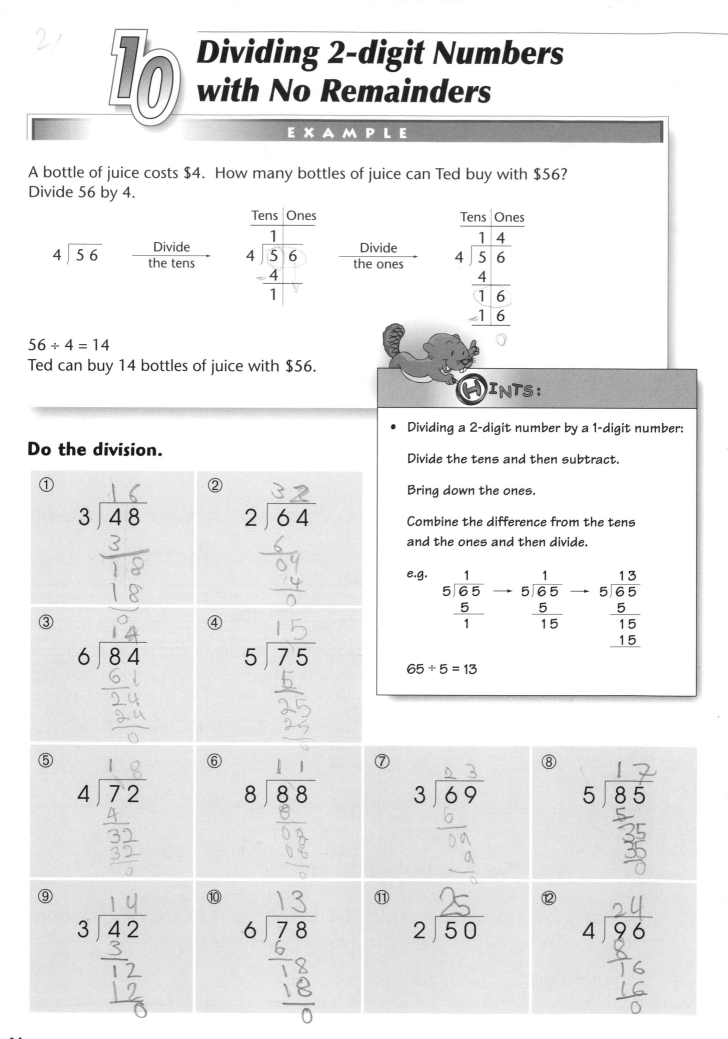

① 3)48

② 2)64

③ 6)84

④ 5)75

⑤ 4)72

⑥ 8)88

⑦ 3)69

⑧ 5)85

⑨ 3)42

⑩ 6)78

⑪ 2)50

⑫ 4)96

⑬
$$\begin{array}{r} 16 \\ 2\overline{)32} \end{array}$$
(scribbled out work below)
12
$\underline{12}$
0

⑭
$$\begin{array}{r} 12 \\ 6\overline{)72} \\ \underline{6} \\ 12 \\ \underline{12} \\ 0 \end{array}$$

⑮
$$\begin{array}{r} 19 \\ 5\overline{)95} \\ \underline{5} \\ 45 \\ \underline{45} \\ 0 \end{array}$$

⑯
$$\begin{array}{r} 12 \\ 7\overline{)84} \\ \underline{7} \\ 14 \\ 14 \\ \underline{} \\ 0 \end{array}$$

⑰
$$\begin{array}{r} 11 \\ 9\overline{)99} \end{array}$$

⑱
$$\begin{array}{r} 12 \\ 8\overline{)96} \end{array}$$

⑲
$$\begin{array}{r} 13 \\ 4\overline{)52} \\ \underline{4} \\ 12 \\ 12 \\ \underline{} \\ 0 \end{array}$$

⑳
$$\begin{array}{r} 21 \\ 3\overline{)63} \\ 6 \\ \underline{} \\ 3 \\ 3 \\ 0 \end{array}$$

㉑
$$\begin{array}{r} 27 \\ 3\overline{)81} \\ 6 \\ \underline{} \\ 21 \\ 21 \\ \underline{} \\ 0 \end{array}$$

㉒
$$\begin{array}{r} 16 \\ 5\overline{)80} \\ 5 \\ \underline{} \\ 30 \\ 30 \\ \underline{} \\ 0 \end{array}$$

㉓
$$\begin{array}{r} 38 \\ 2\overline{)76} \\ 6 \\ \underline{} \\ 16 \\ 16 \\ \underline{} \\ 0 \end{array}$$

㉔
$$\begin{array}{r} 19 \\ 4\overline{)76} \\ 4 \\ \underline{} \\ 36 \\ 36 \\ \underline{} \\ 0 \end{array}$$

㉕
$$\begin{array}{r} 13 \\ 7\overline{)91} \\ 7 \\ \underline{} \\ 21 \\ 21 \\ \underline{} \\ 0 \end{array}$$

㉖
$$\begin{array}{r} 15 \\ 6\overline{)90} \\ 6 \\ \underline{} \\ 30 \\ 30 \\ \underline{} \\ 0 \end{array}$$

㉗
$$\begin{array}{r} 14 \\ 5\overline{)70} \\ 5 \\ \underline{} \\ 20 \end{array}$$

㉘
$$\begin{array}{r} 19 \\ 2\overline{)38} \\ 2 \\ \underline{} \\ 18 \\ 18 \\ \underline{} \\ 0 \end{array}$$

㉙ 87 ÷ 3 = _____

㉚ 74 ÷ 2 = _____

㉛ 60 ÷ 5 = _____

㉜ 68 ÷ 4 = _____

㉝ 78 ÷ 6 = _____

㉞ 39 ÷ 3 = _____

㉟ 82 ÷ 2 = _____

㊱ 95 ÷ 5 = _____

㊲ 78 ÷ 3 = _____

㊳ 98 ÷ 7 = _____

㊴ 84 ÷ 4 = _____

㊵ 84 ÷ 6 = _____

Do the division. Then put the letters in order from the greatest quotient to the smallest.

④①

A. $66 \div 6 =$ __11__

B. $70 \div 5 =$ __14__

C. $51 \div 3 =$ __17__

D. $56 \div 2 =$ __28__

④② The order of the pencils : _____ , _____ , _____ , _____ .

④③

A. $60 \div 4 =$ __26__

B. $84 \div 6 =$ __14__

C. $72 \div 2 =$ __36__

D. $77 \div 7 =$ __11__

④④ The order of the crayons : _____ , _____ , _____ , _____ .

④⑤

A. $58 \div 2 =$ __29__

B. $75 \div 3 =$ __25__

C. $68 \div 4 =$ __17__

D. $80 \div 5 =$ __16__

④⑥ The order of the chocolate bars : _____ , _____ , _____ , _____ .

④⑦

A. $92 \div 2 =$ __46__

B. $88 \div 8 =$ __11__

C. $91 \div 7 =$ __13__

D. $84 \div 3 =$ __28__

④⑧ The order of the puzzles : _____ , _____ , _____ , _____ .

Solve the problems. Show your work.

49 5 children share 70 pencils. How many pencils does each child get?

Each child gets __14__ pencils.

$$5\overline{)70} = 14$$

50 Each bag of chips costs $2. How many bags of chips can Sally buy with $26?

13 chips

$$2\overline{)26} = 13$$

51 Mrs William buys 3 kg of meat for $39. How much does 1 kg of meat cost?

$$3\overline{)39} = 13$$
$$\begin{array}{r} 39 \\ 3 \\ \hline 09 \\ 9 \\ \hline 0 \end{array}$$

52 A ribbon is 96 cm long. Sally cuts it into 4 equal strips. How long is each strip?

$$\begin{array}{r} 24 \\ 4\overline{)96} \\ 8 \\ \hline 16 \end{array}$$

53 84 candies are packed into packets of 7. How many packets of candies are there?

$$\begin{array}{r} 12 \\ 7\overline{)84} \\ 7 \\ \hline 14 \\ 14 \\ \hline 0 \end{array}$$

Just for Fun

Fill in the missing numbers.

①
$$\begin{array}{r} 3\,8 \\ 2\overline{)7\,6} \\ 6 \\ \hline 1\,6 \\ 1\,6 \end{array}$$

②
$$\begin{array}{r} 2\,7 \\ 3\overline{)8\,1} \\ 6 \\ \hline 2\,1 \\ 2\,1 \end{array}$$

③
$$\begin{array}{r} 1\,5 \\ 6\overline{)9\,0} \\ 6 \\ \hline 3\,0 \\ 3\,0 \end{array}$$

Mon

Dividing 3-digit Numbers with No Remainders

EXAMPLE

Each box can hold 6 lollipops. Ted puts 738 lollipops into the boxes. How many boxes does Ted need?

```
      1              1 2              1 2 3
  6) 7 3 8  →    6) 7 3 8   →    6) 7 3 8
     6              6                6
     1              1 3              1 3
                    1 2              1 2
                      1              1 8
                                     1 8
```

bring down the tens

bring down the ones

738 ÷ 6 = 123
Ted needs 123 boxes.

HINTS:

- Dividing a 3-digit number by a 1-digit number :

  1st Divide
  2nd Multiply — repeat these steps until there are no more numbers to bring down
  3rd Subtract
  4th Bring down

- Don't forget to do division from left to right.

- Estimate the quotient to check the answer.

  e.g.   809 ÷ 8 = ?

  estimate   800 ÷ 8 = 100 ← the answer should be close to 100

Do the division.

①
```
     11 9
  4) 4 7 6
     4
     0 7
       4
     3 6
     3 6
     0 0
```

②
```
     1 7 1
  3) 5 1 3
     3
     2 1
     2 1
     0 3
       3
       0
```

③ 684 ÷ 6 = 114

④ 972 ÷ 4 = 243

⑤ 670 ÷ 5 = 138

⑥ 608 ÷ 8 = 751

⑦ 966 ÷ 7 = 138

⑧ 870 ÷ 5 = 174

⑨ 860 ÷ 4 = 215

⑩ 931 ÷ 7 = 133

⑪ 648 ÷ 9 = 72

⑫ 558 ÷ 6 = 96

⑬ 762 ÷ 3 = 254

⑭ 567 ÷ 9 = 63

Estimate by rounding the dividends to the nearest ten or hundred. Then do the division.

⑮ 3⟌747   **estimate** 3⟌750

⑯ 5⟌695   **estimate** 5⟌

⑰ 8⟌792   **estimate** 8⟌

⑱ 6⟌906   **estimate** 6⟌

⑲ 686 ÷ 7 = 98   **estimate** 700 ÷ 7 = 100

⑳ 326 ÷ 2 = 163   **estimate** 300 ÷ 2 = 150

㉑ 788 ÷ 4 = 197   **estimate** 800 ÷ 4 = 200

㉒ 915 ÷ 5 = 183   **estimate** 900 ÷ 5 = 180

㉓ 294 ÷ 6 = 49   **estimate** 300 ÷ 6 = 50

㉔ 416 ÷ 8 = 59   **estimate** 400 ÷ 8 = 50

㉕ 567 ÷ 3 = 219   **estimate** 600 ÷ 3 = 200

㉖ 891 ÷ 9 = 99   **estimate** 900 ÷ 9 = 100

Circle the correct answer(s).

㉗ Which problem has the smallest quotient?

A. 500 ÷ 4   B. (833 ÷ 7)   C. 738 ÷ 6

120   119   123

$$6\overline{)672}$$

㉘ Which problem has the greatest quotient?

A. 912 ÷ 8   B. 882 ÷ 9   C. (672 ÷ 6)

114   98   110

㉙ Which problems have the same quotient?

A. (381 ÷ 3)   B. 936 ÷ 8   C. 548 ÷ 4   D. (762 ÷ 6)

㉚ Which problems have quotients smaller than 100?

A. (917 ÷ 7)   B. 776 ÷ 8   C. 705 ÷ 5   D. (528 ÷ 6)

㉛ Which is the best estimation for 719 ÷ 4 ?

A. 800 ÷ 4   B. 720 ÷ 4   C. (700 ÷ 4)   D. 710 ÷ 4

㉜ What is the difference between 774 ÷ 9 and 882 ÷ 7 ?

A. 50   B. 30   C. (20)   D. 40

㉝ What is the sum of the quotients of 512 ÷ 8 and 693 ÷ 9 ?

A. 141   B. 153   C. 173   D. (151)

㉞ What is the product of the quotients of 261 ÷ 3 and 432 ÷ 6 ?

360

A. 6612   B. 6274   C. 6264   D. 6192

Solve the problems. Show your work.

㉟ Mrs White sold 750 doughnuts in 5 days. How many doughnuts were sold each day?

_____ doughnuts were sold each day.

㊱ Mrs White earned $648 in 8 days. How much did Mrs White earn each day?

㊲ Ted shares 816 g of peanuts with 5 friends. How many grams of peanuts does each child get?

㊳ May uses 973 beads to make 7 bracelets. How many beads does May use to make 1 bracelet?

㊴ Ted uses 528 blocks to build 4 towers. How many blocks are there in each tower?

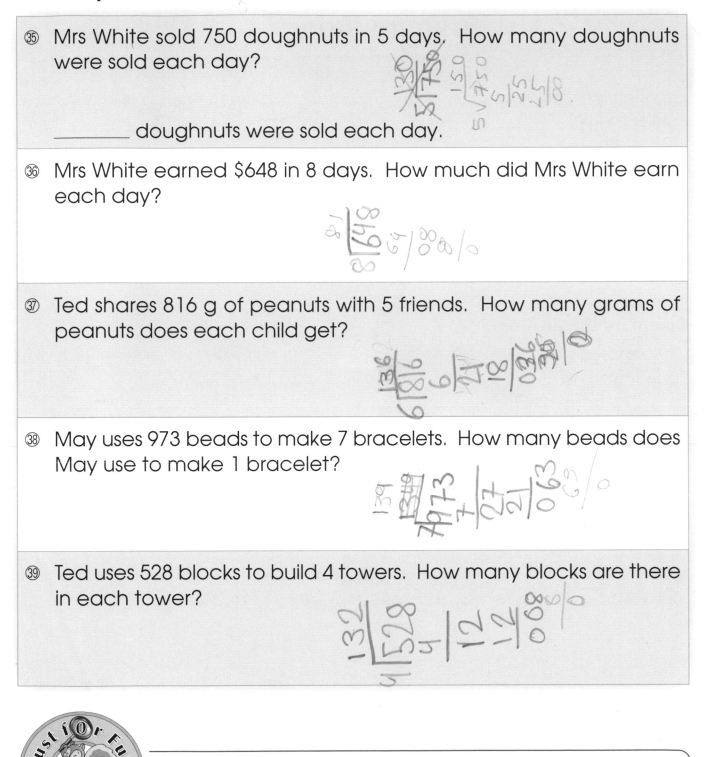

Dividing 2-digit Numbers with Remainders

Sally shares 74 candies with 4 friends. How many candies does each child get? How many candies are left?

74 ÷ 5 = 14R4
↑
14 with remainder 4

Each child gets 14 candies.
4 candies are left.

```
      Tens | Ones
         1 | 4 R 4
      5 | 7 | 4
         5
         2 | 4
         2 | 0
           | 4
```

Complete the division.

HINTS:

- Dividing a 2-digit number by a 1-digit number:

  Divide the tens and then subtract.

  Bring down the ones.

  Combine the difference from the tens and the ones and then divide.

  Write the remainder beside the quotient.

  e.g.
  ```
       1          1          19        19 R 1
   2│3 9  →  2│3 9  →  2│3 9  →  2│3 9
     2          2          2          2
     1          19         19         19
                           18         18
                            1          1
  ```

  39 ÷ 2 = 19R1

①
```
    1 5 R 2
3 │ 4 7
    3
    1 7
    1 5
      2
```

②
```
    1 2 R 3
4 │ 5 1
    4
    1 1
      8
      3
```

③
```
    1 3 R 1
6 │ 7 9
    6
    1 9
    1 8
      1
```

④
```
    1 8 R 1
2 │ 3 7
    2
    1 7
    1 6
      1
```

⑤
```
    1 5 R 1
5 │ 7 6
    5
    2 6
    2 5
      1
```

⑥
```
    1 1 R 5
8 │ 9 3
    8
    1 3
    - 8
      5
```

Do the division. Use R to show remainders.

⑦
11 R5
6)71
6
11
6
5

⑧
14 R1
4)57
4
17
16
1

⑨
16 R1
2)33
2
13
12
1

⑩
29 R2
3)89
6
29
27
2

⑪
12 R4
5)64
5
14
10
4

⑫
13 R3
7)94
7
24
21
3

⑬
14 R1
6)85
6
25
24
1

⑭
12 R3
8)99
8
19
16
3

⑮
38 R1
2)77
6
17
16
1

⑯
14 R3
5)73
5
23
20
3

⑰
13 R3
6)81
6
21
18
3

⑱
14 R3
4)59
4
19
16
3

⑲ $44 \div 3 =$ 14 R6

⑳ $86 \div 5 =$ 17 R1

㉑ $59 \div 4 =$ 14 R6

㉒ $74 \div 6 =$ 12 R2

㉓ $66 \div 5 =$ 13 R1

㉔ $89 \div 7 =$ 12 R5

㉕ $97 \div 4 =$ 24 R1

㉖ $80 \div 3 =$ 26 R2

㉗ $75 \div 2 =$ 37 R1

㉘ $89 \div 5 =$ 17 R4

㉙ $91 \div 8 =$ 11 R3

㉚ $61 \div 4 =$ 15 R1

㉛ $70 \div 6 =$ 11 R4

㉜ $59 \div 2 =$ 29 R1

Do the division. Then find the problems with remainder 1 and write the letters in order in (55) to find what May buys for Ted.

㉝ $5 \overline{)72}$ 14R2 — s	㉞ $4 \overline{)67}$ 16R3 — b	㉟ $3 \overline{)47}$ 15R2 — m	㊱ $2 \overline{)55}$ 27R1 — r
㊲ $5 \overline{)61}$ 12R1 — a	㊳ $7 \overline{)87}$ 12R3 — l	㊴ $8 \overline{)95}$ 11 — t	㊵ $6 \overline{)73}$ 12R1 — d

㊶ 92 ÷ 7 = 13R1 (i)	㊷ 94 ÷ 4 = 23R2 (q)
㊸ 73 ÷ 2 = 36R1 (o)	㊹ 64 ÷ 5 = 12R2 (p)
㊺ 58 ÷ 3 = 19R1 (c)	㊻ 71 ÷ 4 = 17R (h)
㊼ 96 ÷ 5 = 19R1 (a)	㊽ 82 ÷ 7 = 11R (k)
㊾ 98 ÷ 8 = 12R2 (d)	㊿ 74 ÷ 5 = 14R (g)
(51) 90 ÷ 7 = 12R6 (e)	(52) 80 ÷ 6 = 13R (y)
(53) 37 ÷ 2 = 18R1 (r)	(54) 50 ÷ 3 = 16R (f)

(55)

A _ _ _ _ _ _   _ _ _ .

Solve the problems. Show your work.

㊶ Mrs Stanley puts 89 eggs equally in 6 boxes. How many eggs are there in each box? How many eggs are left?

There are ___14___ eggs in each box. ___5___ eggs are left.

㊷ Samantha puts 97 sandwiches equally in 7 bags. How many sandwiches are there in each bag? How many sandwiches are left?

㊸ Ted pours 47 glasses of water equally into 3 buckets. How many glasses of water are there in each bucket? How many glasses of water are left?

㊹ A class of 29 students is divided into 2 groups. How many students are there in each group? How many student is left ?

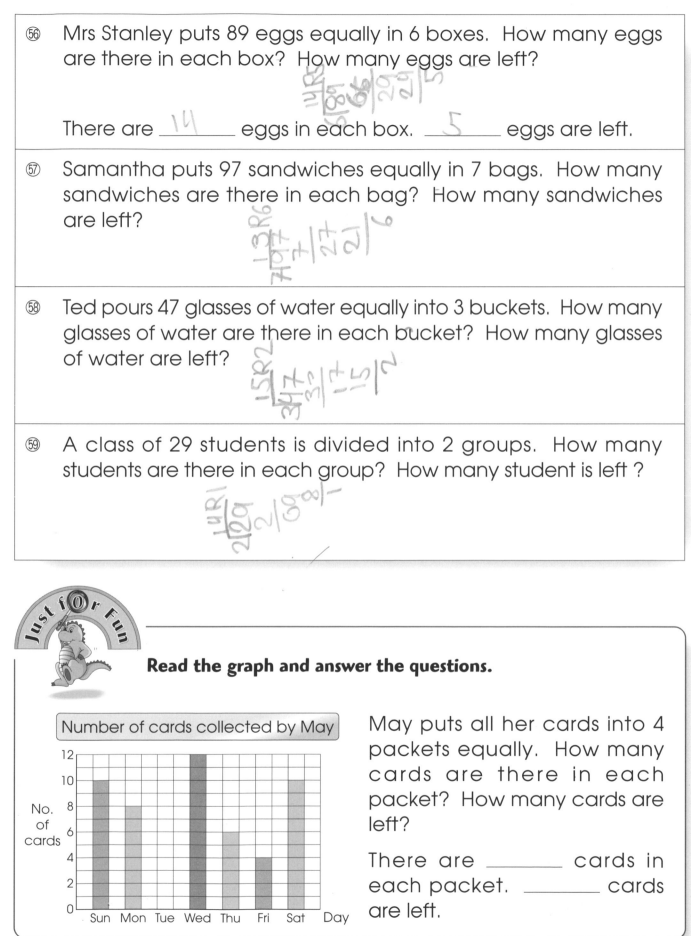

Just for Fun

Read the graph and answer the questions.

Number of cards collected by May

May puts all her cards into 4 packets equally. How many cards are there in each packet? How many cards are left?

There are _____ cards in each packet. _____ cards are left.

13 Dividing 3-digit Numbers with Remainders

Mr Smith divides 538 stickers among 4 classes.
How many stickers are for each class?
How many stickers are left?

```
    1 3 4 R2 ←— remainder
  4)5 3 8
    4
    1 3
    1 2
      1 8
      1 6
        2
```

538 ÷ 4 = 134R2
134 stickers are for each class.
2 stickers are left.

HINTS:

- Follow these steps to do division :

  1st Divide   **2nd** Multiply
  3rd Subtract   **4th** Bring down

- Use the following formula to check answers:

  Q x D + R = Dividend

  Quotient ⌐ ⌐ Remainder
          Divisor

  e.g.   Is 659 ÷ 3 = 219R2 correct?

  check 219 x 3 + 2 = 657 + 2
                   = 659
                   = Dividend

  So, 659 ÷ 3 = 219R2 is correct.

Do the division. Use R to show the remainders.

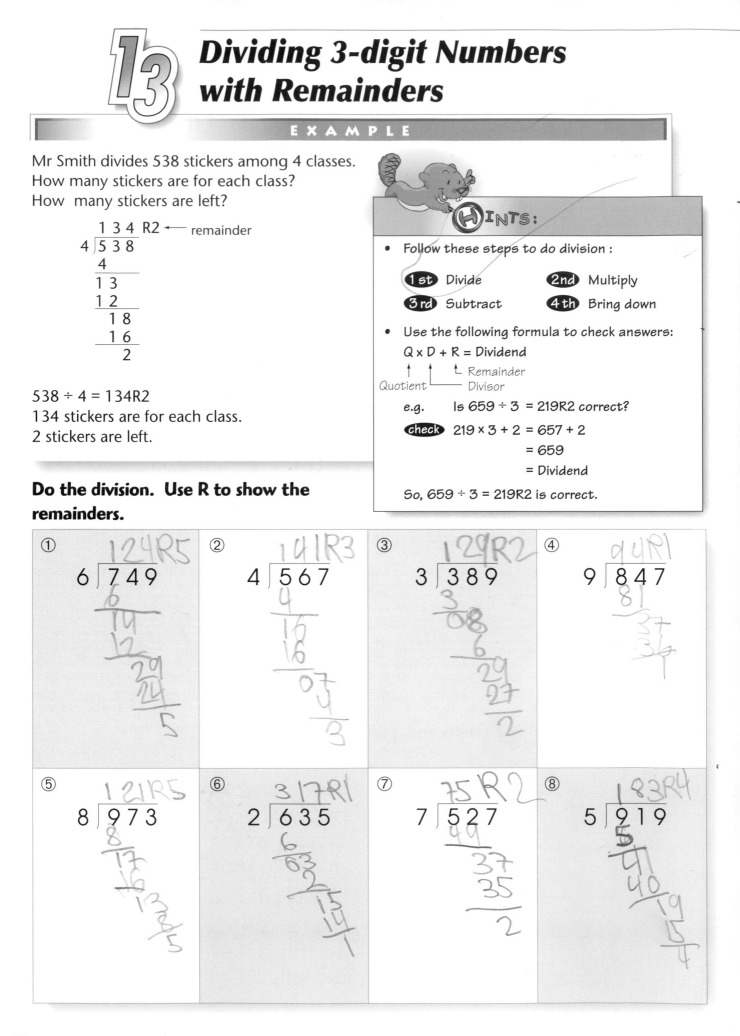

① 6)749

② 4)567

③ 3)389

④ 9)847

⑤ 8)973

⑥ 2)635

⑦ 7)527

⑧ 5)919

⑨ 136 R1
3) 409

⑩ 93 R3
7) 654

⑪ 131 R4
6) 789

⑫ 271 R1
2) 543

⑬ 68 R1
9) 613

⑭ 28 R2
3) 854

⑮ 236 R1
4) 945

⑯ 88 R2
8) 706

⑰ 479 ÷ 5 = 95 R8

⑱ 682 ÷ 6 = 113 R6

⑲ 574 ÷ 3 = 191 R3

⑳ 908 ÷ 8 = 113 R5

㉑ 729 ÷ 4 = 182 R25

㉒ 395 ÷ 7 = 56 R4

㉓ 286 ÷ 5 = 57 R2

㉔ 626 ÷ 4 = 156 R5

㉕ 486 ÷ 7 = 69 R4

㉖ 772 ÷ 3 = 257 R3

㉗ 503 ÷ 4 = 125 R3

㉘ 422 ÷ 9 = 46 R8

㉙ 621 ÷ 5 = 124 R2

㉚ 519 ÷ 2 = 259 R5

㉛ 734 ÷ 6 = 122 R3

㉜ 849 ÷ 7 = 121 R2

㉝ 653 ÷ 8 = 81 R6

㉞ 599 ÷ 6 = 99 R8

Estimate by rounding the dividends to the nearest ten or hundred. Then do the division.

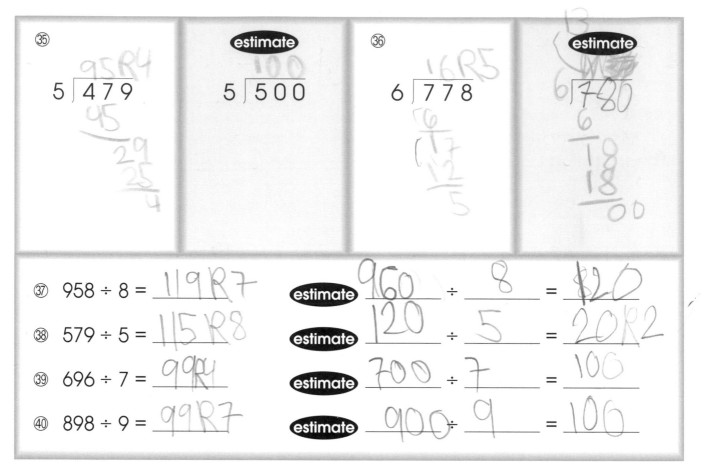

㉟ 95R4
5)479
 45
 29
 25
  4

estimate
100
5)500

㊱ 16R5
6)778
 6
 17
 12
  5

estimate
6)780
 6
 18
 18
  00

㊲ 958 ÷ 8 = __119R7__   estimate __960__ ÷ __8__ = __820__

㊳ 579 ÷ 5 = __115R8__   estimate __120__ ÷ __5__ = __20R2__

㊴ 696 ÷ 7 = __99R4__   estimate __700__ ÷ __7__ = __100__

㊵ 898 ÷ 9 = __99R7__   estimate __900__ ÷ __9__ = __100__

Do the division. Then check the answers.

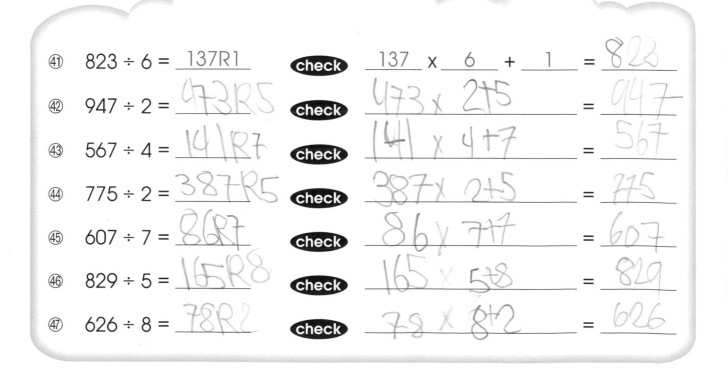

㊶ 823 ÷ 6 = __137R1__   check __137__ x __6__ + __1__ = __822__

㊷ 947 ÷ 2 = __473R5__   check __473__ x __2+5__ = __947__

㊸ 567 ÷ 4 = __141R7__   check __141__ x __4+7__ = __567__

㊹ 775 ÷ 2 = __387R5__   check __387__ x __2+5__ = __775__

㊺ 607 ÷ 7 = __86R7__   check __86__ x __7+7__ = __607__

㊻ 829 ÷ 5 = __165R8__   check __165__ x __5+8__ = __829__

㊼ 626 ÷ 8 = __78R2__   check __78__ x __8+2__ = __626__

Solve the problems. Show your work.

48. There are 748 blocks for 5 children. How many blocks are there for each child? How many blocks are left?

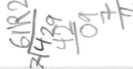

There are _____ blocks for each child. _____ blocks are left.

49. May's mother puts 429 cookies in 7 boxes. How many cookies are there in each box? How many cookies are left?

50. Ted shares 260 grams of golden raisins with 2 friends. How many grams of golden raisins does each child get? How many grams of golden raisins are left?

51. Ted puts 369 baseball cards in 5 boxes. How many baseball cards are there in each box? How many baseball cards are left?

52. Each box of candies costs $8. How many boxes of candies can May buy with $462? How much is left?

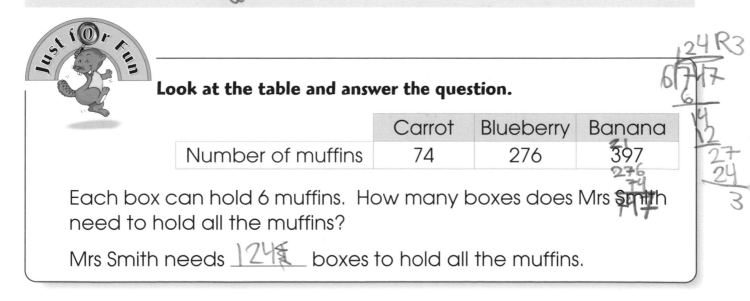

Just for Fun

Look at the table and answer the question.

	Carrot	Blueberry	Banana
Number of muffins	74	276	397

Each box can hold 6 muffins. How many boxes does Mrs Smith need to hold all the muffins?

Mrs Smith needs _____ boxes to hold all the muffins.

14 Zeros in the Quotient

EXAMPLE

3 bags of flour weigh 624 grams. How heavy is 1 bag of flour?

Divide the hundreds:

$$
\begin{array}{r}
2 \\
3\overline{)624} \\
6
\end{array}
$$

Divide the tens:

$$
\begin{array}{r}
20 \\
3\overline{)624} \\
6 \\
\hline
2 \\
0 \\
\hline
2
\end{array}
$$

← no groups of 3 go into 2; put a '0' in the quotient

Divide the ones:

$$
\begin{array}{r}
208 \\
3\overline{)624} \\
6 \\
\hline
2 \\
0 \\
\hline
24 \\
24
\end{array}
$$

$624 \div 3 = 208$

1 bag of flour weighs 208 grams.

Do the division. Use R to show the remainders.

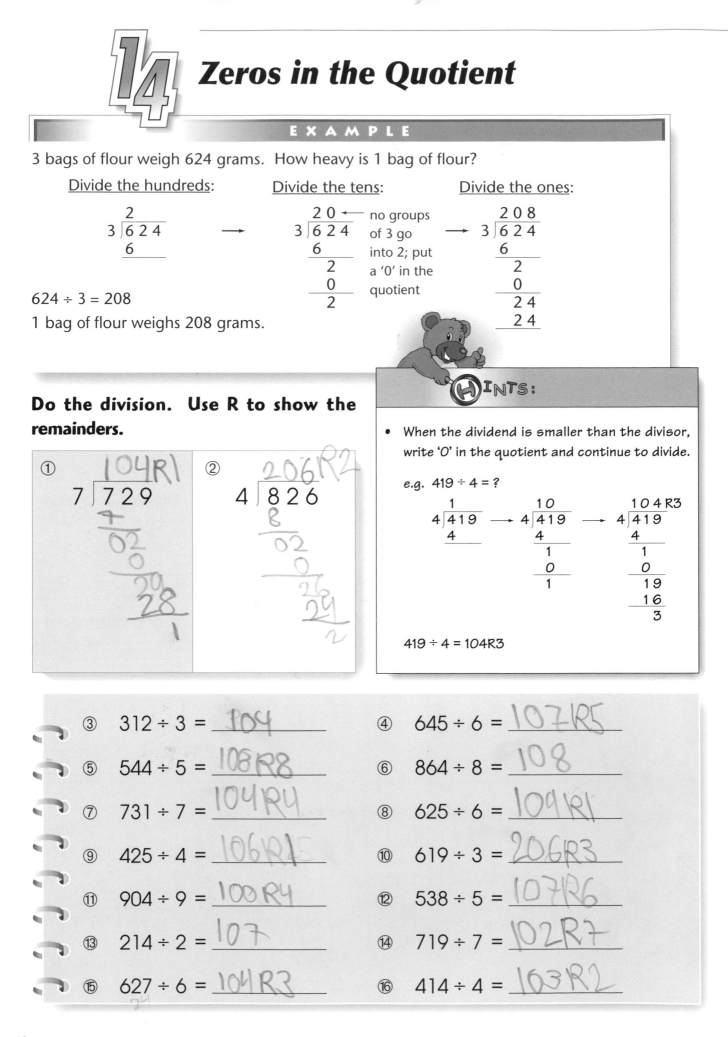

①
$$
\begin{array}{r}
104\text{R}1 \\
7\overline{)729} \\
7 \\
\hline
02 \\
0 \\
\hline
29 \\
28 \\
\hline
1
\end{array}
$$

②
$$
\begin{array}{r}
206\text{R}2 \\
4\overline{)826} \\
8 \\
\hline
02 \\
0 \\
\hline
26 \\
24 \\
\hline
2
\end{array}
$$

HINTS:

- When the dividend is smaller than the divisor, write '0' in the quotient and continue to divide.

e.g. $419 \div 4 = ?$

$$
\begin{array}{r}
1 \\
4\overline{)419} \\
4
\end{array}
\longrightarrow
\begin{array}{r}
10 \\
4\overline{)419} \\
4 \\
\hline
1 \\
0 \\
\hline
1
\end{array}
\longrightarrow
\begin{array}{r}
104\text{R}3 \\
4\overline{)419} \\
4 \\
\hline
1 \\
0 \\
\hline
19 \\
16 \\
\hline
3
\end{array}
$$

$419 \div 4 = 104\text{R}3$

---

③ $312 \div 3 =$ __104__

④ $645 \div 6 =$ __107R5__

⑤ $544 \div 5 =$ __108R8__

⑥ $864 \div 8 =$ __108__

⑦ $731 \div 7 =$ __104R4__

⑧ $625 \div 6 =$ __109R1__

⑨ $425 \div 4 =$ __106R15__

⑩ $619 \div 3 =$ __206R3__

⑪ $904 \div 9 =$ __100R4__

⑫ $538 \div 5 =$ __107R6__

⑬ $214 \div 2 =$ __107__

⑭ $719 \div 7 =$ __102R7__

⑮ $627 \div 6 =$ __104R3__

⑯ $414 \div 4 =$ __103R2__

Help Sally check her answers. If the answer is correct, put a ✓ in the ◯ ; other-wise put a ✗ .

⑰ 709 ÷ 7 = <u>101R3</u> ⓧ **check** <u>101</u> × <u>7</u> + <u>3</u> = <u>710</u>

⑱ 627 ÷ 6 = <u>104R3</u> ✓ **check** 104 × 6 + 3 = 627

⑲ 539 ÷ 5 = <u>106R4</u> ⓧ **check** 106 × 5 + 4 = 534

⑳ 423 ÷ 4 = <u>105R3</u> ✓ **check** 105 × 4 + 3 = 423

㉑ 976 ÷ 9 = <u>108R4</u> ✓ **check** 108 × 9 + 4 = 976

㉒ 874 ÷ 8 = <u>109R6</u> ⓧ **check** 109 × 8 + 6 = 878

㉓ 626 ÷ 3 = <u>208R2</u> ✓ **check** 208 × 3 + 2 = 626

Do the division. Then check the answers.

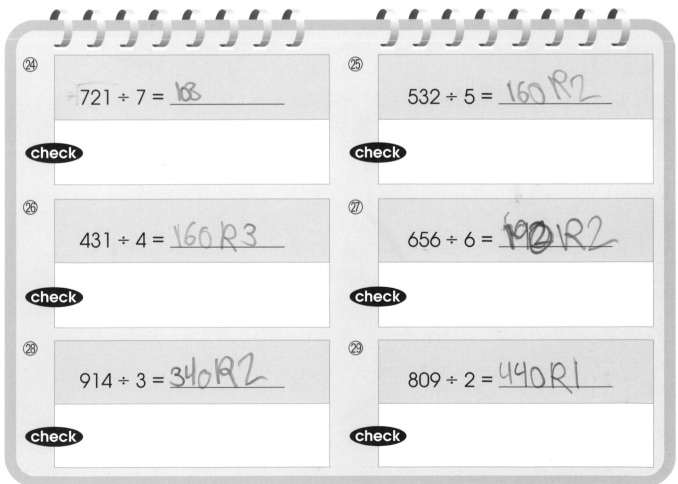

㉔ 721 ÷ 7 = <u>108</u>

check

㉕ 532 ÷ 5 = <u>160 R2</u>

check

㉖ 431 ÷ 4 = <u>160 R3</u>

check

㉗ 656 ÷ 6 = <u>109 R2</u>

check

㉘ 914 ÷ 3 = <u>340 R2</u>

check

㉙ 809 ÷ 2 = <u>440 R1</u>

check

In each group, use 4 of the numbers to complete the division.

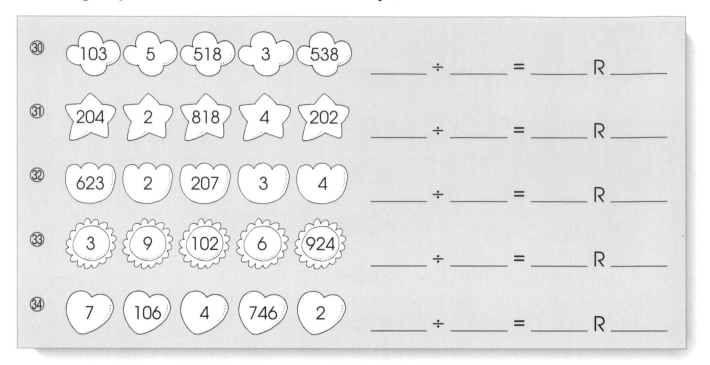

30 103 5 518 3 538

_____ ÷ _____ = _____ R _____

31 204 2 818 4 202

_____ ÷ _____ = _____ R _____

32 623 2 207 3 4

_____ ÷ _____ = _____ R _____

33 3 9 102 6 924

_____ ÷ _____ = _____ R _____

34 7 106 4 746 2

_____ ÷ _____ = _____ R _____

Match the division sentences that have the same answers. Write the letters in the rings.

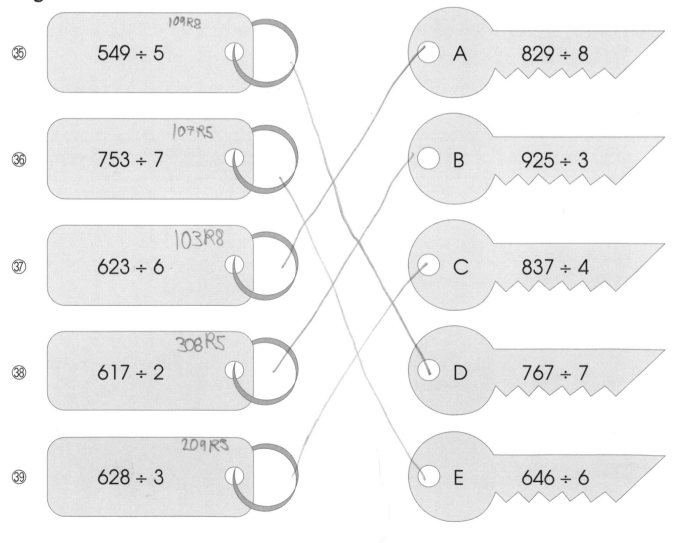

35 549 ÷ 5   109R8

36 753 ÷ 7   107R5

37 623 ÷ 6   103R8

38 617 ÷ 2   308R5

39 628 ÷ 3   209R5

A   829 ÷ 8

B   925 ÷ 3

C   837 ÷ 4

D   767 ÷ 7

E   646 ÷ 6

Solve the problems. Show your work.

㊵ Ted puts 632 marbles in 6 jars. How many marbles are there in each jar? How many marbles are left?

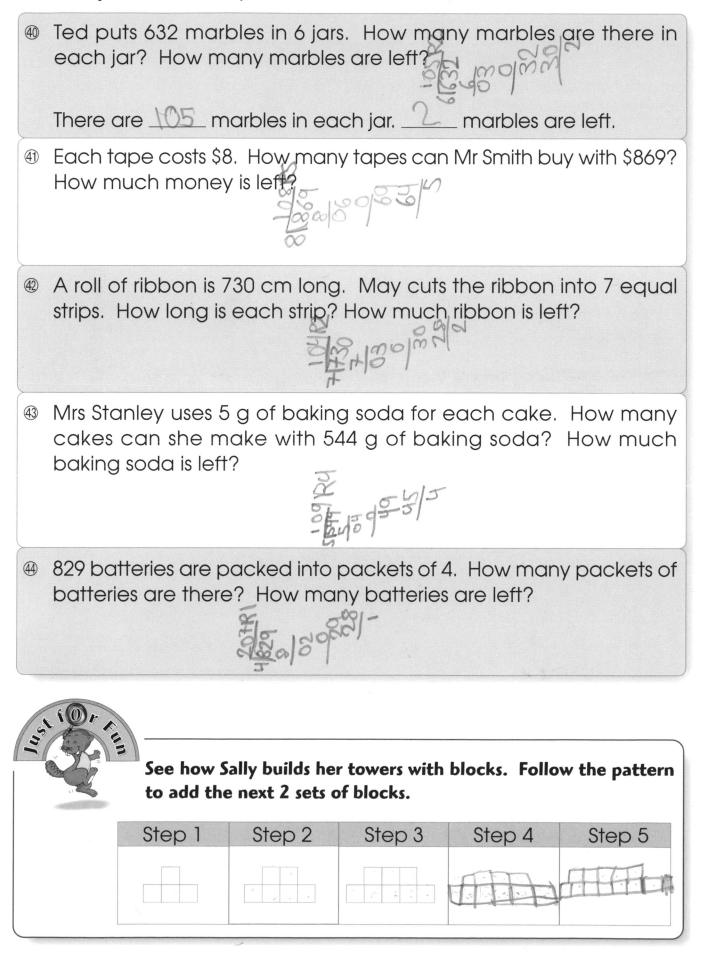

There are __105__ marbles in each jar. __2__ marbles are left.

㊶ Each tape costs $8. How many tapes can Mr Smith buy with $869? How much money is left?

㊷ A roll of ribbon is 730 cm long. May cuts the ribbon into 7 equal strips. How long is each strip? How much ribbon is left?

㊸ Mrs Stanley uses 5 g of baking soda for each cake. How many cakes can she make with 544 g of baking soda? How much baking soda is left?

㊹ 829 batteries are packed into packets of 4. How many packets of batteries are there? How many batteries are left?

Just for Fun

See how Sally builds her towers with blocks. Follow the pattern to add the next 2 sets of blocks.

Step 1	Step 2	Step 3	Step 4	Step 5

Dividing 4-digit Numbers

Uncle Sam puts 4268 oranges into 8 boxes. How many oranges are there in each box? How many oranges are left?

Divide the thousands:	Divide the hundreds:	Divide the tens:	Divide the ones:	Write the remainder:

$$8\overline{)4268}$$

no groups of 8 in 4; move to the right and try with a bigger number

$$8\overline{)\begin{array}{c}5\\4268\\40\\\hline 2\end{array}}$$

$$8\overline{)\begin{array}{c}53\\4268\\40\\\hline 26\\24\\\hline 2\end{array}}$$

$$8\overline{)\begin{array}{c}533\\4268\\40\\\hline 26\\24\\\hline 28\\24\\\hline 4\end{array}}$$

$$8\overline{)\begin{array}{c}533\,R\,4\\4268\\40\\\hline 26\\24\\\hline 28\\24\\\hline 4\end{array}}$$

There are 533 oranges in each box.
4 oranges are left.

Do the division.

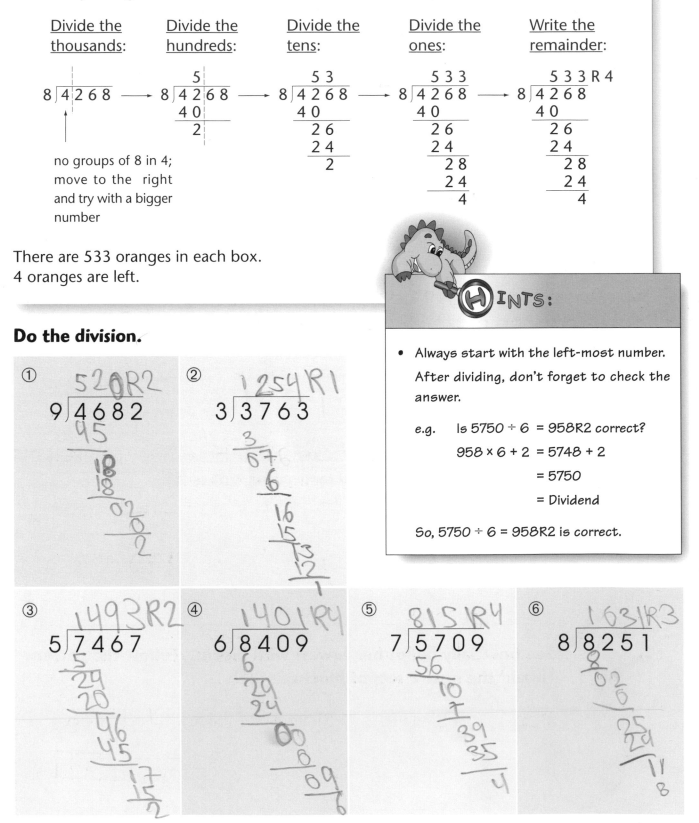

①
$$9\overline{)4682}$$
520 R2

②
$$3\overline{)3763}$$
1254 R1

③
$$5\overline{)7467}$$
1493 R2

④
$$6\overline{)8409}$$
1401 R4

⑤
$$7\overline{)5709}$$
815 R4

⑥
$$8\overline{)8251}$$
1031 R3

HINTS:

- Always start with the left-most number. After dividing, don't forget to check the answer.

  e.g. Is 5750 ÷ 6 = 958R2 correct?

  958 × 6 + 2 = 5748 + 2

  = 5750

  = Dividend

  So, 5750 ÷ 6 = 958R2 is correct.

⑦

1415 R3

$$4 \overline{) 5803}$$

⑧

1495 R3

$$5 \overline{) 7478}$$

⑨

129 R4

$$7 \overline{) 9074}$$

⑩

491

$$8 \overline{) 3982}$$

64

⑪ $2095 ÷ 3 =$ 698 R3

⑫ $6874 ÷ 5 =$ 1374 R8

⑬ $4105 ÷ 8 =$ 513 R1

⑭ $8753 ÷ 9 =$ 972 R5

⑮ $6582 ÷ 7 =$ 940 R2

⑯ $7742 ÷ 4 =$ 1935 R5

⑰ $3394 ÷ 6 =$ 565 R6

⑱ $5680 ÷ 8 =$ 710

⑲ $5217 ÷ 2 =$ 2608 R5

⑳ $4094 ÷ 7 =$ 584 R8

㉑ $8753 ÷ 4 =$ 2188 R2

㉒ $3299 ÷ 5 =$ 659 R8

㉓ $2574 ÷ 9 =$ 286

㉔ $2980 ÷ 6 =$ 496 R6

㉕ $8061 ÷ 5 =$ 1612 R2

㉖ $6524 ÷ 3 =$ 2174 R6

㉗ $7206 ÷ 8 =$ 900 R7

㉘ $8219 ÷ 9 =$ 913 R2

㉙ $4020 ÷ 6 =$ 670

㉚ $3742 ÷ 7 =$ 534 R5

㉛ $9224 ÷ 9 =$ 1024 R8

㉜ $5073 ÷ 4 =$ 1268 R2

㉝ $4316 ÷ 3 =$ 1438 R6

㉞ $1085 ÷ 9 =$ 120 R5

See how May stores her things. Complete the table.

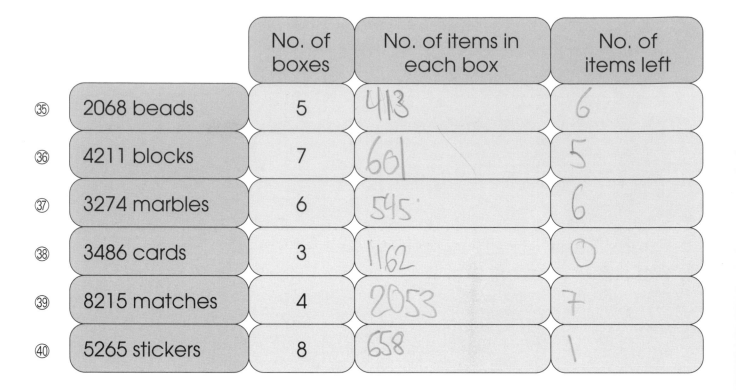

		No. of boxes	No. of items in each box	No. of items left
㉟	2068 beads	5	413	6
㊱	4211 blocks	7	601	5
㊲	3274 marbles	6	545	6
㊳	3486 cards	3	1162	0
㊴	8215 matches	4	2053	7
㊵	5265 stickers	8	658	1

Do the division. Then find the problems with no remainders and write the letters in order in �51 to complete what Sally says.

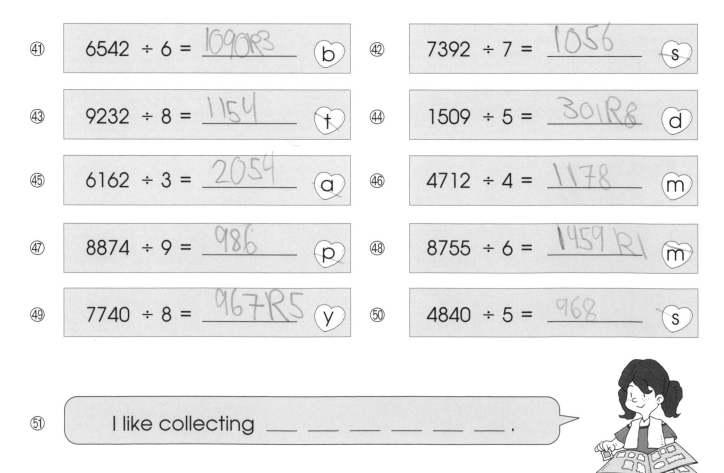

㊶ 6542 ÷ 6 = 1090R3 (b)

㊷ 7392 ÷ 7 = 1056 (s)

㊸ 9232 ÷ 8 = 1154 (t)

㊹ 1509 ÷ 5 = 301R8 (d)

㊺ 6162 ÷ 3 = 2054 (a)

㊻ 4712 ÷ 4 = 1178 (m)

㊼ 8874 ÷ 9 = 986 (p)

㊽ 8755 ÷ 6 = 1459 R1 (m)

㊾ 7740 ÷ 8 = 967R5 (y)

㊿ 4840 ÷ 5 = 968 (s)

(51) I like collecting ___ ___ ___ ___ ___ ___ .

Solve the problems. Show your work.

52 3265 cookies were sold in 5 days. How many cookies were sold each day?

_____ cookies were sold each day.

53 Ted can go 7560 cm in 7 minutes. How far can he go in 1 minute?

54 May uses 8 strips of ribbon for each craft item. How many craft items can she make with 8268 strips of ribbon? How many strips of ribbon are left?

55 Mr Smith puts 4286 doughnuts into boxes of 6 doughnuts. How many boxes of doughnuts are there? How many doughnuts are left?

56 May uses 9 beads to make a bracelet. How many bracelets can she make with 2086 beads? How many beads are left?

Just for Fun

Draw the top, front and side view of the tower in the space below to show how it looks.

Top view

Side view

Front view

Top view	Side view	Front view
. . . . .	. . . . .	. . . . .
. . . . .	. . . . .	. . . . .
. . . . .	. . . . .	. . . . .
. . . . .	. . . . .	. . . . .

More Multiplying and Dividing

EXAMPLE

5 children share 8 boxes of chocolate each containing 89 chocolates. How many chocolates does each child get? How many chocolates are left?

89 x 8 = 712   ←   **1st** Use multiplication to find the total number of chocolates.

712 ÷ 5 = 142 R2   ←   **2 nd** Use division to find the number of chocolates each child gets and the number of chocolates left.

Each child gets 142 chocolates.
2 chocolates are left.

Find the answers.

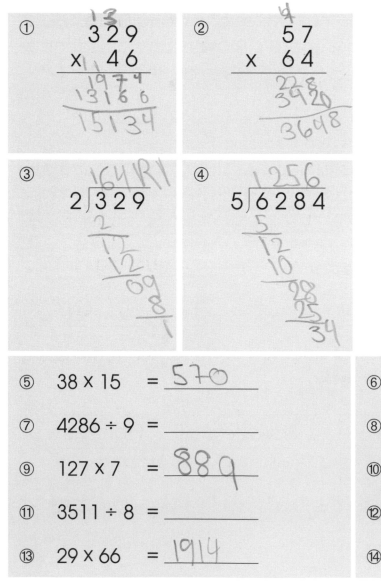

①
$$329 \times 46$$
```
    1 3
    3 2 9
  x   4 6
  1 9 7 4
1 3 1 6 6
1 5 1 3 4
```

②
$$57 \times 64$$
```
     4
     5 7
   x 6 4
   2 2 8
 3 9 2 0
 3 6 4 8
```

③
```
    1 6 4 R1
 2 ) 3 2 9
    2
    1 2
    1 2
      0 9
        8
        1
```

④
```
    1 2 5 6
 5 ) 6 2 8 4
    5
    1 2
    1 0
      2 8
      2 5
        3 4
```

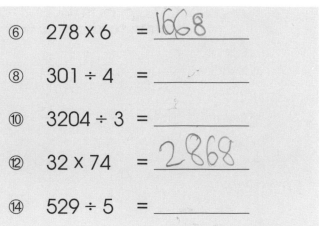

- Don't think that every problem needs one operation only. Sometimes more than one operation is needed. Try to write two appropriate number sentences to solve a two-step problem.

  e.g. Sam earned $735 in a week. How much did Sam earn in 3 days?

  735 ÷ 7 = 105 ← earnings per day
  105 x 3 = 315 ← earnings in 3 days

  Sam earned $315 in 3 days.

⑤ 38 X 15 = 570

⑥ 278 X 6 = 1668

⑦ 4286 ÷ 9 = _____

⑧ 301 ÷ 4 = _____

⑨ 127 X 7 = 889

⑩ 3204 ÷ 3 = _____

⑪ 3511 ÷ 8 = _____

⑫ 32 X 74 = 2868

⑬ 29 X 66 = 1914

⑭ 529 ÷ 5 = _____

Circle the correct answers.

⑮ Which number sentences have the same product?

   A. 44×25 B. 221×5 C. 74×15 D. 22×50

⑯ Which number sentences have the same quotient?

   A. $407 \div 6$ B. $527 \div 8$ C. $267 \div 4$ D. $592 \div 9$

⑰ Which number sentences have the same remainder?

   A. $1068 \div 9$ B. $1159 \div 8$ C. $3758 \div 7$ D. $813 \div 6$

⑱ Which numbers, when divided by 8, have a remainder of 3?

   A. 3899   B. 8753   C. 6822   D. 9395

⑲ Which numbers, when divided by 7, have a quotient of 106?

   A. 739   B. 743   C. 746   D. 749

⑳ Which numbers are divisible by 6?

   A. 8492   B. 784   C. 7650   D. 8184

㉑ Which number sentences have a product greater than 6000?

   A. 849×8 B. 54×99 C. 74×88 D. 65×74

㉒ Which number sentences have a product that is a multiple of 10?

   A. 426×5 B. 126×9 C. 75×81 D. 85×44

㉓ Which number sentences have the same answer?

   A. 24×36 B. 16×37 C. $2368 \div 4$ D. $2593 \div 3$

Solve the problems. Show your work.

㉔ Each basket holds 26 apples. How many apples are there in 16 baskets?

There are _____ apples in 16 baskets.

㉕ Each basket of apples costs $7. How many baskets of apples can John buy with $200? How much money is left?

㉖ May buys 8 bags of candies each containing 128 candies. How many candies does May buy?

㉗ May shares her candies with 4 friends. How many candies does each child get? How many candies are left?

㉘ Aunt Pam sold 882 pizzas in 6 days. How many pizzas were sold each day?

㉙ Each pizza costs $4. How much money did Aunt Pam get for selling pizzas each day?

㉚ Aunt Pam uses 9 g of pepper for each pizza. How many g of pepper does she need to make 75 pizzas?

Write two number sentences to solve each problem. Show your work.

③① 4 girls share 6 boxes of gumballs each containing 325 gumballs. How many gumballs does each girl get? How many gumballs are left?

_____ X _____ = _____

_____ ÷ _____ = _____

Each girl gets _____ gumballs. _____ gumballs are left.

③② There are 484 sheets of paper in 2 packs. How many sheets of paper are there in 7 packs?

③③ Mrs Stanley gives a box of stickers to her class of 36 students. Each student gets 48 stickers. If only 7 students share the stickers, how many stickers does each student get? How many stickers are left?

③④ The total weight of 6 sacks of soil is 5910 grams. What is the total weight of 9 sacks of soil?

Just for Fun

Find the answers.

① ▲ + ● − ▲ = 9   ● = _____

② ■ ÷ ■ + ■ ÷ ■ = ?   ? = _____

Final Review

Do the division. Then find the problems with remainder 1 and write the letters in order in ㉓ to complete what May says.

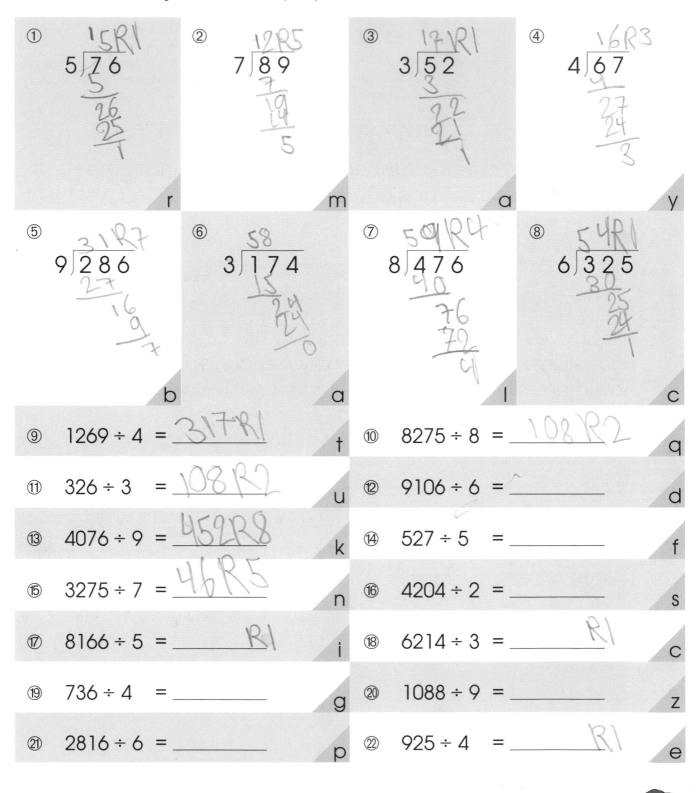

① 5)76 15R1   r

② 7)89 12R5   m

③ 3)52 17R1   a

④ 4)67 16R3   y

⑤ 9)286 31R7   b

⑥ 3)174 58   a

⑦ 8)476 59R4   l

⑧ 6)325 54R1   c

⑨ 1269 ÷ 4 = 317R1   t

⑩ 8275 ÷ 8 = 108R2   q

⑪ 326 ÷ 3 = 108R2   u

⑫ 9106 ÷ 6 = _____   d

⑬ 4076 ÷ 9 = 452R8   k

⑭ 527 ÷ 5 = _____   f

⑮ 3275 ÷ 7 = 46R5   n

⑯ 4204 ÷ 2 = _____   s

⑰ 8166 ÷ 5 = ____R1   i

⑱ 6214 ÷ 3 = ____R1   c

⑲ 736 ÷ 4 = _____   g

⑳ 1088 ÷ 9 = _____   z

㉑ 2816 ÷ 6 = _____   p

㉒ 925 ÷ 4 = ____R1   e

㉓ P r a c t i c e makes perfect!

Do the division. Then check the answers.

㉔ 276 ÷ 9 = _____ (check) _____ X _____ + _____ = _____

㉕ 1294 ÷ 5 = _____ (check) _____ X _____ + _____ = _____

㉖ 3266 ÷ 4 = _____ (check) _____ X _____ + _____ = _____

㉗ 825 ÷ 7 = _____ (check) _____ X _____ + _____ = _____

㉘ 7086 ÷ 8 = _____ (check) _____ X _____ + _____ = _____

㉙ 6283 ÷ 6 = _____ (check) _____ X _____ + _____ = _____

㉚ 5774 ÷ 3 = _____ (check) _____ X _____ + _____ = _____

Do the multiplication.

㉛
```
  564
x   9
_____
```

㉜
```
  876
x   3
_____
```

㉝
```
  298
x   4
_____
```

㉞
```
  763
x   5
_____
```

㉟
```
   28
x  45
_____
```

㊱
```
   37
x  82
_____
```

㊲
```
   66
x  53
_____
```

㊳
```
   21
x  78
_____
```

㊴ 64 X 18 = _____

㊵ 389 X 8 = _____

㊶ 612 X 7 = _____

㊷ 34 X 34 = _____

㊸ 371 X 6 = _____

㊹ 287 X 2 = _____

㊺ 58 X 26 = _____

㊻ 49 X 51 = _____

Complete the multiplication and division sentences using each group of numbers.

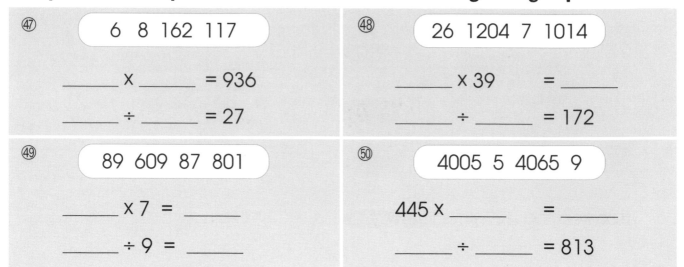

47 6 8 162 117

_____ × _____ = 936

_____ ÷ _____ = 27

48 26 1204 7 1014

_____ × 39 = _____

_____ ÷ _____ = 172

49 89 609 87 801

_____ × 7 = _____

_____ ÷ 9 = _____

50 4005 5 4065 9

445 × _____ = _____

_____ ÷ _____ = 813

Fill in the missing numbers.

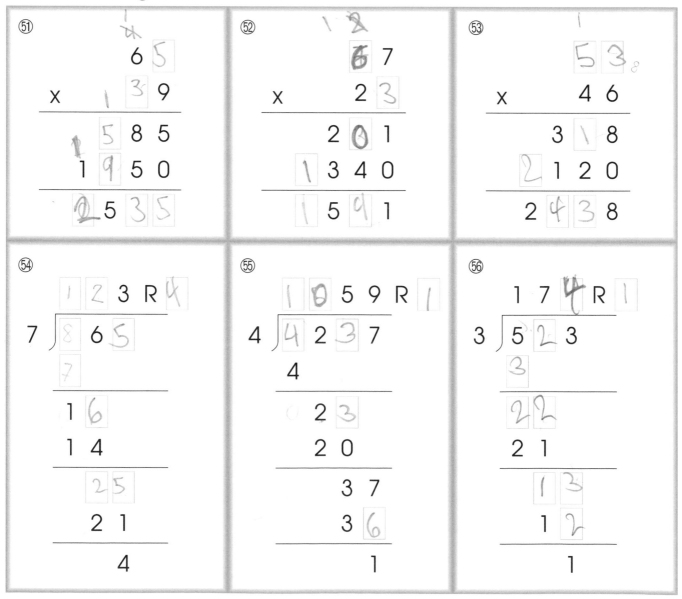

51

```
        6 5
  x   1 3 9
  ─────────
      5 8 5
  1 9 5 0
  ─────────
  2 5 3 5
```

52

```
      6 7
  x   2 3
  ───────
    2 0 1
  1 3 4 0
  ───────
  1 5 9 1
```

53

```
      5 3
  x   4 6
  ───────
    3 1 8
  2 1 2 0
  ───────
  2 4 3 8
```

54

```
        1 2 3 R 4
    7 ) 8 6 5
        7
        ───
        1 6
        1 4
        ───
          2 5
          2 1
          ───
            4
```

55

```
        1 0 5 9 R 1
    4 ) 4 2 3 7
        4
        ───
          2 3
          2 0
          ───
            3 7
            3 6
            ───
              1
```

56

```
        1 7 4 R 1
    3 ) 5 2 3
        3
        ───
        2 2
        2 1
        ───
          1 3
          1 2
          ───
            1
```

Solve the problems. Show your work.

57 A roll of string is 4206 cm long. Bill cuts the string into 8 equal strips. How long is each strip? How much string is left?

Each strip is __525__ cm long. __6__ cm of string is left.

58 Each magazine costs $5. How much money does Mr Smith get from selling 427 magazines?

59 Aunt Pam puts 826 flowers equally in 6 baskets. How many flowers are there in each basket? How many flowers are left?

60 The total weight of 7 bags of sugar is 1995 grams. How heavy is 1 bag of sugar?

61 Ted buys 5 boxes of marbles. Each box has 123 marbles. How many marbles does Ted buy altogether?

62 Ted puts his marbles equally in 6 bags. How many marbles are there in each bag? How many marbles are left?

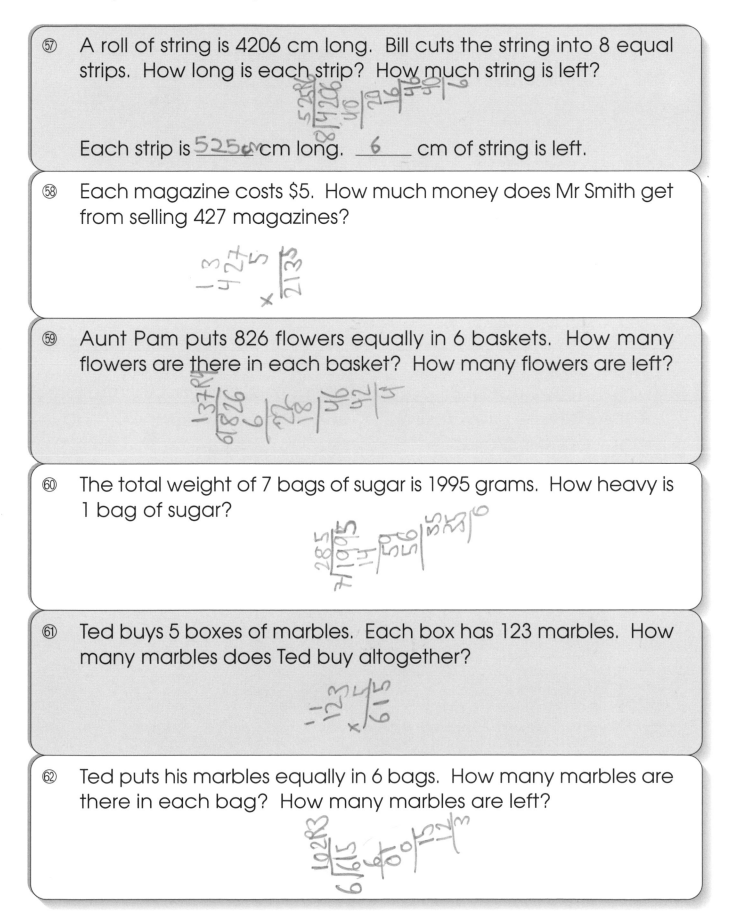

Write two number sentences to solve each problem.

63. There are 275 mL of juice in one box. May pours 6 boxes of juice equally into 4 bottles. How much juice does each bottle hold? How much juice is left?

$$\underline{275} \times \underline{6} = \underline{1650} \qquad \underline{1650} \div \underline{4} = \underline{412 \text{ R} 2}$$

Each bottles holds $\underline{412}$ mL of juice. $\underline{2}$ mL of juice is left.

64. David and Ted have the same number of stamps making a total of 826 stamps. George has 4 times as many stamps as David. How many stamps does George have?

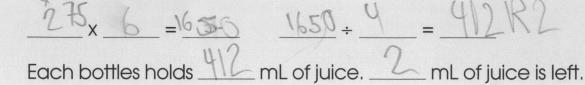

65. Mrs Stanley bought 86 dozens of pencils. She gave 5 pencils to each student. How many students can get the pencils? How many pencils are left?

66. The total weight of 8 boxes of crackers is 3640 grams. What is the total weight of 7 boxes of crackers?

67. Ted's mother wants to bake 56 cakes. Her oven can only bake 4 cakes every 2 hours. How long will it take her to bake all the cakes?

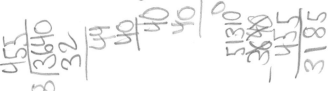

Overview

In Section I, students practised multiplication and division of whole numbers. In Section II, these skills are built upon. Students also work with fractions and decimals.

In the Geometry units, they learn to draw and analyse 3-D shapes. The study of 2-D shapes includes different types of quadrilaterals.

In units involving simple measurements, students learn to measure and calculate the area of different shapes, and to determine the volume of different structures.

Graphing includes bar graphs as well as plotting coordinates as points on a grid. The concepts of number patterns and simple equations are introduced.

Money applications include finding sale prices in dollars and cents.

Throughout the book, there is an emphasis on developing the ability to estimate an answer before calculating it.

eighteen#

Find the sums or differences.

| ① $\begin{array}{r} 627 \\ +\ 346 \\ \hline \end{array}$ | ② $\begin{array}{r} 545 \\ -\ 248 \\ \hline \end{array}$ | ③ $\begin{array}{r} 402 \\ +\ \ 87 \\ \hline \end{array}$ | ④ $\begin{array}{r} 913 \\ -\ \ 54 \\ \hline \end{array}$ |

⑤ $692 - 354 \ =$ _____ ⑥ $329 + 463 \ =$ _____

⑦ $291 + 482 \ =$ _____ ⑧ $842 - 786 \ =$ _____

⑨ $142 + 35 \ =$ _____ ⑩ $510 - 73 \ =$ _____

Fill in the missing numbers.

⑪ $4 +$ _____ $= 18$ ⑫ $33 -$ _____ $= 26$

⑬ $25 +$ _____ $= 32$ ⑭ _____ $+ 17 = 31$

⑮ _____ $- 9 \ = 29$ ⑯ _____ $+ 6 \ = 18$

Do the multiplication or division.

⑰ $\begin{array}{r} 8 \\ \times\ \ 9 \\ \hline \end{array}$	⑱ $\begin{array}{r} 6 \\ \times\ \ 7 \\ \hline \end{array}$	⑲ $\begin{array}{r} 4 \\ \times\ \ 5 \\ \hline \end{array}$	⑳ $\begin{array}{r} 9 \\ \times\ \ 3 \\ \hline \end{array}$
㉑ $3\overline{)12}$	㉒ $9\overline{)27}$	㉓ $7\overline{)35}$	㉔ $6\overline{)48}$
㉕ $8\overline{)26}$	㉖ $5\overline{)47}$	㉗ $9\overline{)46}$	㉘ $4\overline{)34}$

㉙ $2 \times 8 \ =$ _____ ㉚ $7 \times 5 \ =$ _____ ㉛ $3 \times 4 \ =$ _____

㉜ $40 \div 8 \ =$ _____ ㉝ $45 \div 6 \ =$ _____ ㉞ $32 \div 5 \ =$ _____

80 COMPLETE MATHSMART (GRADE 4)

Choose the most appropriate unit to measure each of the following lengths. Write cm, m, or km.

㉟ The length of this book _____

㊱ The width of your bedroom _____

㊲ The distance from your home to your school _____

㊳ The height of a giraffe _____

㊴ The distance from Vancouver to Toronto _____

Choose the most appropriate unit to measure each of the following masses. Write kg or g. Then put them in order from lightest to heaviest.

㊵

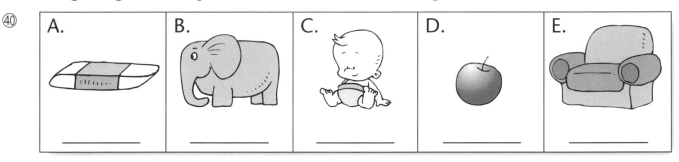

A. _____ B. _____ C. _____ D. _____ E. _____

㊶ From lightest to heaviest : _____

Write the times to the nearest minutes.

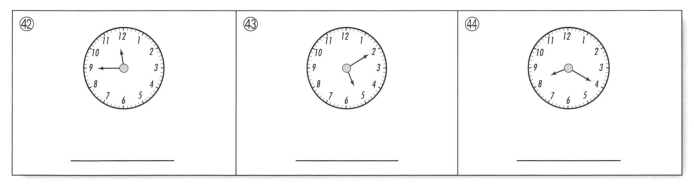

㊷ _____ ㊸ _____ ㊹ _____

Write the number of lines of symmetry for each picture.

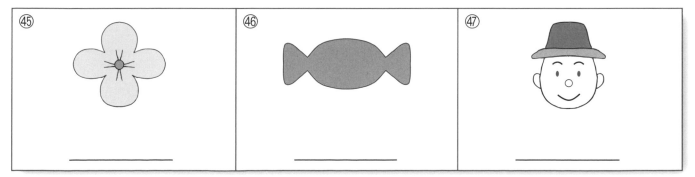

㊺ _____ ㊻ _____ ㊼ _____

Review

2015 watch work start

Write a fraction for the shaded parts in each diagram.

(48) 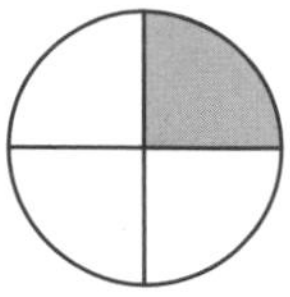 $\frac{1}{4}$

(49) 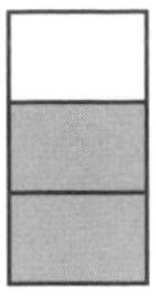 $\frac{2}{3}$

(50) 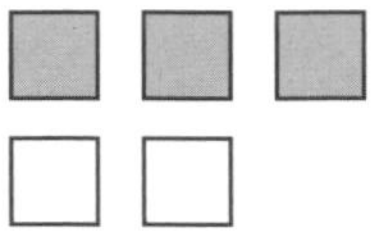 $\frac{3}{5}$

(51) 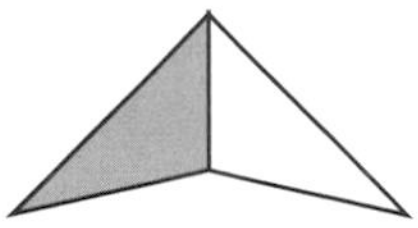 $\frac{1}{2}$

(52) 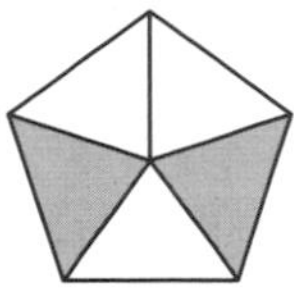 $\frac{2}{5}$

(53) 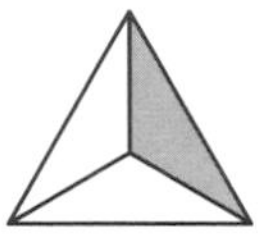 $\frac{1}{3}$

Find the perimeters of the shapes. Then put them in order. Write their representing letters only.

(54)

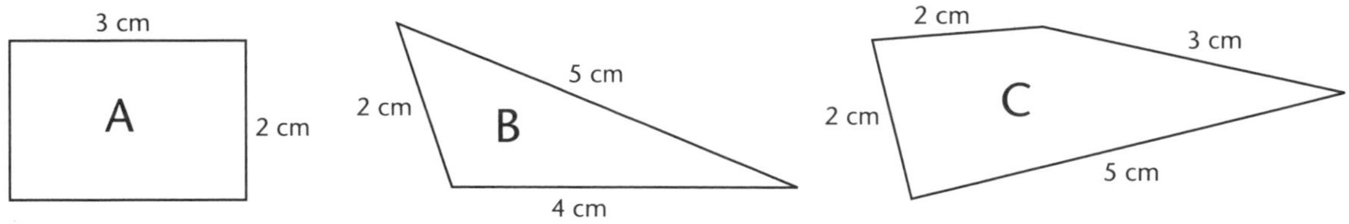

Shape	A	B	C
Perimeter (cm)	10	11	12

(55) From the one with greatest perimeter to the one with least :

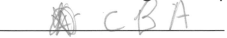

C B A

Look at the first picture. Then write 'reflection', 'rotation', or 'translation' to indicate how it is transformed.

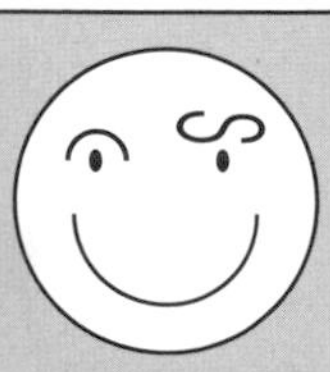

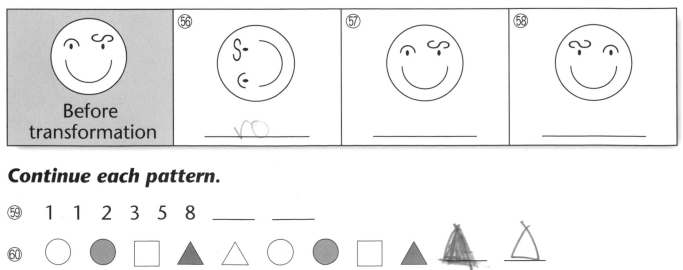

Before transformation

(56) 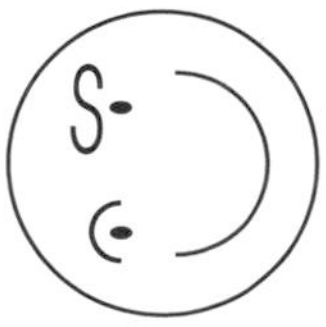 ro

(57)  ______

(58)  ______

Continue each pattern.

(59) 1 1 2 3 5 8 ____ ____

(60) 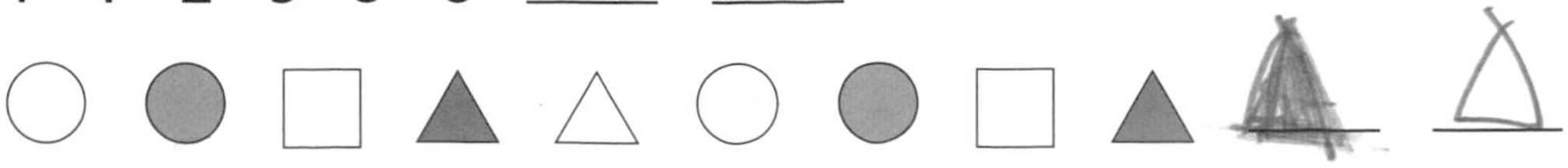

Name the solids and complete the table.

A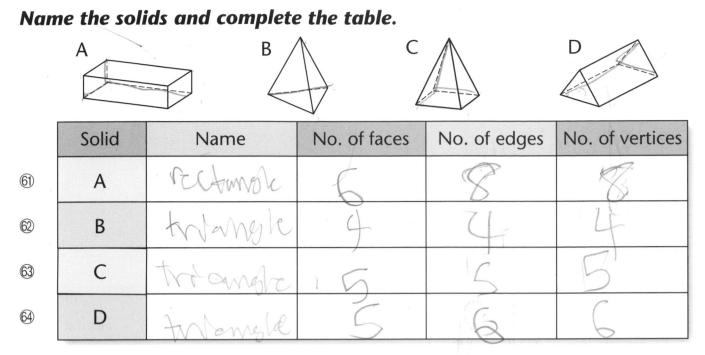
B
C
D

Solid	Name	No. of faces	No. of edges	No. of vertices
⑥¹ A	rectangle	6	8	8
⑥² B	triangle	4	4	4
⑥³ C	triangle	5	5	5
⑥⁴ D	triangle	5	6	6

This graph shows the favourite foods of the students in Ms. Smith's class. Read the graph and answer the questions.

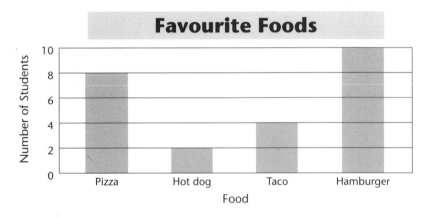

Favourite Foods

⑥⁵ Which food do most students like?   Hamburgers

⑥⁶ How many more students like hamburgers than hot dogs?   8

⑥⁷ Which food is half as much as pizza?   Taco

Answer the questions.

⑥⁸ Anna bought a bag of chips for 99¢ and a chocolate bar for $1.25. How much money did Anna spend? $ 2.24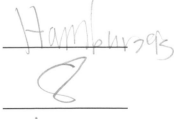

⑥⁹ Michael had $5.25. He bought a magazine for $4.50. How much money does Michael have now? $ 75¢

⑦⁰ What are the total possible outcomes if you roll a dice?   change to get 1,2,3,4,5,6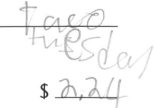

1 Numbers to 10 000

Write the number shown by each group of blocks in numerals.

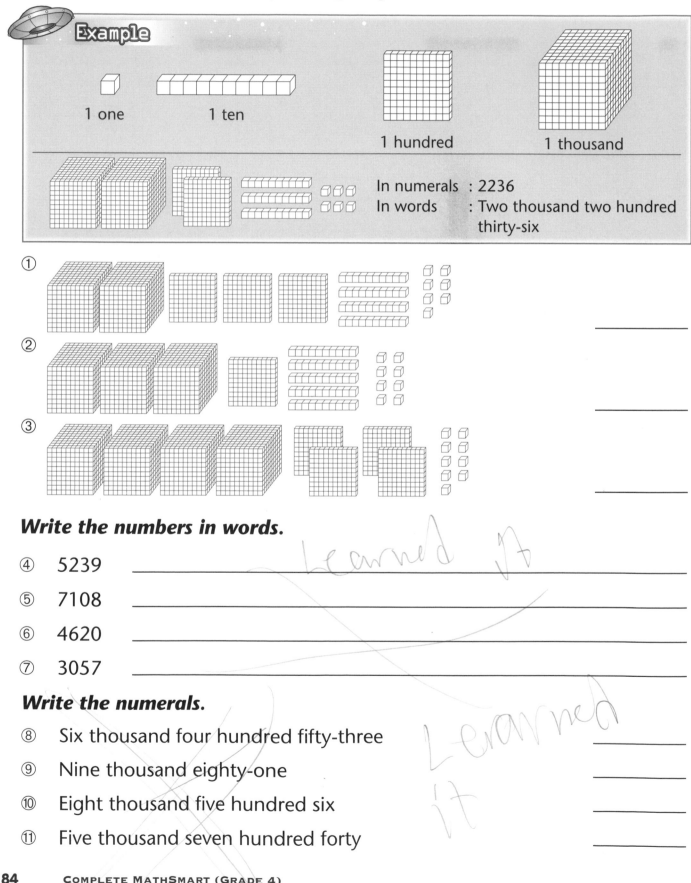

Example

1 one   1 ten   1 hundred   1 thousand

In numerals : 2236
In words   : Two thousand two hundred thirty-six

① _____

② _____

③ _____

Write the numbers in words.

④ 5239 _____

⑤ 7108 _____

⑥ 4620 _____

⑦ 3057 _____

Write the numerals.

⑧ Six thousand four hundred fifty-three   _____

⑨ Nine thousand eighty-one   _____

⑩ Eight thousand five hundred six   _____

⑪ Five thousand seven hundred forty   _____

Write the numbers.

⑫ 5 thousands 7 hundreds 4 ones

_5704_

⑬ 1 thousand 8 hundreds 2 tens 9 ones

_1829_

⑭ 3 thousands 6 tens 5 ones   _3065_

⑮ 9 thousands 4 hundreds 2 tens   _9420_

Fill in the correct digits.

⑯ 2680 | 2 | thousands | 6 | hundreds | 8 | tens | 0 | ones |

⑰ 7963 | 7 | thousands | 9 | hundreds | 6 | tens | 3 | ones |

⑱ 4226 | 4 | thousands | 2 | hundreds | 2 | tens | 6 | ones |

Write the expanded form or standard form of each number.

⑲ 9586   = 9000 + _500_ + _80_ + _6_

⑳ 2955   = _2000_ + 900 + _50_ + _5_

㉑ 8473   = _8000_ + _4_ + 70 + _3_

㉒ _3267_   = 3000 + 200 + 60 + 7

㉓ _6038_ = 6000 + 30 + 8

㉔ _5740_ = 5000 + 700 + 40

Write the place value of each underlined digit.

㉕ 8<u>3</u>26   _300_

㉖ 49<u>1</u>0   _10_

㉗ <u>5</u>741   _5000_

㉘ 604<u>9</u>   _9_

Aunt Anna sells candies and toys. Help her colour the candies or toys.

㉙ Colour the candies with the greatest numbers in stock.

a. 8794   8974   8947   8749

b. 2130   2301   2310   2103

㉚ Colour the toys with the smallest numbers in stock.

a. 3653   4019   3982   4125

b. 1930   2047   1989   2107

Fill in the missing numbers.

㉛ 6093 _____ 5893 5793 _____ _____

㉜ 2102 3102 _____ _____ 6102 _____

㉝ 5264 _____ _____ 5564 5664 _____

The children take turns to pick 4 digits from a bag, and an instruction from a box. Help the children form the 4-digit numbers following the instructions and answer the questions.

		Instruction	Digits picked	Number formed
㉞	Janice	The greatest possible number	2 , 3 , 0 , 1	
㉟	Pete	The smallest possible number	4 , 7 , 3 , 5	
㊱	Marie	The smallest odd number	3 , 8 , 1 , 6	
㊲	Tom	The greatest even number	5 , 9 , 4 , 2	

㊳ Who forms the greatest number? _____

㊴ Who forms the smallest number? _____

The counter of a photocopier records the number of copies made. Look at the counter readings of five photocopiers and answer the questions.

7463   6436   9536

7536   6843

㊵ Which reading shows the most copies made? _____

㊶ Which reading shows the fewest copies made? _____

㊷ Which reading is seven hundred greater than 6143? _____

㊸ Which reading is four hundred smaller than 7863? _____

㊹ Which readings have 4 in the hundreds place? _____

㊺ Which readings have 7 in the thousands place? _____

㊻ Which two readings differ from 8536 by 1000? _____

㊼ Which two readings differ by 1 thousand 1 hundred? _____

㊽ Put the readings in order from smallest to greatest.

_____

MIND BOGGLER

What is the message?

Uncle Tim sent a message to Danny. Put the numbers in order from greatest to smallest, and write their representing letters. Then read the message.

E 7931   K 4386   T 5913   G 9317   R 4638   W 5319   A 7319   O 4678   R 9127

___ ___ ___ ___ ___ ___ ___   ___ ___ ___ ___!

2 Addition and Subtraction

Do the addition. Follow the path of the sums greater than 7600 to help Janice find her toy.

Quick Tip

To do vertical addition, align all the numbers on the right. Add the ones first. Remember to add the digit carried over from the right.

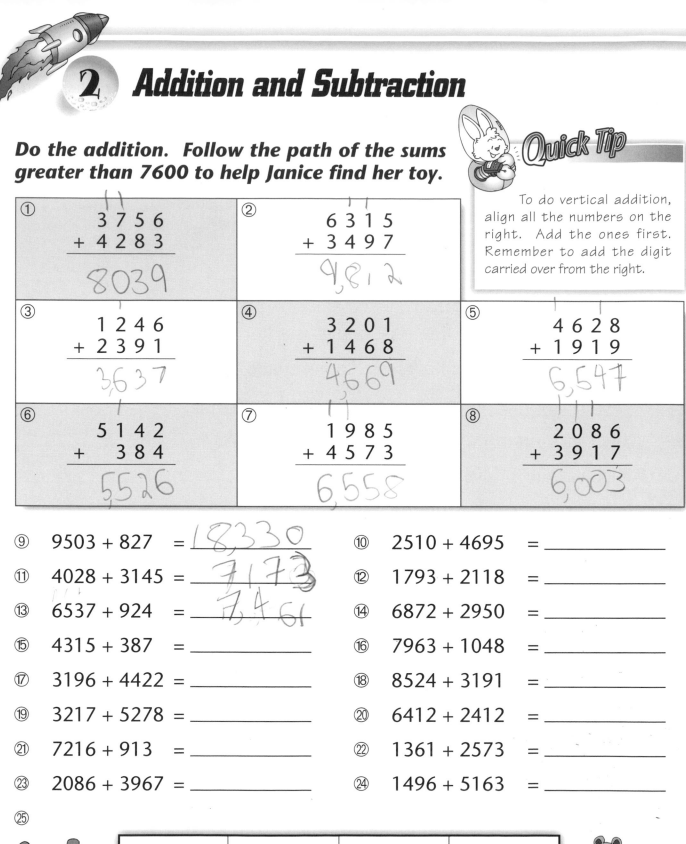

①
$$3756 + 4283 = 8039$$

②
$$6315 + 3497 = 9812$$

③
$$1246 + 2391 = 3637$$

④
$$3201 + 1468 = 4669$$

⑤
$$4628 + 1919 = 6547$$

⑥
$$5142 + 384 = 5526$$

⑦
$$1985 + 4573 = 6558$$

⑧
$$2086 + 3917 = 6003$$

⑨ $9503 + 827 = 18,330$

⑩ $2510 + 4695 = $ _____

⑪ $4028 + 3145 = 7173$

⑫ $1793 + 2118 = $ _____

⑬ $6537 + 924 = 7,461$

⑭ $6872 + 2950 = $ _____

⑮ $4315 + 387 = $ _____

⑯ $7963 + 1048 = $ _____

⑰ $3196 + 4422 = $ _____

⑱ $8524 + 3191 = $ _____

⑲ $3217 + 5278 = $ _____

⑳ $6412 + 2412 = $ _____

㉑ $7216 + 913 = $ _____

㉒ $1361 + 2573 = $ _____

㉓ $2086 + 3967 = $ _____

㉔ $1496 + 5163 = $ _____

㉕

8039	8761	8824	8129
9812	7905	8495	7620
10 330	9822	11 715	9133
8213	9011	7618	8765

Do the subtraction.

㉖ 7321 − 879	㉗ 4821 − 398	
㉘ 9873 − 538	㉙ 6423 − 946	
㉚ 3271 − 974	㉛ 7408 − 293	㉜ 4620 − 979

Quick Tip

To do vertical subtraction, align all the numbers on the right. Subtract the ones first. If you can't take away, borrow 1 from the left.

㉝ 5206 – 378 = ________ ㉞ 6087 – 558 = ________

㉟ 2576 – 827 = ________ ㊱ 4538 – 814 = ________

㊲ 4398 – 673 = ________ ㊳ 3879 – 609 = ________

㊴ 9260 – 859 = ________ ㊵ 5842 – 462 = ________

Round the following numbers to the nearest hundred.

Example

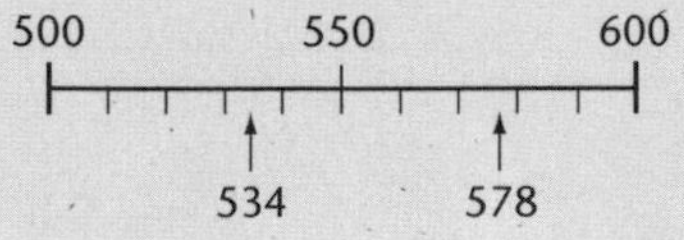
500
550
600
534
578

534 is closer to 500 while 578 is closer to 600, so 534 is rounded to 500 and 578 is rounded to 600. 550 is halfway between 500 and 600. It is rounded up to 600.

㊶ 294 → 300 ㊷ 315 → 300

㊸ 450 → 500 ㊹ 182 → 200

㊺ 537 → 500 ㊻ 128 → 100

Round the following numbers to the nearest thousand.

㊼ 7148 → 7,000 ㊽ 4803 → 5000

㊾ 1963 → 2,000 ㊿ 6530 → 7000

(51) 5298 → 5,000 (52) 8345 → 8000

Estimate the sums or differences by rounding the 4-digit numbers to the nearest thousand and the 3-digit numbers to the nearest hundred. Then find the exact answers.

Quick Tip

Check if your answer is reasonable by rounding the numbers and estimating the answer.

53   7499 + 2501   = _____   **Estimate**   _____ + _____ = _____

54   6269 + 2721   = _____   **Estimate**   _____ + _____ = _____

55   6548 – 613   = _____   **Estimate**   _____ – _____ = _____

56   2138 + 1048   = _____   **Estimate**   _____ + _____ = _____

57   9236 – 703   = _____   **Estimate**   _____ – _____ = _____

58   5211 + 3650   = _____   **Estimate**   _____ + _____ = _____

59   7710 – 439   = _____   **Estimate**   _____ – _____ = _____

60   4721 + 1875   = _____   **Estimate**   _____ + _____ = _____

61   1030 – 250   = _____   **Estimate**   _____ – _____ = _____

Answer the questions.

62   What number is 268 greater than 4735?   _____

63   What is the number if 6739 is reduced by 215?   _____

64   How much is the difference between $1650 and $450?   _____

65   What is the digit in the tens place when you add 3829 and 2958?   _____

66   What is the digit in the hundreds place when you subtract 978 from 2218?   _____

67   What is the difference between the smallest 4-digit odd number and the greatest 3-digit number?   _____

68   What is the sum of the greatest 3-digit even number and the smallest 4-digit odd number?   _____

Solve the problems. Show your work.

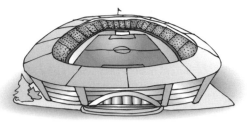

69 A football stadium has 970 seats in the red section, 1125 seats in the green section, and 2540 seats in the yellow section.

a. How many seats are in the green and yellow sections altogether?

_____ = 3665 seats

_____ seats are in the green and yellow sections altogether.

b. How many more seats are in the yellow section than the red section?

_____ = _____

_____ more seats are in the yellow section than the red section.

70 Cameron helps out in the school library. The library has 3411 storybooks, 2936 picture books, and 424 French books.

a. How many storybooks and picture books are there in the library?

_____ = _____

There are _____ storybooks and picture books in the library.

b. How many more storybooks are there than French books?

_____ = _____

There are _____ more storybooks than French books.

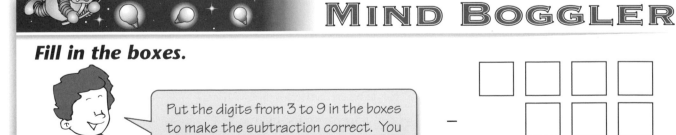

MIND BOGGLER

Fill in the boxes.

Put the digits from 3 to 9 in the boxes to make the subtraction correct. You can only use each digit once.

```
    □ □   □ □
  −      □   □ □
  ─────────────
    8 7   8 3
```

3 Multiplication

Find the products mentally.

① 100 x 7 = _____

② 9 x 10 = _____

③ 8 x 1000 = _____

④ 10 x 5 = _____

⑥ 6 x 100 = _____

⑧ 12 x 100 = _____

Quick Tip

When you multiply a number by 10, just add 1 zero to the number. Add 2 zeros when you multiply it by 100, and 3 zeros when you multiply it by 1000.

⑤ 1000 x 2 = _____

⑦ 3 x 1000 = _____

⑨ 1000 x 15 = _____

Examples

① 2 x 20 = 2 x 2 x 10
= 4 x 10
= 40

② 300 x 4 = 100 x 3 x 4
= 100 x 12
= 1200

Find the products.

⑩ 3 x 80 = _____

⑫ 4 x 600 = _____

⑭ 400 x 3 = _____

⑯ 400 x 7 = _____

⑱ 9 x 20 = _____

⑳ 8 x 70 = _____

㉒ 60 x 6 = _____

㉔ 200 x 8 = _____

㉖ 500 x 6 = _____

㉘ 3000 x 9 = _____

⑪ 50 x 4 = _____

⑬ 2 x 3000 = _____

⑮ 2000 x 4 = _____

⑰ 2 x 5000 = _____

⑲ 5 x 400 = _____

㉑ 90 x 5 = _____

㉓ 700 x 9 = _____

㉕ 4000 x 2 = _____

㉗ 40 x 7 = _____

㉙ 900 x 4 = _____

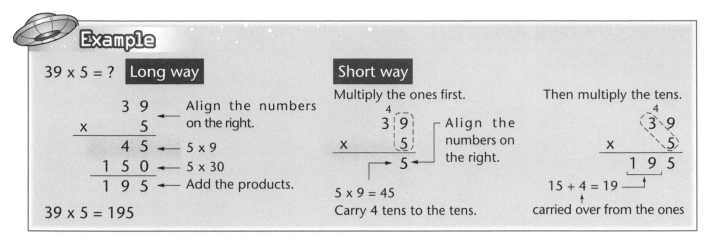

Example

39 x 5 = ?   **Long way**

```
        3 9
    x     5
    ─────────
        4 5  ← 5 x 9
      1 5 0  ← 5 x 30
    ─────────
      1 9 5  ← Add the products.
```

Align the numbers on the right.

39 x 5 = 195

Short way

Multiply the ones first.

```
      4
    3⌐9�
  x   ⌊5⌋
  ─────────
      5
```

Align the numbers on the right.

5 x 9 = 45
Carry 4 tens to the tens.

Then multiply the tens.

```
      4
    3 9
  x   5
  ─────────
  1 9 5
```

15 + 4 = 19
carried over from the ones

Multiply the long way.

③⓪
```
      1 6
  x     7
  ┌──────┐
  │      │
  └──────┘
  ┌──────┐
  │      │
  └──────┘
  ──────────
  ┌──────┐
  │      │
  └──────┘
```

③①
```
      4 3
  x     5
  ┌──────┐
  │      │
  └──────┘
  ┌──────┐
  │      │
  └──────┘
  ──────────
  ┌──────┐
  │      │
  └──────┘
```

③②
```
      2 5
  x     8
  ┌──────┐
  │      │
  └──────┘
  ┌──────┐
  │      │
  └──────┘
  ──────────
  ┌──────┐
  │      │
  └──────┘
```

③③
```
      5 2
  x     4
  ┌──────┐
  │      │
  └──────┘
  ┌──────┐
  │      │
  └──────┘
  ──────────
  ┌──────┐
  │      │
  └──────┘
```

Multiply the short way.

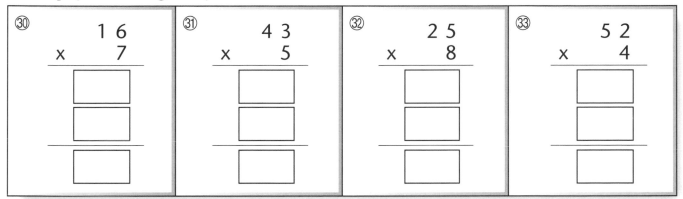

③④
```
      7 2
  x     6
  ─────────
```

③⑤
```
      9 4
  x     5
  ─────────
```

③⑥
```
      2 8
  x     7
  ─────────
```

③⑦
```
      5 7
  x     8
  ─────────
```

③⑧
```
      4 6
  x     3
  ─────────
```

③⑨
```
      3 8
  x     4
  ─────────
```

④⓪
```
      6 8
  x     9
  ─────────
```

④①
```
      9 2
  x     7
  ─────────
```

④② 28 x 9 = _____

④③ 36 x 9 = _____

④④ 76 x 8 = _____

④⑤ 43 x 5 = _____

④⑥ 53 x 6 = _____

④⑦ 81 x 7 = _____

④⑧ 25 x 3 = _____

④⑨ 4 x 68 = _____

⑤⓪ 5 x 62 = _____

⑤① 6 x 17 = _____

⑤② 3 x 72 = _____

⑤③ 8 x 53 = _____

⑤④ 9 x 34 = _____

⑤⑤ 7 x 46 = _____

Quick Tip

Though the order of multiplication has changed, the product is still the same.
e.g. 4 x 68 = 68 x 4

Multiply the long way.

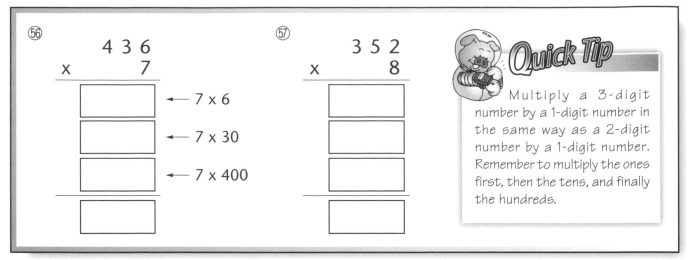

⑤⑥
```
    4 3 6
x         7
```
⬜ ← 7 x 6

⬜ ← 7 x 30

⬜ ← 7 x 400

⬜

⑤⑦
```
    3 5 2
x         8
```
⬜

⬜

⬜

⬜

Quick Tip

Multiply a 3-digit number by a 1-digit number in the same way as a 2-digit number by a 1-digit number. Remember to multiply the ones first, then the tens, and finally the hundreds.

Multiply the short way.

⑤⑧ $\begin{array}{r} 2\ 9\ 6 \\ \times\quad\ 7 \\ \hline \end{array}$	⑤⑨ $\begin{array}{r} 4\ 7\ 8 \\ \times\quad\ 5 \\ \hline \end{array}$	⑥⓪ $\begin{array}{r} 6\ 3\ 9 \\ \times\quad\ 9 \\ \hline \end{array}$	⑥① $\begin{array}{r} 7\ 6\ 4 \\ \times\quad\ 3 \\ \hline \end{array}$
⑥② 847 x 2 = _____	⑥③ 729 x 4 = _____		⑥④ 352 x 9 = _____
⑥⑤ 4 x 526 = _____	⑥⑥ 925 x 6 = _____		⑥⑦ 8 x 648 = _____
⑥⑧ 7 x 388 = _____	⑥⑨ 509 x 2 = _____		⑦⓪ 5 x 183 = _____

Aunt Mary bought a lot of things. Help her find the total amount.

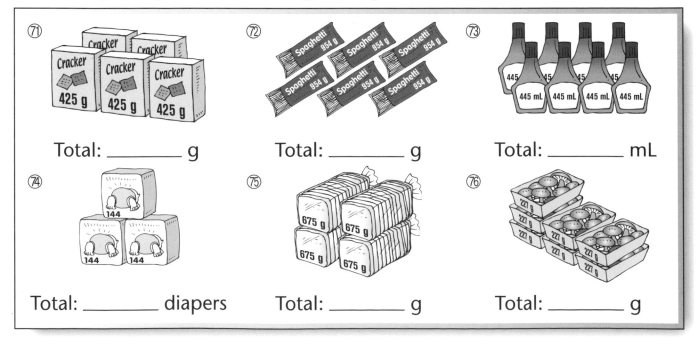

⑦① Cracker 425 g

Total: _____ g

⑦② Spaghetti 954 g

Total: _____ g

⑦③ 445 mL

Total: _____ mL

⑦④ 144

Total: _____ diapers

⑦⑤ 675 g

Total: _____ g

⑦⑥ 227 g

Total: _____ g

Solve the problems.

⑦ Daniel and Michelle went apple-picking. They filled 7 baskets with 275 apples each. How many apples did they pick?

⑦ Julian's school bus can carry 55 students each time. The bus is filled 6 times a day. How many students have been on the bus in one day?

⑦ The bleachers of Julian's school have 5 sections. Each section can seat 125 people . How many people can sit in the bleachers?

⑧ Amanda has 7 boxes of cookies for sale in a fundraising event. Each box contains 24 packages of cookies. How many packages of cookies will Amanda have to sell?

MIND BOGGLER

What number am I?

I'm a 2-digit number smaller than 50. When I'm multiplied by 7, the product is greater than 200. The sum of my digits is 5.

You are _____ .

4 Division I

Fill in the missing numbers.

① 80 ÷ 2 = _____ tens ÷ 2

= _____ tens

= _____

② 900 ÷ 3 = _____ hundreds ÷ 3

= _____ hundreds

= _____

③ 160 ÷ 4 = _____ tens ÷ 4

= _____ tens

= _____

④ 450 ÷ 5 = _____ tens ÷ 5

= _____ tens

= _____

⑤ 360 ÷ 6 = _____ tens ÷ 6

= _____ tens

= _____

⑥ 700 ÷ 7 = _____ hundreds ÷ 7

= _____ hundred

= _____

Do the division.

⑦ 160 ÷ 2 = _____

⑧ 90 ÷ 3 = _____

⑨ 50 ÷ 5 = _____

⑩ 80 ÷ 4 = _____

⑪ 560 ÷ 8 = _____

⑫ 900 ÷ 9 = _____

⑬ 630 ÷ 7 = _____

⑭ 350 ÷ 5 = _____

⑮ 180 ÷ 6 = _____

⑯ 140 ÷ 7 = _____

⑰ 240 ÷ 8 = _____

⑱ 450 ÷ 9 = _____

Round the dividends to the nearest ten. Then estimate the quotients.

⑲ 62 ÷ 3 Estimate ▶ _____ ÷ 3

= _____

⑳ 78 ÷ 4 Estimate ▶ _____ ÷ 4

= _____

㉑ 47 ÷ 5 Estimate ▶ _____ ÷ 5

= _____

㉒ 303 ÷ 6 Estimate ▶ _____ ÷ 6

= _____

㉓ 81 ÷ 2 Estimate ▶ _____ ÷ 2

= _____

㉔ 804 ÷ 8 Estimate ▶ _____ ÷ 8

= _____

㉕ 346 ÷ 7 Estimate ▶ _____ ÷ 7

= _____

㉖ 537 ÷ 9 Estimate ▶ _____ ÷ 9

= _____

Divide the 2-digit numbers.

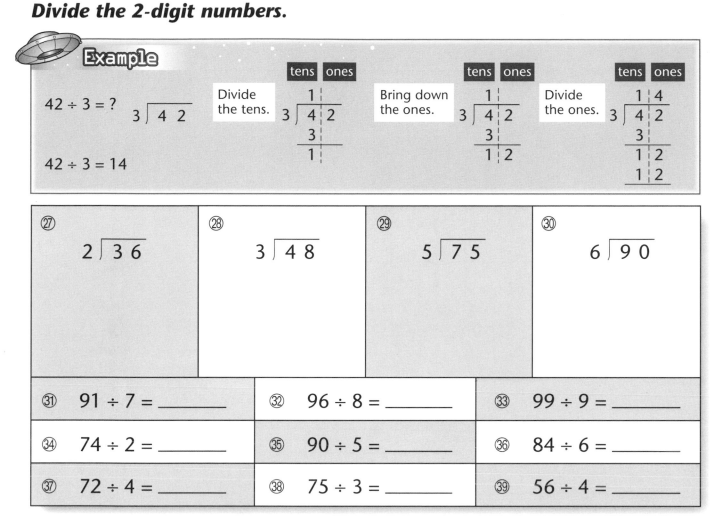

Example

$42 \div 3 = ?$

$3\overline{)42}$

$42 \div 3 = 14$

	tens	ones
Divide the tens.

| | tens | ones |
Bring down the ones.

Divide the ones.

㉗ $2\overline{)36}$

㉘ $3\overline{)48}$

㉙ $5\overline{)75}$

㉚ $6\overline{)90}$

㉛ $91 \div 7 =$ _____

㉜ $96 \div 8 =$ _____

㉝ $99 \div 9 =$ _____

㉞ $74 \div 2 =$ _____

㉟ $90 \div 5 =$ _____

㊱ $84 \div 6 =$ _____

㊲ $72 \div 4 =$ _____

㊳ $75 \div 3 =$ _____

㊴ $56 \div 4 =$ _____

See how Aunt Anna put the food equally into the bags and containers. Help her find the number of things in each bag or container.

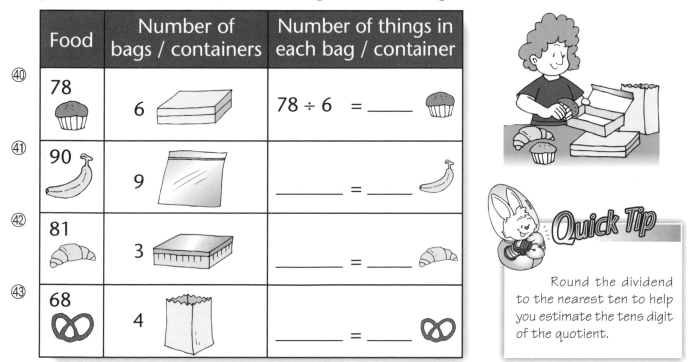

	Food	Number of bags / containers	Number of things in each bag / container
㊵	78	6	$78 \div 6$ = _____
㊶	90	9	_____ = _____
㊷	81	3	_____ = _____
㊸	68	4	_____ = _____

Quick Tip

Round the dividend to the nearest ten to help you estimate the tens digit of the quotient.

Do the division. Write the letters representing the division sentences with remainder 2 in order. Find out what fruit Janice likes most.

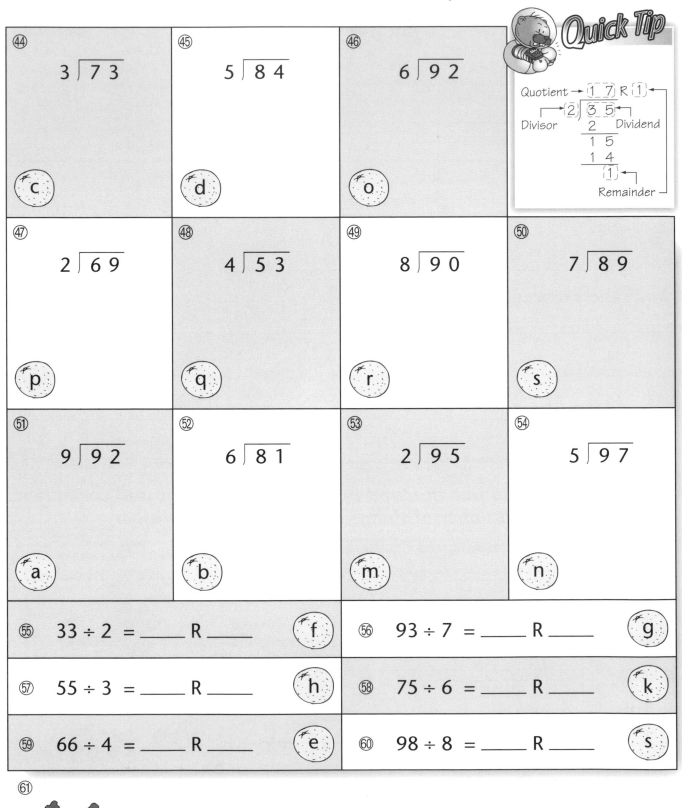

㊹

$3\overline{)73}$

c

㊺

$5\overline{)84}$

d

㊻

$6\overline{)92}$

o

Quick Tip

Quotient → 1 7 R 1

2)3 5

Divisor   2   Dividend

1 5

1 4

1

Remainder

㊼

$2\overline{)69}$

p

㊽

$4\overline{)53}$

q

㊾

$8\overline{)90}$

r

㊿

$7\overline{)89}$

s

51

$9\overline{)92}$

a

52

$6\overline{)81}$

b

53

$2\overline{)95}$

m

54

$5\overline{)97}$

n

55   33 ÷ 2 = ____ R ____   f

56   93 ÷ 7 = ____ R ____   g

57   55 ÷ 3 = ____ R ____   h

58   75 ÷ 6 = ____ R ____   k

59   66 ÷ 4 = ____ R ____   e

60   98 ÷ 8 = ____ R ____   s

61

I like ___ ___ ___ ___ ___ ___ ___ .

Complete the table. You can use a calculator to complete the last column. Then answer the question.

	Division	Divisor	Quotient	Divisor x Quotient
⑥②	5⟌7 0			
⑥③	4⟌8 4			
⑥④	3⟌6 9			
⑥⑤	6⟌9 6			

⑥⑥ What conclusion can you draw?

_____ .

Solve the problems. Show your work.

⑥⑦ Ryan earned $96 in 4 weeks from delivering newspapers. How much money did he earn in one week?

_____ = _____

He earned $ _____ in one week.

⑥⑧ Janice puts 92 lollipops equally into 6 jars. How many lollipops are there in each jar? How many lollipops are left behind?

_____ = _____

There are _____ lollipops in each jar. _____ lollipops are left behind.

MIND BOGGLER

How many bags?

Ryan put 95 cupcakes equally into 7 bags. He then put 1 more cupcake from the leftovers into each bag until there are no more leftovers. How many bags will have 1 more cupcake than the others?

_____ bags will have 1 more cupcake than the others.

5 Division II

Do the division.

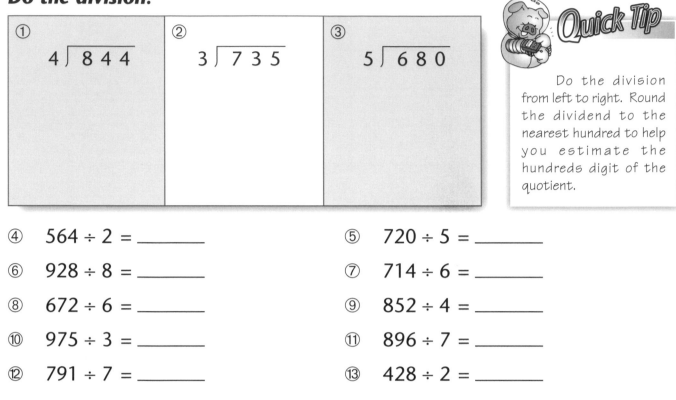

① 4) 8 4 4

② 3) 7 3 5

③ 5) 6 8 0

Quick Tip

Do the division from left to right. Round the dividend to the nearest hundred to help you estimate the hundreds digit of the quotient.

④ 564 ÷ 2 = _____

⑤ 720 ÷ 5 = _____

⑥ 928 ÷ 8 = _____

⑦ 714 ÷ 6 = _____

⑧ 672 ÷ 6 = _____

⑨ 852 ÷ 4 = _____

⑩ 975 ÷ 3 = _____

⑪ 896 ÷ 7 = _____

⑫ 791 ÷ 7 = _____

⑬ 428 ÷ 2 = _____

Divide the 3-digit numbers.

⑭ 6) 1 8 6

⑮ 9) 3 7 8

⑯ 7) 4 5 5

Quick Tip

If the first digit of the 3-digit dividend is smaller than the 1-digit divisor, the quotient is a 2-digit number.

⑰ 255 ÷ 5 = _____

⑱ 288 ÷ 9 = _____

⑲ 304 ÷ 4 = _____

⑳ 252 ÷ 3 = _____

㉑ 296 ÷ 8 = _____

㉒ 186 ÷ 2 = _____

㉓ 315 ÷ 7 = _____

㉔ 396 ÷ 6 = _____

㉕ 198 ÷ 9 = _____

㉖ 240 ÷ 5 = _____

㉗ 448 ÷ 8 = _____

㉘ 273 ÷ 7 = _____

㉙ 150 ÷ 6 = _____

㉚ 666 ÷ 9 = _____

Match the division sentences with the same quotient. Help the children get their favourite toys.

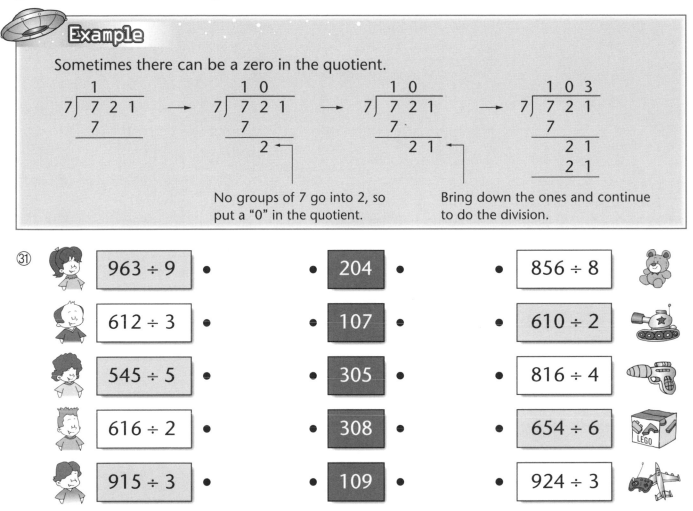

Example

Sometimes there can be a zero in the quotient.

```
      1                    1 0                   1 0                  1 0 3
  7) 7 2 1      →      7) 7 2 1      →      7) 7 2 1      →      7) 7 2 1
     7                    7                    7                    7
  _____          _____           _____         _____
                          2                      2 1                 2 1
                                                                     2 1
                                                                  _____
```

No groups of 7 go into 2, so   Bring down the ones and continue
put a "0" in the quotient.   to do the division.

㉛

963 ÷ 9	•	• 204 •	•	856 ÷ 8
612 ÷ 3	•	• 107 •	•	610 ÷ 2
545 ÷ 5	•	• 305 •	•	816 ÷ 4
616 ÷ 2	•	• 308 •	•	654 ÷ 6
915 ÷ 3	•	• 109 •	•	924 ÷ 3

Use multiplication to check each of the following division sentences. Check ✔ the box if the quotient is correct; otherwise, write the correct quotient in the box.

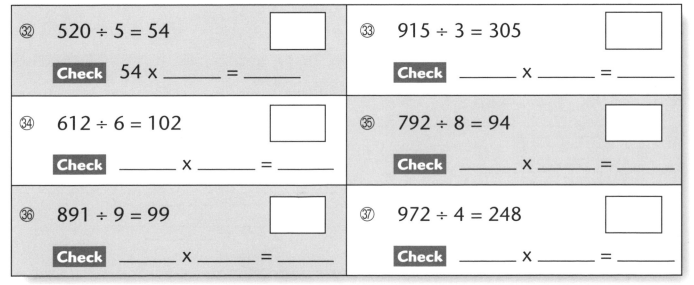

㉜ 520 ÷ 5 = 54   [   ]

Check 54 x _____ = _____

㉝ 915 ÷ 3 = 305   [   ]

Check _____ x _____ = _____

㉞ 612 ÷ 6 = 102   [   ]

Check _____ x _____ = _____

㉟ 792 ÷ 8 = 94   [   ]

Check _____ x _____ = _____

㊱ 891 ÷ 9 = 99   [   ]

Check _____ x _____ = _____

㊲ 972 ÷ 4 = 248   [   ]

Check _____ x _____ = _____

Do the division and use R to show the remainders.

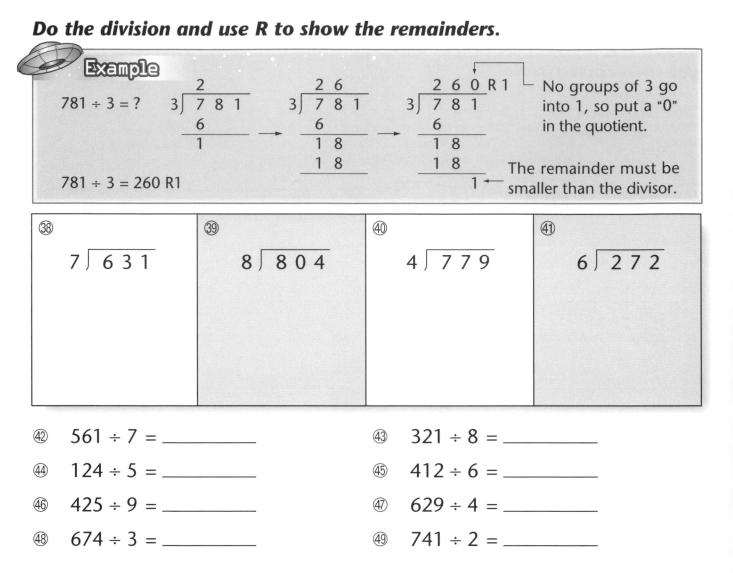

Example

$781 \div 3 = ?$

$$\begin{array}{r} 2 \\ 3\overline{)781} \\ 6 \\ \hline 1 \end{array} \rightarrow \begin{array}{r} 26 \\ 3\overline{)781} \\ 6 \\ \hline 18 \\ 18 \end{array} \rightarrow \begin{array}{r} 260 \text{ R }1 \\ 3\overline{)781} \\ 6 \\ \hline 18 \\ 18 \\ \hline 1 \end{array}$$

No groups of 3 go into 1, so put a "0" in the quotient.

$781 \div 3 = 260$ R1

The remainder must be smaller than the divisor.

③⑧
$$7\overline{)631}$$

③⑨
$$8\overline{)804}$$

④⓪
$$4\overline{)779}$$

④①
$$6\overline{)272}$$

④② $561 \div 7 =$ _____

④③ $321 \div 8 =$ _____

④④ $124 \div 5 =$ _____

④⑤ $412 \div 6 =$ _____

④⑥ $425 \div 9 =$ _____

④⑦ $629 \div 4 =$ _____

④⑧ $674 \div 3 =$ _____

④⑨ $741 \div 2 =$ _____

Follow Janice's instructions to complete the table with a calculator. Write a conclusion for what you can observe.

Step 1
Multiply the quotient by the divisor.

Step 2
Add the remainder to the product.

Step 3
Write down the sum in the last column of the table.

	Division	Divisor	Quotient	Remainder	Sum
⑤⓪	$405 \div 4$				
⑤①	$397 \div 7$				
⑤②	$721 \div 5$				
⑤③	$643 \div 8$				

⑤④ Conclusion : _____

Help Uncle Tim put the stationery equally in the boxes. Check ✓ the boxes in the last column for the division with no remainders. Then circle the correct numbers.

	Number of boxes used	Number of pens in each box	Number of pens left	With or without remainder
⑤⑤ Pencils	6			
⑤⑥ Ball-points	6			
⑤⑦ Felt-pens	6			
⑤⑧ Pencils	7			
⑤⑨ Ball-points	7			
⑥⓪ Felt-pens	7			
⑥① Pencils	8			
⑥② Ball-points	8			
⑥③ Felt-pens	8			

⑥④ To use the smallest number of boxes without any pens left unpacked, Uncle Tim should use 6 / 7 / 8 boxes to pack the pencils, 6 / 7 / 8 boxes to pack the ball-points, and 6 / 7/ 8 boxes to pack the felt-pens.

MIND BOGGLER

How many packs ?

Uncle Tim now puts half dozen of pencils in each box, and sells them in packs of 2 boxes. How many packs of pencils are available for sale?

_____ packs are available.

6 Fractions

Janice has a bagel with white and black sesame seeds. See how Janice has cut it. Answer the questions.

① What fraction of the bagel has sesame seeds? _____ $\frac{3}{4}$

② What fraction of the bagel has no sesame seeds? _____ $\frac{1}{4}$

③ What fraction of the bagel has black sesame seeds only? $\frac{1}{4}$ _____

④ What fraction of the bagel has both black and white sesame seeds? $\frac{1}{4}$ _____

⑤ What fraction of the sesame seeds are black? $\frac{1}{4}$ _____

⑥ What fraction of the sesame seeds are white? $\frac{1}{4}$ _____

⑦ Janice shares her bagel with her friends. What fraction of the bagel does each child have?

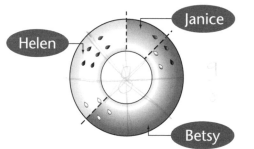

Helen   Janice   Betsy

a. Janice has _____ of the bagel.

b. Betsy has __ $\frac{4}{8}$ $\frac{1}{2}$ __ of the bagel.

c. Helen has _____ of the bagel.

Help Janice colour the bagels with a proper fraction green, those with an improper fraction yellow, and those with a mixed number red.

⑧

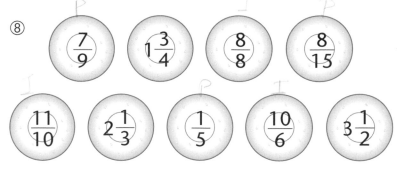

$\frac{7}{9}$ $1\frac{3}{4}$ $\frac{8}{8}$ $\frac{8}{15}$

$\frac{11}{10}$ $2\frac{1}{3}$ $\frac{1}{5}$ $\frac{10}{6}$ $3\frac{1}{2}$

Write the mixed number represented by each group of diagrams.

⑨ 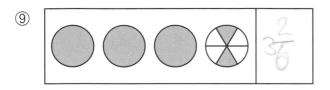 $3\frac{2}{6}$

⑩ $2\frac{5}{12}$

Write the improper fraction represented by each group of diagrams.

⑪ $\frac{16}{8} = \frac{2}{8}$

⑫ $1\frac{1}{4} = \frac{5}{4}$

⑬ $1\frac{5}{10}$

Colour the diagram to show each fraction. Then put the fractions in order from least to greatest.

⑭ a.
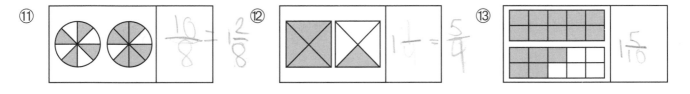

$\frac{3}{5}$ $\frac{1}{5}$ $\frac{4}{5}$

b. $\frac{1}{5} < \frac{3}{5} < \frac{4}{5}$

⑮ a.

$\frac{2}{8}$ $\frac{7}{8}$ $\frac{5}{8}$

b. $\frac{2}{8}$ $\frac{5}{8}$ $\frac{7}{8}$

Compare the fractions. Write > or < in the boxes.

⑯ $\frac{7}{6}$ $\boxed{>}$ $\frac{3}{6}$

⑰ $2\frac{3}{8}$ $\boxed{<}$ $2\frac{5}{8}$

⑱ $3\frac{1}{7}$ $\boxed{<}$ $4\frac{1}{7}$

⑲ $\frac{8}{9}$ $\boxed{>}$ $\frac{2}{9}$

⑳ $\frac{5}{3}$ $\boxed{>}$ $\frac{4}{3}$

㉑ $5\frac{1}{10}$ $\boxed{>}$ $4\frac{1}{2}$

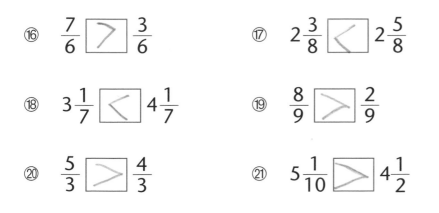

> **Quick Tip**
>
> To compare fractions with the same denominator, compare their numerators.
> e.g. $\frac{3}{4} > \frac{2}{4}$ because 3 > 2
> To compare mixed numbers with the same denominator, compare the whole numbers first. If they are the same, compare their numerators.
> e.g. $3\frac{2}{4} > 3\frac{1}{4}$ because 2 > 1
> $5\frac{2}{4} > 3\frac{2}{4}$ because 5 > 3

Put the fractions in order from greatest to least.

㉒ $\frac{7}{12}$ $\frac{13}{12}$ $\frac{11}{12}$

$\frac{13}{12}$ $\frac{11}{12}$ $\frac{7}{12}$

㉓ $3\frac{1}{5}$ $3\frac{4}{5}$ $2\frac{1}{5}$

$3\frac{4}{5}$ $3\frac{1}{5}$ $2\frac{1}{5}$

Draw pictures to show each set.

㉔ Janice has 9 cubes.

$\frac{5}{9}$ of the cubes are red.

$\frac{4}{9}$ of the cubes are blue.

㉕ Danny has 15 crayons.

$\frac{6}{15}$ of the crayons are red.

$\frac{5}{15}$ of the crayons are blue.

$\frac{4}{15}$ of the crayons are green.

㉖ Uncle Tim has 12 balloons.

$\frac{3}{12}$ of the balloons are yellow.

$\frac{5}{12}$ of the balloons are blue.

The rest of the balloons are red.

Draw a set of pictures for each question to help find the missing numerator.

㉗ Aunt Anna is watering her flowers.

$\frac{5}{8}$ of her flowers are red.

$\frac{3}{8}$ of her flowers are not red.

㉘ Some students are doing math.

$\frac{3}{5}$ of them are boys.

$\frac{2}{5}$ of them are girls.

㉙ Pete has a box of marbles.

$\frac{3}{10}$ of the marbles are red.

$\frac{4}{10}$ of the marbles are blue.

$\frac{3}{10}$ of the marbles are white.

$$\frac{3}{5} = \frac{6}{10} = 0.6$$

Write a fraction and a decimal number to show the shaded parts in each diagram.

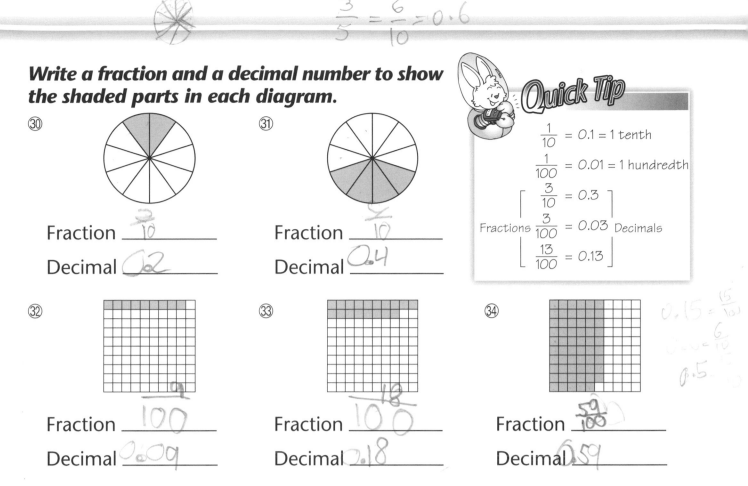

㉚ Fraction ___$\frac{3}{10}$___

Decimal ___0.2___

㉛ Fraction ___$\frac{5}{10}$___

Decimal ___0.4___

㉜ Fraction ___$\frac{9}{100}$___

Decimal ___0.09___

㉝ Fraction ___$\frac{18}{100}$___

Decimal ___0.18___

㉞ Fraction ___$\frac{59}{100}$___

Decimal ___0.59___

$0.15 = \frac{15}{100}$

0.5

Colour the diagrams to show the fractions. Then write the decimals.

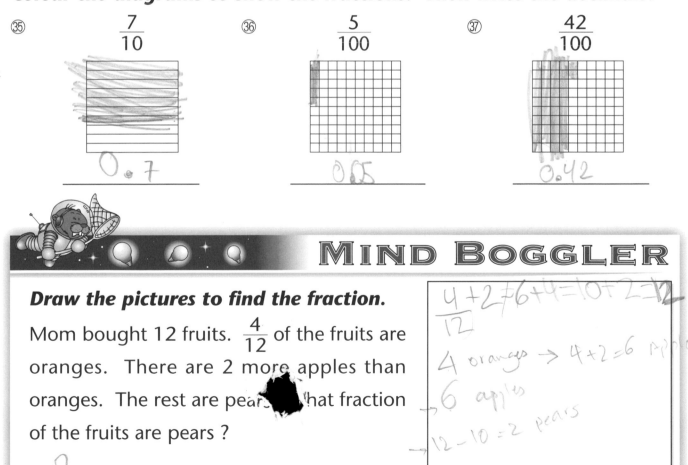

㉟ $\dfrac{7}{10}$

___0.7___

㊱ $\dfrac{5}{100}$

___0.05___

㊲ $\dfrac{42}{100}$

___0.42___

MIND BOGGLER

Draw the pictures to find the fraction.

Mom bought 12 fruits. $\dfrac{4}{12}$ of the fruits are oranges. There are 2 more apples than oranges. The rest are pears. What fraction of the fruits are pears ?

___$\frac{2}{12}$___ of the fruits are pears.

$\frac{4+2 \neq 6 + 4 = 10 + 2 = 12}{12}$

4 oranges → 4+2=6 apples

6 apples

12 − 10 = 2 pears

7 Decimals

Write each decimal number in words.

① 0.2 __two tenths__

② 0.05 __five hundred__

③ 0.74 __seventy four hundred__

④ 0.91 __niny one hundred__

Write as a decimal number.

⑤ Four tenths __0.4__

⑥ Eight hundredths __0.08__

⑦ Twelve hundredths __0.12__

⑧ Sixty-seven hundredths __0.67__

Write each decimal number on the place value chart.

		tens	ones	tenths	hundredths
⑨	5.2			5	2
⑩	7.49		7	4	9
⑪	58.1		5	8	1

Write the place value and meaning of each underlined digit.

2.4
0.44
0.06

⑫ 2.4<u>6</u> place value __hundredths__ means __0.06__

⑬ 1.<u>4</u>2 place value __thents__ means __0.40__

⑭ <u>7</u>.12 place value __one__ means __7.00__

⑮ 8.5<u>9</u> place value __hundredths__ means __0.09__

Help Janice compare the prices of candies in two stores. Write > or < in the boxes.

⑯ $0.42 > $0.39

⑰ $2.15 < $2.24

⑱ $0.87 < $1.01

⑲ $1.03 < $1.30

$\frac{1}{10}$ 0.1 = 0.10 → $\frac{10}{100}$ 00010

Write the numbers in order from least to greatest.

⑳   0.10   0.07   1.40   0.1   0.07   1.4

㉑   2.20   2.02   20.20   2.02   2.20   20.2 ✓

㉒   3.42   3.04   4.32   3.04   3.42   4.32 ✓

Use the number line below to help round the decimals to the nearest whole number.

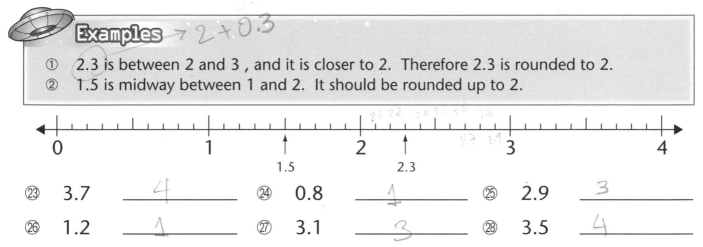

Examples → 2 + 0.3

① 2.3 is between 2 and 3 , and it is closer to 2. Therefore 2.3 is rounded to 2.
② 1.5 is midway between 1 and 2. It should be rounded up to 2.

0 ——— 1 ——↑— 2 ——↑— 3 ——— 4
          1.5   2.3

㉓   3.7   __4__   ㉔   0.8   __1__   ㉕   2.9   __3__

㉖   1.2   __1__   ㉗   3.1   __3__   ㉘   3.5   __4__

Write the decimals and complete the addition or subtraction sentences to match the pictures.

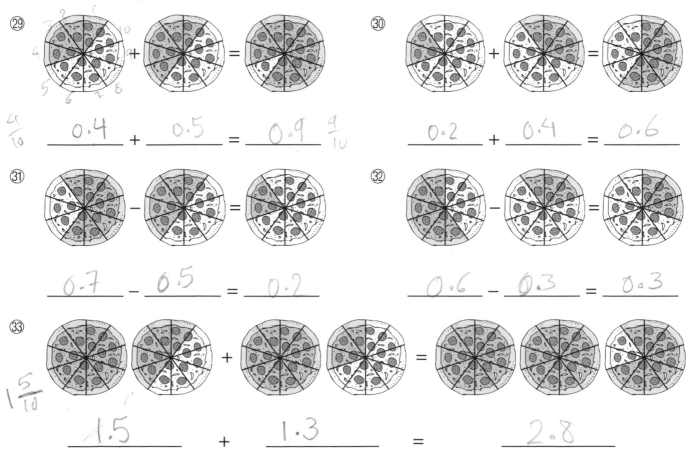

㉙ $\frac{4}{10}$ __0.4__ + __0.5__ = __0.9__ $\frac{9}{10}$

㉚   __0.2__ + __0.4__ = __0.6__

㉛   __0.7__ − __0.5__ = __0.2__

㉜   __0.6__ − __0.3__ = __0.3__

�33 $1\frac{5}{10}$ __1.5__ + __1.3__ = __2.8__

Do the addition.

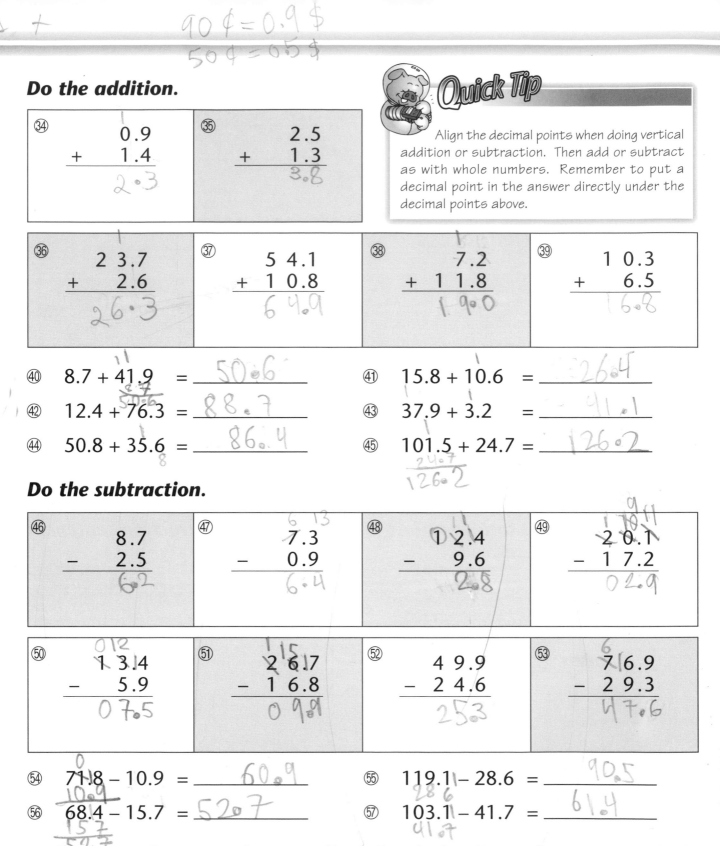

㉞
```
    0.9
+   1.4
    2.3
```

㉟
```
    2.5
+   1.3
    3.8
```

㊱
```
  2 3.7
+   2.6
  2 6.3
```

㊲
```
  5 4.1
+ 1 0.8
  6 4.9
```

㊳
```
    7.2
+ 1 1.8
  1 9.0
```

㊴
```
  1 0.3
+   6.5
  1 6.8
```

㊵ 8.7 + 41.9 = __50.6__

㊶ 15.8 + 10.6 = __26.4__

㊷ 12.4 + 76.3 = __88.7__

㊸ 37.9 + 3.2 = __41.1__

㊹ 50.8 + 35.6 = __86.4__

㊺ 101.5 + 24.7 = __126.2__

Do the subtraction.

㊻
```
    8.7
−   2.5
    6.2
```

㊼
```
    7.3
−   0.9
    6.4
```

㊽
```
  1 2.4
−   9.6
    2.8
```

㊾
```
  2 0.1
− 1 7.2
  0 2.9
```

㊿
```
  1 3.4
−   5.9
  0 7.5
```

(51)
```
  2 6.7
− 1 6.8
  0 9.9
```

(52)
```
  4 9.9
− 2 4.6
  2 5.3
```

(53)
```
  7 6.9
− 2 9.3
  4 7.6
```

(54) 71.8 − 10.9 = __60.9__

(55) 119.1 − 28.6 = __90.5__

(56) 68.4 − 15.7 = __52.7__

(57) 103.1 − 41.7 = __61.4__

Estimate each answer by rounding the decimals to the nearest whole number. Then find the exact answer.

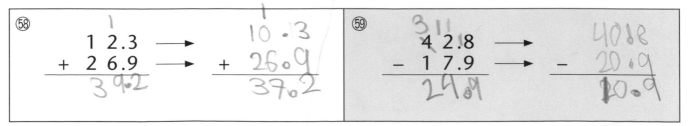

(58)
```
  1 2.3   ⟶     1 0.3
+ 2 6.9   ⟶   + 2 6.9
  3 9.2         3 7.2
```

(59)
```
  4 2.8   ⟶     4 0.8
− 1 7.9   ⟶   − 2 0.9
  2 9.9         2 0.9
```

Look at the locations of the children's homes and solve the problems.

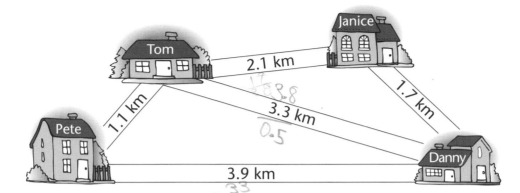

Tom — 2.1 km — Janice
1.1 km
1.7 km
3.3 km
0.5
Pete
3.9 km — Danny

60 Tom went to meet Janice at her house. Then he walked to Danny's home. How many km did Tom walk altogether?

2.1 + 1.7 = 38   38 km altogether

61 If Tom goes directly to Danny's house, by how many km will the route be shorter?

3.8 - 3.3 = 0.5   0.5 km

62 How many km does Pete walk if he goes to Danny's house via Tom's house?

_____ = _____   _____ km

63 How many more km will Pete walk if he goes by the route in 62 instead of the direct route?

_____ = _____   _____ km more

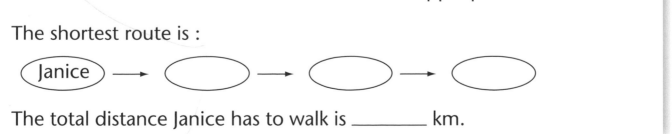

MIND BOGGLER

Fill in the names and complete the sentence.

Janice is going to give each of her three friends an apple pie. She will walk to her friends' houses and her father will drive her home later. Janice wants to take the shortest route to deliver the apple pies.

The shortest route is :

(Janice) → (____) → (____) → (____)

The total distance Janice has to walk is _____ km.

Progress Test

Complete the table to show the place value and the meaning of the grey digit in each number.

Number	0.53	4230	21.7	6.19	7528
① Place value					
② Meaning					

Write the numbers.

③ 6 thousands 3 hundreds 5 tens   _____

④ Seven thousand eight hundred twenty-nine   _____

⑤ Forty-two hundredths   _____

⑥ Two thousand three   _____

⑦ 36 and 9 hundredths   _____

Write each number in words.

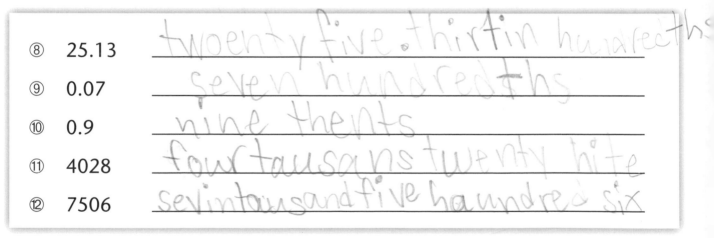

⑧ 25.13   *twoenty five thirtin hundrecths*

⑨ 0.07   *seven hundredths*

⑩ 0.9   *nine thents*

⑪ 4028   *four tausans twenty hite*

⑫ 7506   *sevintausand five haundred six*

Fill in the correct numbers.

⑬ 6793 = 6000 + *700* + *90* + *3*

⑭ 3075 = *3* thousands *0* hundreds *7* tens *5* ones

⑮ *5089* = 5000 + 80 + 9

⑯ *4605* = 4 thousands 6 hundreds 5 ones

⑰ *3019* = 3 tens and 19 hundredths   *30.19*

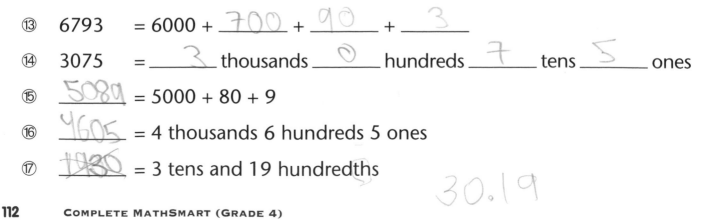

Fill in the missing numbers.

⑱ 4993   5093   _5193_   _5293_   5393   _5493_

⑲ 9080   _8080_   7080   _6080_   _5080_   4080

⑳ 0.19   0.29   _0.39_   _0.49_   0.59   _0.69_

Put the numbers in order.

㉑ 1.3   1.03   1.33 $1.33 > 1.03 > 1.30$

㉒ 5.46   5.64   5.06 $5.64 > 5.46 > 5.06$

㉓ 8736   9736   8973 $9736 > 8973 > 8736$

㉔ $\frac{11}{15}$ $\frac{17}{15}$ $\frac{3}{15}$ $\frac{9}{15}$ $\frac{3}{15} < \frac{9}{15} < \frac{11}{15} < \frac{17}{15}$

㉕ $2\frac{3}{9}$ $2\frac{7}{9}$ $1\frac{3}{9}$ $1\frac{1}{9}$ $2\frac{7}{9} > 2\frac{3}{9} > 1\frac{3}{9} > 1\frac{1}{9}$

Write a fraction and a decimal number for the shaded parts of the diagram in ㉖ and colour the diagrams to show the fractions or decimal numbers in ㉗ and ㉘. Fill in the missing numbers.

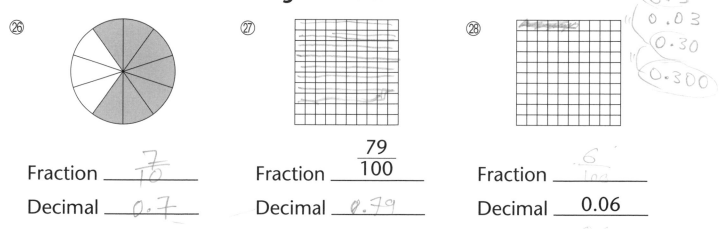

0.3
0.03
0.30
0.300

㉖ Fraction _$\frac{7}{10}$_

Decimal _0.7_

㉗ Fraction _$\frac{79}{100}$_

Decimal _0.79_

㉘ Fraction _$\frac{6}{100}$_

Decimal _0.06_

0.06

Fill in the boxes with 'P' to represent proper fractions, 'I' to represent improper fractions, and 'M' to represent mixed numbers.

0.84

㉙ $\frac{14}{14}$ [I]   ㉚ $3\frac{6}{9}$ [M]   ㉛ $\frac{7}{18}$ [P]   ㉜ $\frac{17}{11}$ [I]

㉝ $5\frac{7}{12}$ [M]   ㉞ $\frac{15}{8}$ [I]   ㉟ $\frac{4}{7}$ [P]   ㊱ $\frac{9}{13}$ [P]

Progress Test

Calculate.

㊲ 6473 − 948	㊳ 36 × 9	㊴ 943 × 8	㊵ 2564 + 4795
㊶ 4)243	㊷ 5)86	㊸ 6)756	㊹ 7)248
㊺ 3.6 + 21.8	㊻ 39.5 + 16.4	㊼ 46.9 − 2.7	㊽ 23.4 − 19.8

㊾ 9.2 + 45.9 = ________ ㊿ 23.1 – 9.8 = ________

(51) 72 x 6 = ________ (52) 805 x 7 = ________

(53) 96 ÷ 8 = ________ (54) 864 ÷ 8 = ________

(55) 542 x 6 = ________ (56) 7203 – 874 = ________

Draw pictures to help complete the sentences.

(57) Janice has a collection of  stickers. $\frac{3}{12}$ of the stickers are red. $\frac{4}{12}$ of the stickers are blue. The rest are yellow.

a. $\frac{\square}{12}$ of the stickers are yellow.

b. Most of the stickers are ________ .

c. ________ stickers are the fewest.

The children are playing computer games. Help them solve the problems.

⑤⑧ Sam scored 3468 points in 6 rounds. If he got the same points in each round, what was his score in each round?

_____ = _____

His score in each round was _____ points.

⑤⑨ Sam scored 1020 points in the 7th round. What was his total score in 7 rounds?

_____ = _____

His total score in 7 rounds was _____ points.

⑥⓪ Edith scored 615 points fewer than Sam. What was her total score?

_____ = _____

Her total score was _____ points.

⑥① Tom scored 837 points in each of the first 4 rounds. What was his total score in the first 4 rounds?

_____ = _____

His total score in the first 4 rounds was _____ points.

⑥② Sam took 1.2 hours to finish the first 6 rounds and 0.4 hour to finish the 7th round. How much time did he use to finish the game?

_____ = _____

He used _____ hours to finish the game.

⑥③ Tom took 0.5 hour more than Sam to finish the game and Edith took 0.2 hour less than Tom. How long did Edith take to finish the game?

_____ = _____

Edith took _____ hours to finish the game.

8 Geometry I

Identify each set of lines and write the letter in the box.

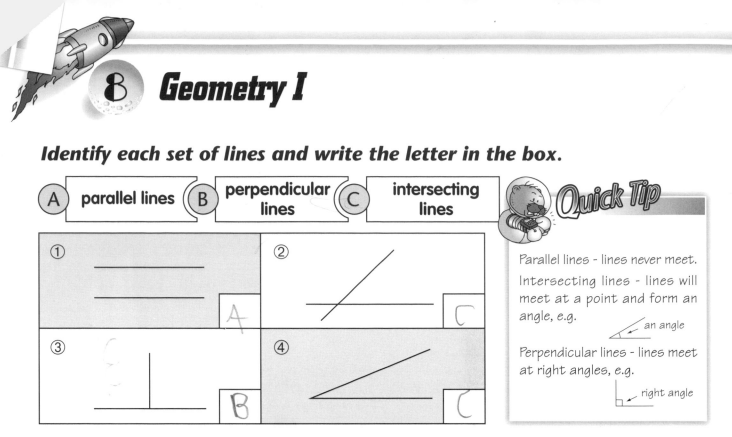

| A | parallel lines | B | perpendicular lines | C | intersecting lines |

Quick Tip

Parallel lines - lines never meet.

Intersecting lines - lines will meet at a point and form an angle, e.g. *an angle*

Perpendicular lines - lines meet at right angles, e.g. *right angle*

① A
② C
③ B
④ C

Identify the angles formed by the clock hands. Write their representing letters in the right boxes.

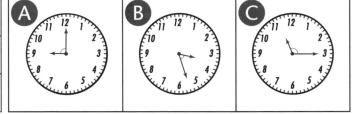

⑤	A right angle	A
⑥	Greater than a right angle	C
⑦	Smaller than a right angle	B

Measure the following angles using a protractor.

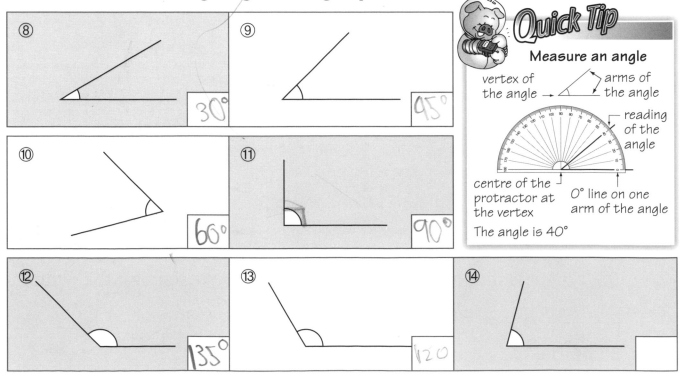

Quick Tip

Measure an angle

vertex of the angle → *arms of the angle*

reading of the angle

centre of the protractor at the vertex — 0° line on one arm of the angle

The angle is 40°

⑧ 30°
⑨ 45°
⑩ 60°
⑪ 90°
⑫ 135°
⑬ 120

Colour the quadrilaterals.

⑮

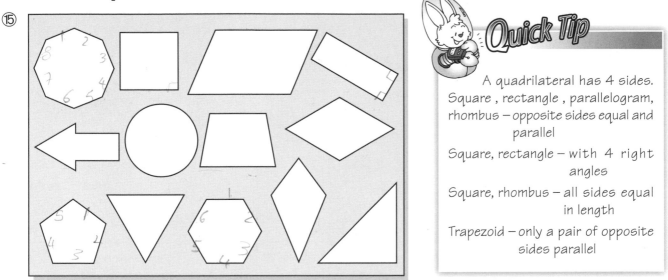

Quick Tip

A quadrilateral has 4 sides.
Square , rectangle , parallelogram, rhombus — opposite sides equal and parallel
Square, rectangle — with 4 right angles
Square, rhombus — all sides equal in length
Trapezoid — only a pair of opposite sides parallel

Write the name of each shape. Then check ✔ the boxes to show its properties.

⑯

A	B	C	D	E
Trapezoid	Square	Rhombus	Rectangle	Parallelogram

Property / Shape	A	B	C	D	E
⑰ 4 equal sides		✓	✓		
⑱ 2 pairs of equal sides				✓	✓
⑲ 2 pairs of parallel sides		✓	✓	✓	✓
⑳ 1 pair of parallel sides only	✓				
㉑ 4 right angles		✓		✓	

What shapes are they? Write their names in the boxes.

㉒ It has 2 pairs of equal sides and 4 right angles. Rectangle

㉓ It has 2 pairs of parallel sides and all sides are equal. Rhombus

㉔ It has only 1 pair of parallel sides. Trapezoid

㉕ It has 2 pairs of equal sides and no right angles. Parallelogram

㉖ It has 4 equal sides and 4 right angles. Square

Write the name of each shape and sketch its faces.

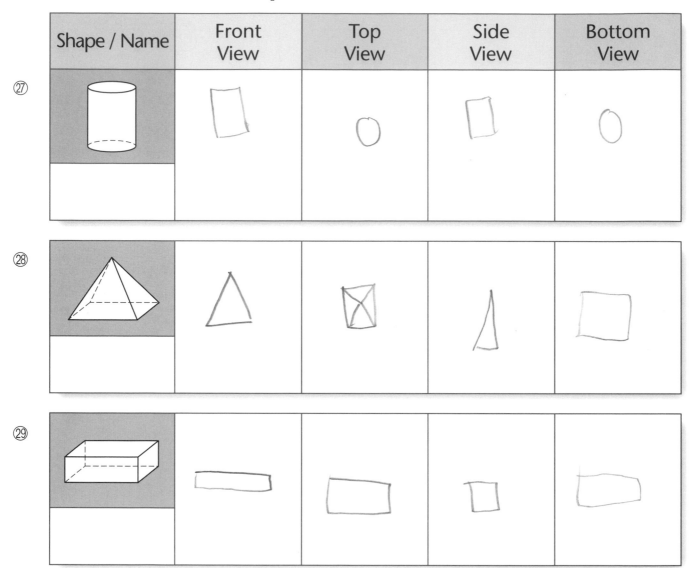

Shape / Name	Front View	Top View	Side View	Bottom View
㉗				
㉘				
㉙				

Janice makes the skeletons of some 3-D shapes with straws and marshmallows. Help her complete the skeletons and fill in the missing numbers.

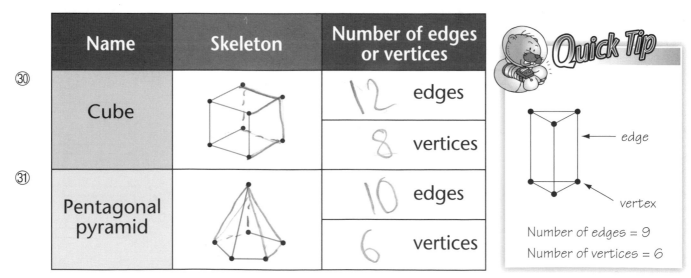

Name	Skeleton	Number of edges or vertices	
㉚ Cube		12	edges
		8	vertices
㉛ Pentagonal pyramid		10	edges
		6	vertices

Quick Tip

edge

vertex

Number of edges = 9
Number of vertices = 6

Find the congruent and similar shapes. Write the letters in the right boxes.

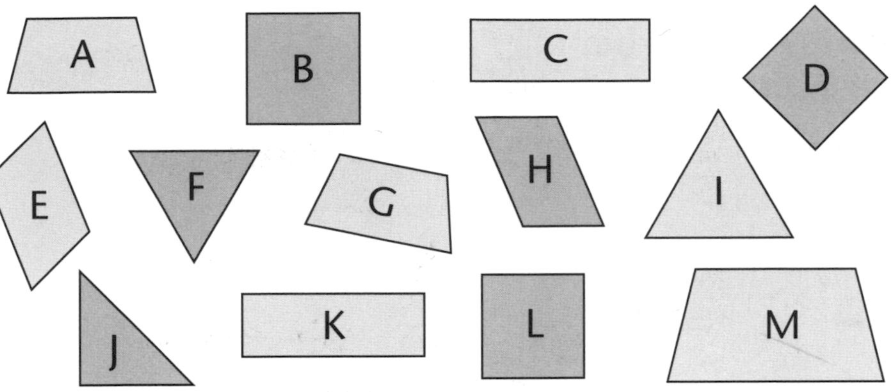

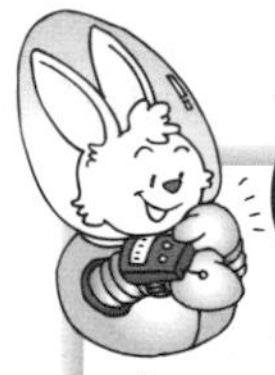

Quick Tip

Congruent figures have the same size and shape. Similar figures have the same shape but different sizes.

e.g. 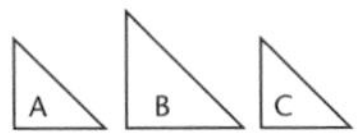

A and C – congruent
A and B } similar
B and C } similar

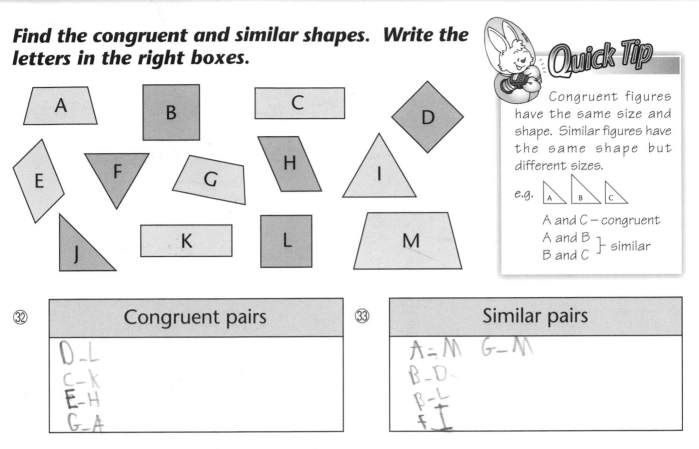

㉜ Congruent pairs
D–L C–K E–H G–A

㉝ Similar pairs
A–M G–M B–D B–L F–I

Draw a similar figure and a congruent figure for the shape.

㉞

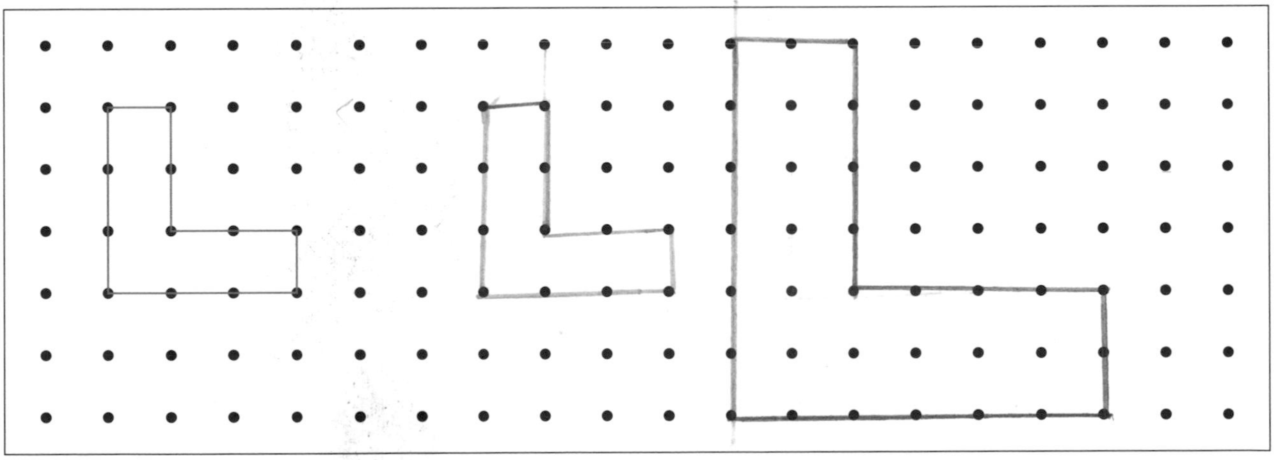

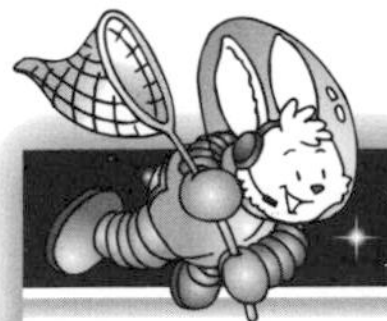

MIND BOGGLER

Use the geoboard to help you draw a congruent figure of the 3-D shape.

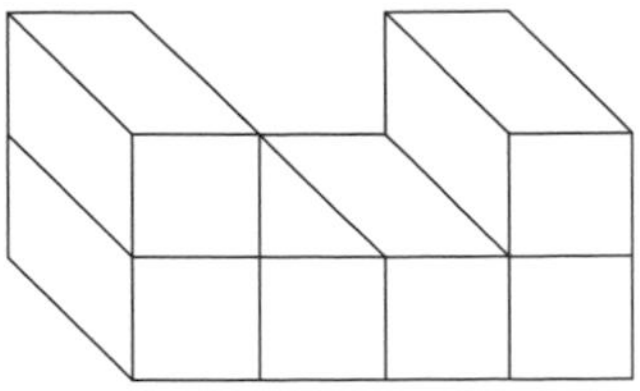

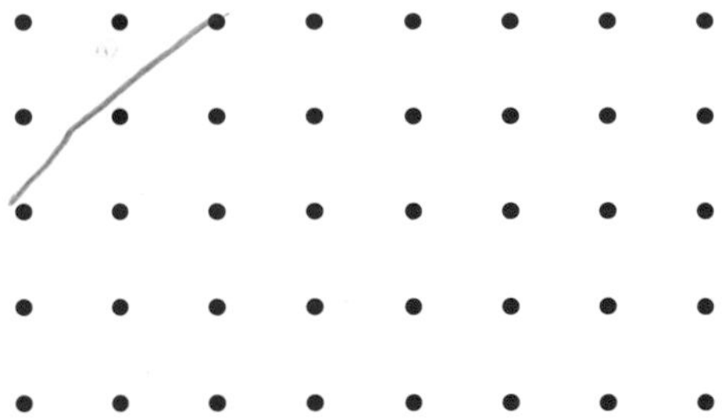

9 Units of Measure

Write the most appropriate unit you would use to measure each object.

① Your pencil _____ cm

② Distance from home to school _____ Km

③ Your height _____ m & cm

④ The height of the door _____ m

⑤ A worm _____ cm

⑥ Your desk _____ cm

⑦ An ant _____ mm

Janice has several pencils. Help her measure the length of each pencil in mm. Then write the length in cm.

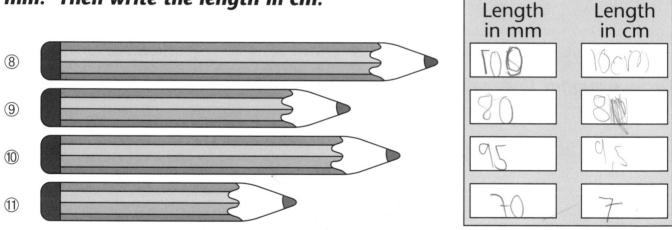

	Length in mm	Length in cm
⑧	100	10cm
⑨	80	8
⑩	95	9.5
⑪	70	7

Draw pictures following the instructions.

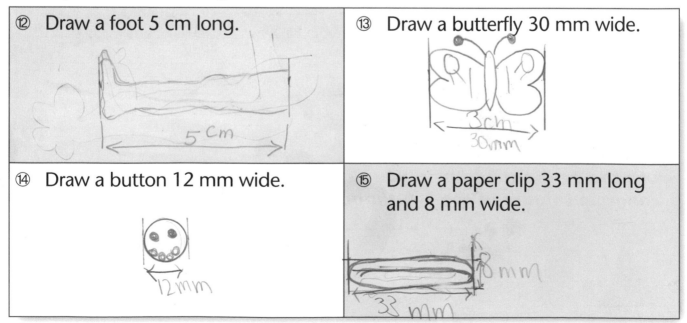

⑫ Draw a foot 5 cm long.

5 Cm

⑬ Draw a butterfly 30 mm wide.

3cm
30mm

⑭ Draw a button 12 mm wide.

12mm

⑮ Draw a paper clip 33 mm long and 8 mm wide.

8 mm
33 mm

Janice was celebrating her tenth birthday with her friends. Help the children fill in the missing numbers in the game card.

Quick Tip

1 decade = 10 years

1 century = 100 years or 10 decades

1 millennium = 1000 years or 100 decades

⑯ 20 years are __2__ decades.

⑰ 500 years are __5__ centuries.

⑱ 3000 years are __3__ millenniums.

⑲ 800 years are __80__ decades.

⑳ There are __50__ years in half a century.

㉑ There are __250__ years in a quarter of a millennium.

㉒ Canada was 134 years old in the year 2001. Her age was __1__ century __3__ decades and __4__ years.

The children were playing computer games. See when each child started and finished the game. Complete the table and sentences.

㉓

	Janice	Pete	Marie	Joey	Tom	Sam
Starting time	2:29	2:54	3:27	3:58	4:18	4:50
Finishing time	2:54	3:27	3:58	4:18	4:50	5:20
Time used (min)	25 min	33 min	31 min	20 min	32 min	30 min

㉔ __Joey__ used the shortest time to finish the game.

㉕ __Pete__ used the longest time to finish the game.

㉖ Janice used __5__ min longer than Joey.

㉗ Sam used 1 min shorter than __Marie__

㉘ Time used by Joey and __Sam__ differed by 10 min.

㉙ Time used by __Sam__ and __pete__ differed by 3 min.

Quick Tip

To determine time intervals, trade 1 hour for 60 minutes if necessary, e.g. the time interval between 2:12 and 1:49 can be calculated by

$$\begin{array}{r} 2:12 \\ -1:49 \end{array} \quad \begin{array}{r} 1:72 \\ -1:49 \\ \hline 23 \end{array}$$

Time interval is 23 min.

The children were each given $50 to buy their favourite toys. See what they bought and write the change they got in the boxes. Then answer the questions.

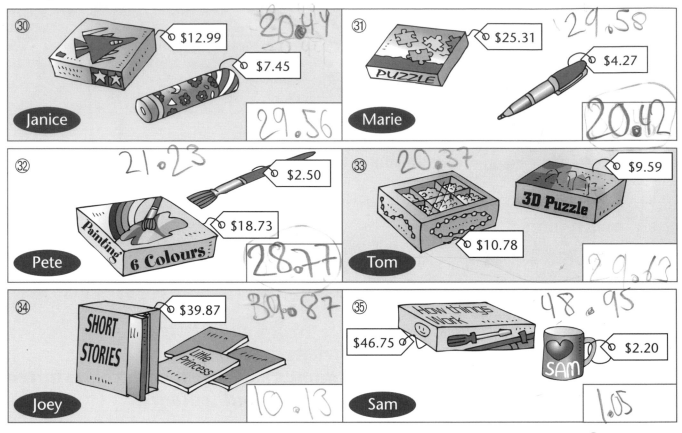

30. Janice — $12.99, $7.45 — *20.44* — 29.56

31. Marie — $25.31, $4.27 — *29.58* — 20.42

32. Pete — $2.50, $18.73 — *21.23* — 28.77

33. Tom — $9.59, $10.78 — *20.37* — 29.63

34. Joey — $39.87 — *39.87* — 10.13

35. Sam — $46.75, $2.20 — *48.95* — 1.05

36. Who spent the most money? Sam

37. Who got the most change? tom

The numbers of bills and coins are shown in the circles. Find the total amount in each group.

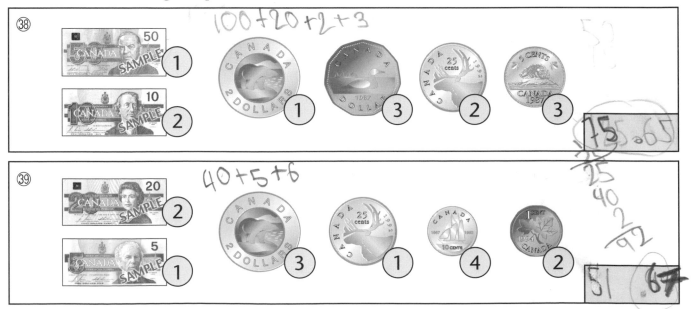

38. 50 (1), 10 (2); 2 dollars (1), 1 dollar (3), 25 cents (2), 5 cents (3)
100 + 20 + 2 + 3   *50*   *75.65*   *25 40 2 92*

39. 20 (2), 5 (1); 2 dollars (3), 25 cents (1), 10 cents (4), 1 cent (2)
40 + 5 + 6   *51.67*

Look at the prices and help the children solve the problems. Show your work.

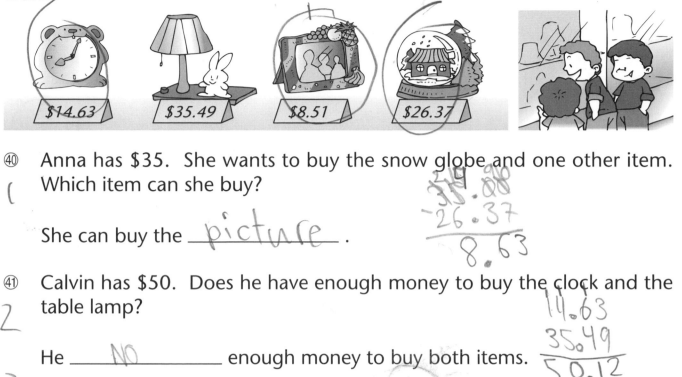

$14.63 $35.49 $8.51 $26.37

⑩ Anna has $35. She wants to buy the snow globe and one other item. Which item can she buy?

She can buy the ___picture___ .

$$\begin{array}{r} 35.00 \\ -26.37 \\ \hline 8.63 \end{array}$$

㊶ Calvin has $50. Does he have enough money to buy the clock and the table lamp?

He ___NO___ enough money to buy both items.

$$\begin{array}{r} 14.63 \\ 35.49 \\ \hline 50.12 \end{array}$$

㊷ Michelle has $40. If she wants to buy the table lamp and the photo frame, how much more money does she need?

She needs $ ___4$___ more.

$$\begin{array}{r} 35.49 \\ +8.51 \\ \hline 44.00 \end{array}$$

㊸ Julie has $50 and she wants to buy as many items as she can. Which items can she buy?

She can buy ___clocke_photo frame_clobe___

_____ .

MIND BOGGLER

Cindy bought 3 of the above items and got a change of $4.63 from $75. What did she buy?

Cindy bought ___lamp frame globe___

_____ .

10 Perimeter and Area

Check ✔ the circle to show whether you would consider the 'perimeter' or 'area' in each case. Then select the most appropriate unit of measure. Write cm, m, cm², or m² on the line.

① The carpet for covering the floor of the family room

○ perimeter ✓ area ___m²___

② The flower chain for decorating the tack board

✓ perimeter ○ area ___cm___

③ The fencing around the backyard

✓ perimeter ○ area ___m___

④ The treated planks for building a deck

○ perimeter ✓ area ___m²___

⑤ The decorating paper for wrapping up a storybook

○ perimeter ✓ area ___cm²___

> **Quick Tip**
>
> Centimetres (cm) and square centimetres (cm²) are for measuring the perimeter and area of a small thing. Metres (m) and square metres (m²) are for measuring a large thing.

Help Janice measure the sides and find the perimeter (P) of each sticker. Then answer the questions.

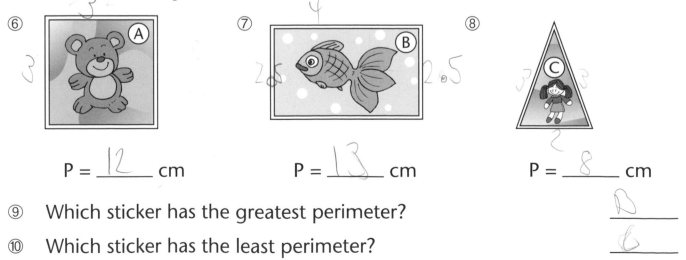

⑥ P = __12__ cm

⑦ P = __13__ cm

⑧ P = __8__ cm

⑨ Which sticker has the greatest perimeter? ___B___

⑩ Which sticker has the least perimeter? ___C___

Janice cut out different shapes for her art project. Help her calculate the perimeter of each shape.

⑪	Perimeter
A	19 cm
B	24 cm
C	26 cm
D	67 cm
E	30 cm
F	36 cm

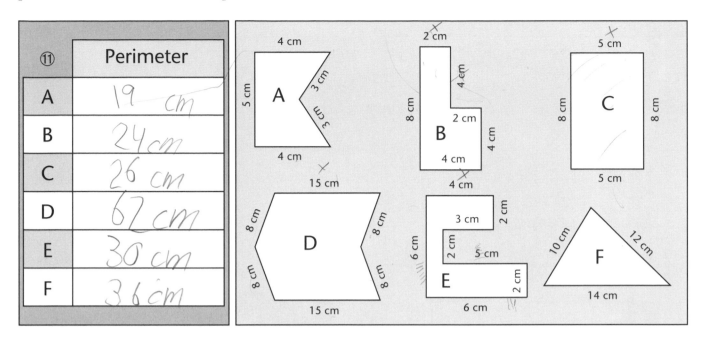

Pete drew some shapes on the centimetre grid paper. Help him find the perimeter and area of each shape.

3 cm × 3 cm = 9 cm²

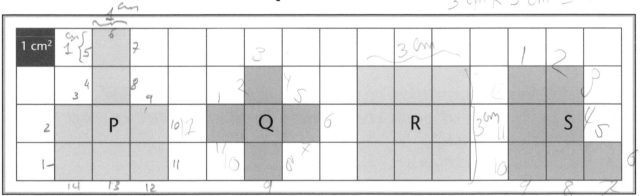

		P	Q	R	S
⑫	Perimeter	14 cm	12 cm	12 cm	12 cm
⑬	Area	8 cm²	5 cm²	9 cm²	7 cm²

⑭ Which shape has the greatest perimeter? ___P___

⑮ Which shape has the greatest area? ___R___

⑯ Does the shape with the greatest perimeter have

the greatest area? ___NO___

Estimate the area of each polygon on the centimetre grid paper.

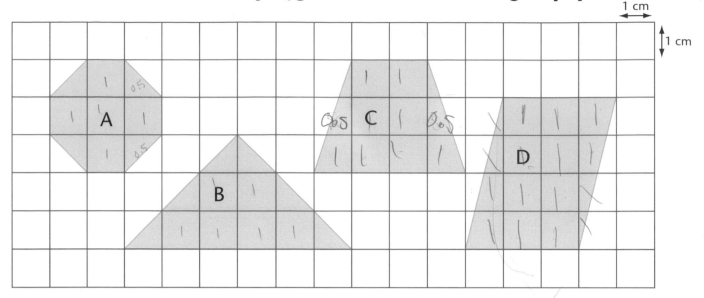

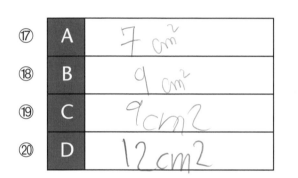

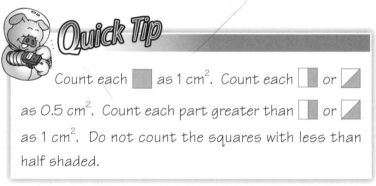

⑰	A	7 cm²
⑱	B	9 cm²
⑲	C	9 cm2
⑳	D	12 cm2

Draw 3 different rectangles each having an area of 12 cm². Count and label the perimeter of each rectangle. Then circle the correct word to complete the sentence.

�21

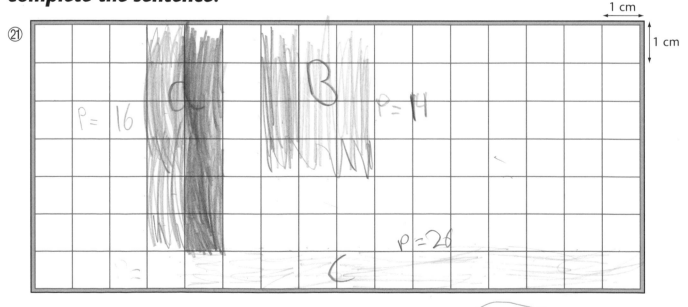

P = 16

B P = 14

P = 20

�22 The perimeters of the rectangles are the same / different .

Draw 3 different shapes each having a perimeter of 16 cm on the centimetre dot paper. Count and label the area of each shape. Then circle the correct word to complete the sentence.

㉓

1 cm²

㉔ The areas of the shapes are the same / different .

MIND BOGGLER

Draw Marie's bookmarks.

Marie has designed a rectangular bookmark with an area of 27 cm² and a perimeter of 24 cm. Help her design and draw 2 more bookmarks so that one has a greater area but a smaller perimeter than A while the other has a smaller area but a greater perimeter than A. Label the area and the perimeter of each bookmark.

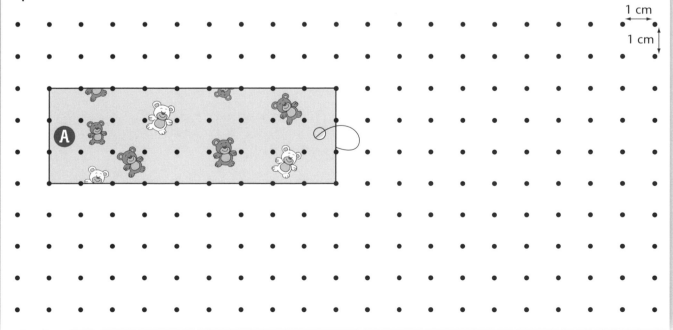

1 cm

1 cm

A

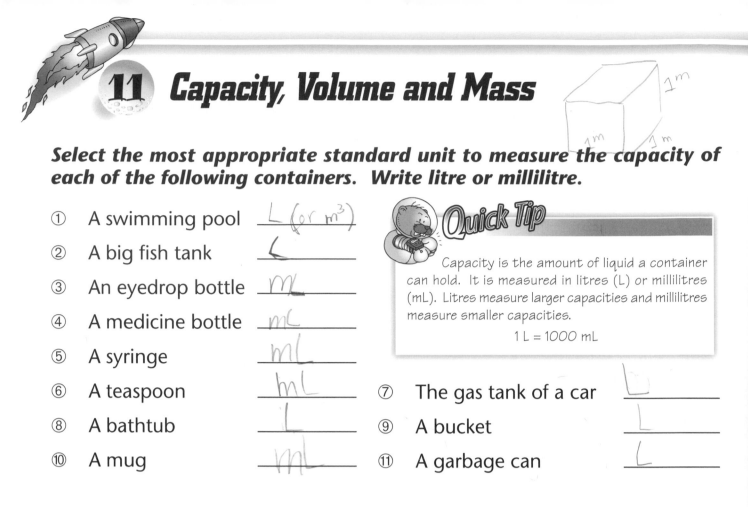

11 Capacity, Volume and Mass

Select the most appropriate standard unit to measure the capacity of each of the following containers. Write litre or millilitre.

① A swimming pool _L (or m³)_

② A big fish tank _L_

③ An eyedrop bottle _mL_

④ A medicine bottle _mL_

⑤ A syringe _mL_

⑥ A teaspoon _mL_

⑧ A bathtub _L_

⑩ A mug _mL_

⑦ The gas tank of a car _L_

⑨ A bucket _L_

⑪ A garbage can _L_

Quick Tip

Capacity is the amount of liquid a container can hold. It is measured in litres (L) or millilitres (mL). Litres measure larger capacities and millilitres measure smaller capacities.

1 L = 1000 mL

Pete is comparing the capacity of the containers he found at home. Look at the containers and answer the questions.

250 mL — Milk 1L — Detergent 750 mL — Syrup 500 mL — 3 L

⑫ How many mugs of water can fill up 1 milk carton? ___4___ mugs

⑬ How many bottles of syrup can fill up 1 milk carton? ___2___ bottles

⑭ How many mugs of water can fill up 1 detergent bottle? ___3___ mugs

⑮ How many cartons of milk can fill up 1 bucket? ___3___ cartons

⑯ How many bottles of syrup can fill up 1 bucket? ___6___ bottles

⑰ How many bottles of detergent can fill up 1 bucket? ___4___ bottles

⑱ List the containers in order from the one with least capacity to the one with greatest.

mug Syrup Detergent milk

Bucket 750 mL × 4 = 3000 mL

Michelle uses centimetre cubes to build the following structures. Count the number of cubes used to determine the volume of each structure.

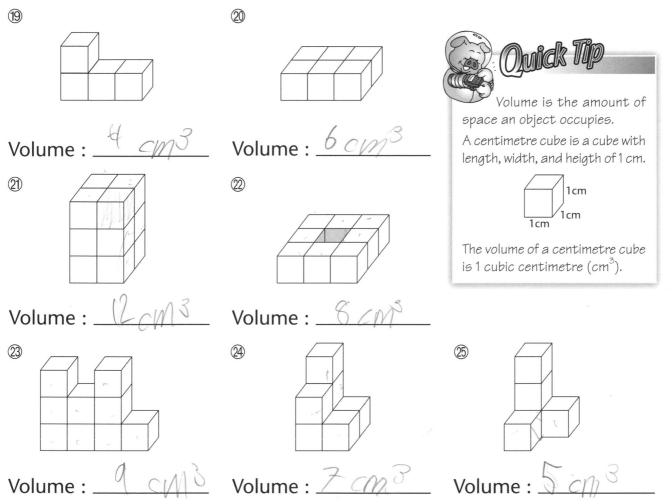

⑲ Volume : _____4_____ cm³

⑳ Volume : _____6 cm³_____

㉑ Volume : _____12 cm³_____

㉒ Volume : _____8 cm³_____

㉓ Volume : _____9 cm³_____

㉔ Volume : _____7 cm³_____

㉕ Volume : _____5 cm³_____

Use 16 centimetre cubes to build 2 different prisms. Draw them and answer the questions.

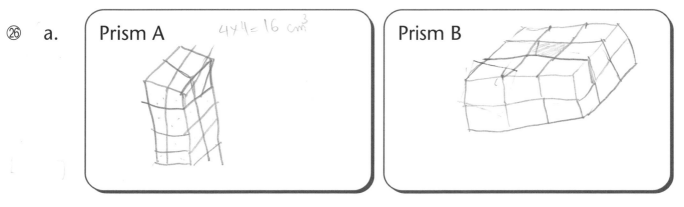

㉖ a.

Prism A   4×4 = 16 cm³

Prism B

b. Do the prisms have the same volume? _____Yes_____

c. Do the prisms have the same height? _____No_____

d. Do the prisms have the same length and width? _____No_____

Select the most appropriate standard unit to measure the mass of each of the following items. Write kilogram, gram, or milligram.

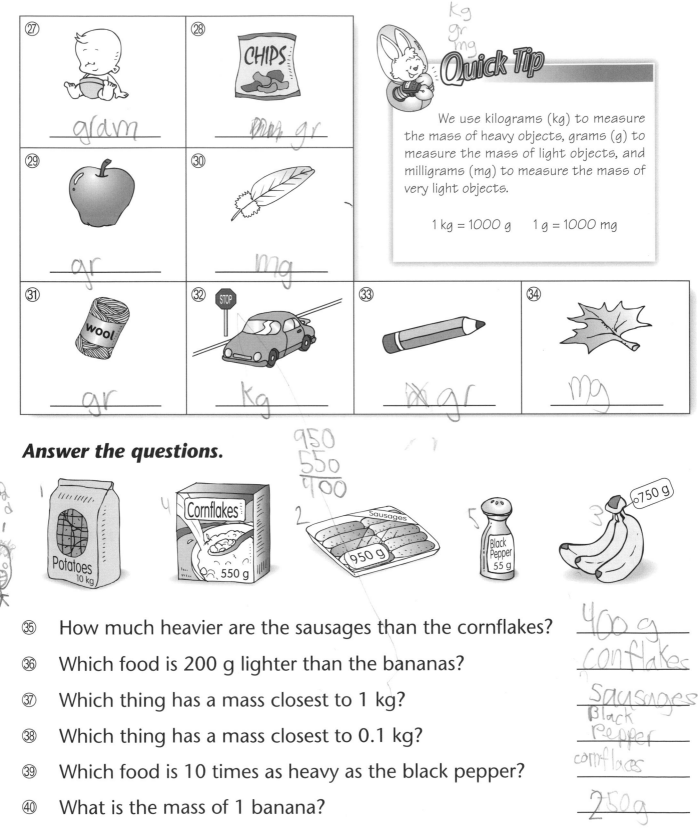

㉗ gram

㉘ ~~mg~~ gr

Quick Tip

We use kilograms (kg) to measure the mass of heavy objects, grams (g) to measure the mass of light objects, and milligrams (mg) to measure the mass of very light objects.

1 kg = 1000 g   1 g = 1000 mg

㉙ gr

㉚ mg

㉛ gr

㉜ kg

㉝ ~~mg~~ gr

㉞ mg

Answer the questions.

Potatoes 10 kg

Cornflakes 550 g

Sausages 950 g

Black Pepper 55 g

750 g

950
550
400

㉟ How much heavier are the sausages than the cornflakes?   400 g

㊱ Which food is 200 g lighter than the bananas?   cornflakes

㊲ Which thing has a mass closest to 1 kg?   sausages

㊳ Which thing has a mass closest to 0.1 kg?   Black Pepper

㊴ Which food is 10 times as heavy as the black pepper?   cornflakes

㊵ What is the mass of 1 banana?   250 g

㊶ List the masses in order from heaviest to lightest.

Potatoes, sausages, Banana, cornflakes, Black-pepper

Check ✔ the most reasonable estimate for the mass of each item.

㊷ a loonie		
A✔ less than 10 g	B 10 to 50 g	C over 50 g

㊸ an adult		
A less than 40 kg	B✔ 40 to 100 kg	C over 150 kg

㊹ a piano		
A✔ less than 100 kg	B 100 to 250 kg	C over 250 kg

Circle the correct mass in each question.

㊺ The greater mass 　(3.5 kg)　or　350 g

㊻ The lighter mass 　1 kg　or　(900 g)

㊼ The mass that is closer to 2 kg 　(2100 g)　or　1800 g

Janice has written some sentences about her things. Help her make each sentence reasonable by filling in kg, g, or mg.

㊽ My mass is about 30 000 ~~kg~~ .　　30 kg = 30,000 gr

㊾ The bit of nail clipped from my thumb is about 20 mg .

㊿ I have a table tennis ball of mass about 2 g .

51 Yesterday, I bought a 1- kg bag of sugar for Mom.

MIND BOGGLER

Look at the pictograph that shows the masses of different animals compared with the average mass of a man. Answer the questions.

① How many pigs will weigh the same as a horse?　　4

② What is the smallest number of calves, pigs, and tigers together to weigh as a horse?

1 Calf + 1 Pig + 1 Tiger

Mass of Animals Compared with the Mass of Man

☺ stands for 1 man

Calf	☺
Pig	☺ ☺
Tiger	☺ ☺ ☺ ☺ ☺
Horse	☺ ☺ ☺ ☺ ☺ ☺ ☺ ☺

12 Geometry II

Describe the transformations with 'Translation', 'Reflection', or 'Rotation'.

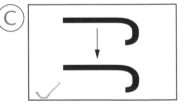

Transformation
The change of position and orientation of an object

Examples

Translation (Slide) F → F

Reflection (Flip) F Ⅎ
line of reflection

Rotation (Turn) F ⊤
centre of rotation

① Reflection

② Translation

③

Draw the reflection images of these letters.

④ J | L
⑤ K | ⟩
⑥ N | И

Which diagrams below show a translation? Check ✔ the letter.

⑦ Ⓐ E E ✓

Ⓑ

Ⓒ ✓

In each set, check ✔ the one that shows a rotation image of the shape on the left.

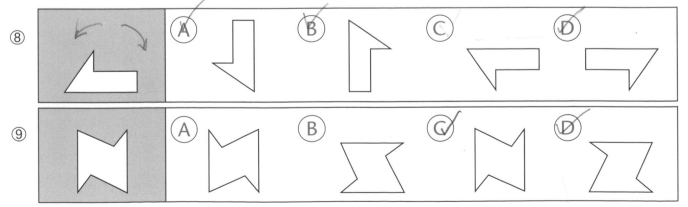

⑧ Ⓐ Ⓑ Ⓒ Ⓓ

⑨ Ⓐ Ⓑ Ⓒ ✓ Ⓓ

Draw an image of each shape for each type of transformation.

		Translation	Reflection	Rotation
⑩		a.	b.	c.
⑪		a.	b.	c.

Describe how the shape is translated in each case. Write the numbers and circle the correct words.

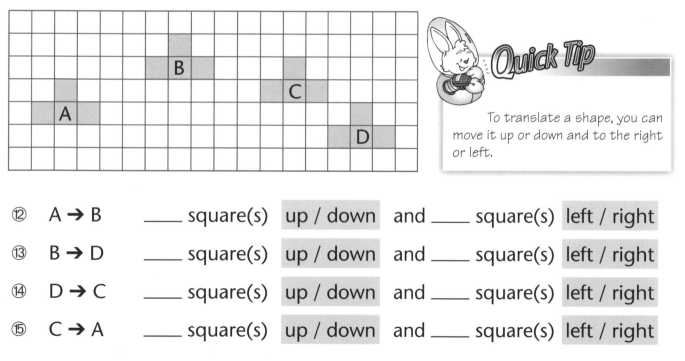

Quick Tip

To translate a shape, you can move it up or down and to the right or left.

⑫   A ➜ B   _____ square(s)   up / down   and _____ square(s)   left / right

⑬   B ➜ D   _____ square(s)   up / down   and _____ square(s)   left / right

⑭   D ➜ C   _____ square(s)   up / down   and _____ square(s)   left / right

⑮   C ➜ A   _____ square(s)   up / down   and _____ square(s)   left / right

Write 'quarter', 'half', or 'full' to show how letter 'Q' is rotated in a clockwise direction.

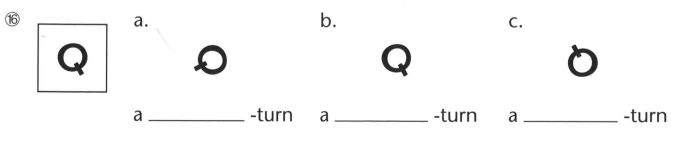

⑯   a.   b.   c.

a _____ -turn   a _____ -turn   a _____ -turn

COMPLETE MATHSMART (GRADE 4)   133

Use a ruler to draw the lines of symmetry.

⑰

Complete the symmetrical diagrams. (⟷) represents the line of symmetry.

⑱ ⑲ ⑳ ㉑

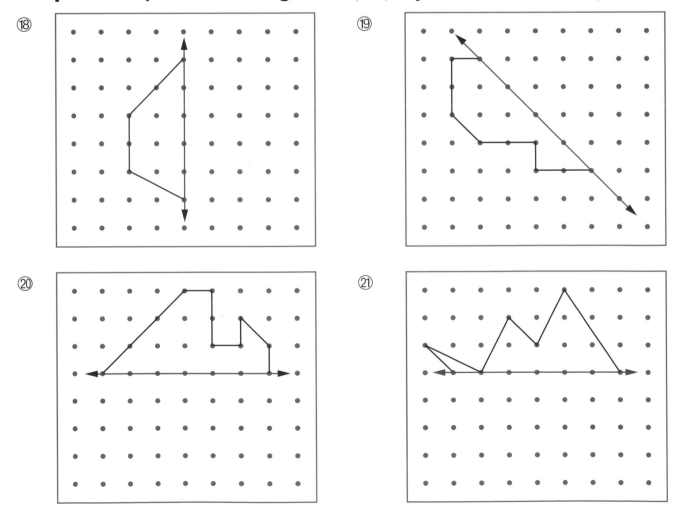

Sam is in Ferns Park. Look at the map and guide him through the Park.

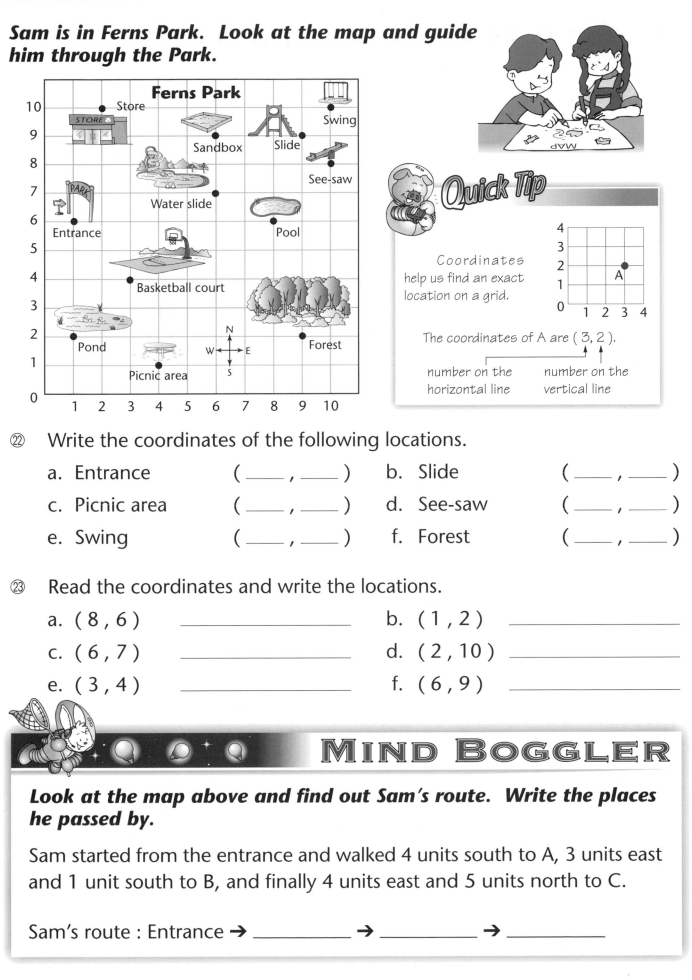

㉒ Write the coordinates of the following locations.

a. Entrance (___ , ___) b. Slide (___ , ___)

c. Picnic area (___ , ___) d. See-saw (___ , ___)

e. Swing (___ , ___) f. Forest (___ , ___)

㉓ Read the coordinates and write the locations.

a. (8 , 6) _____ b. (1 , 2) _____

c. (6 , 7) _____ d. (2 , 10) _____

e. (3 , 4) _____ f. (6 , 9) _____

MIND BOGGLER

Look at the map above and find out Sam's route. Write the places he passed by.

Sam started from the entrance and walked 4 units south to A, 3 units east and 1 unit south to B, and finally 4 units east and 5 units north to C.

Sam's route : Entrance → _____ → _____ → _____

13 Patterns and Simple Equations

Continue each skip counting pattern by filling in the missing numbers.

①	12	15	18	21					
②	44	48	52	56					
③	70	65	60			45			
④	60	54	48			30			
⑤	14	21	28			49			
⑥	8	16	24				56		
⑦	90	81	72	63					
⑧	20	30			60		80		

Draw the next two shapes in each pattern.

⑨

⑩

⑪

⑫

Quick Tip

There may be changes in two or more attributes of the shapes, e.g. size, shape, orientation, pattern.

Look for the patterns and complete the sentences.

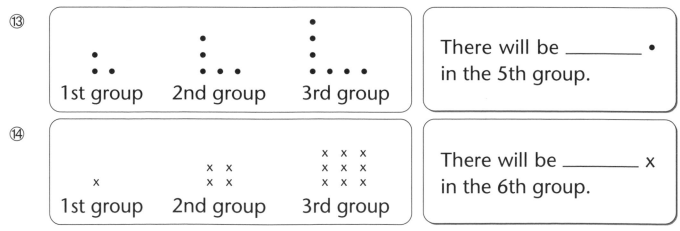

⑬

1st group   2nd group   3rd group

There will be _____ •
in the 5th group.

⑭

1st group   2nd group   3rd group

There will be _____ x
in the 6th group.

Finish each number pattern by writing the next 3 numbers. Then give the rule of each pattern.

> **Example**
>
> Write the next 3 numbers of the number pattern 39, 41, 40, 42, 41,...
>
> 39   41   40   42   41   43   42   44   Rule : Add 2, minus 1.
>   +2   −1   +2   −1   +2   −1   +2

⑮ 49   53   57   61   65   _____ _____ _____

  [Rule] _____

⑯ 86   79   72   65   58   _____ _____ _____

  [Rule] _____

⑰ 61   67   59   65   57   _____ _____ _____

  [Rule] _____

⑱ 96   95   93   90   86   _____ _____ _____

  [Rule] _____

⑲ 2   4   8   16   32   _____ _____ _____

  [Rule] _____

⑳ 3   6   12   21   33   _____ _____ _____

  [Rule] _____

Complete the table to show the pattern and solve the problem.

㉑ Joanne baked 7 cookies and 3 doughnuts on Monday, 10 cookies and 6 doughnuts on Tuseday, and 13 cookies and 9 doughnuts on Wednesday. Following this pattern, how many cookies and doughnuts did she bake on Friday?

a.

	Monday	Tuesday	Wednesday	Thursday	Friday
No. of cookies					
No. of doughnuts					

b. Joanne baked _____ cookies and _____ doughnuts on Friday.

Ms. Beatty's class sew duvet covers to raise money for the Children Cancer Fund. Look at the designs and complete the tables.

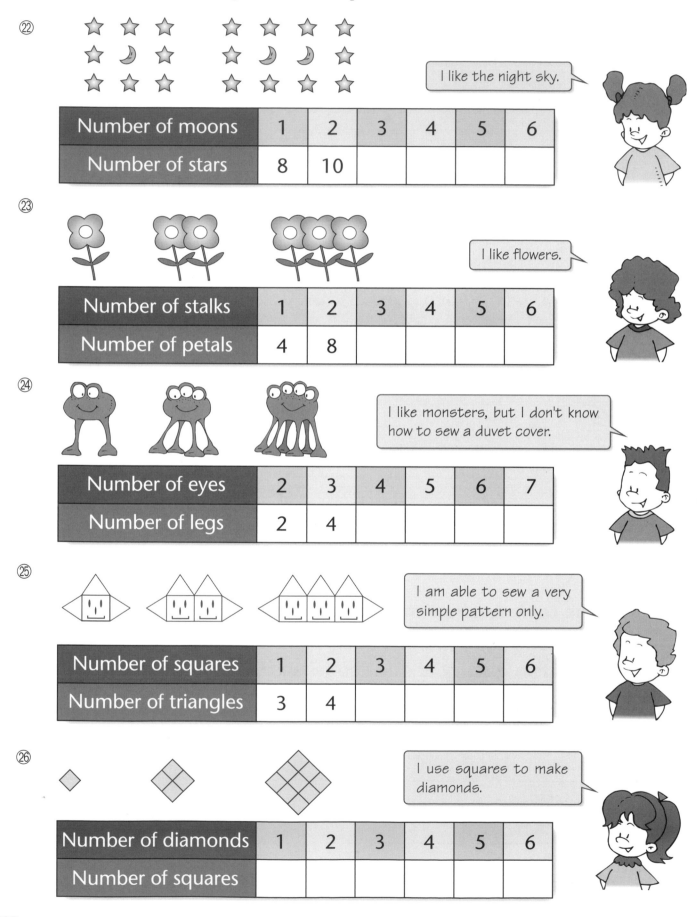

㉒

I like the night sky.

Number of moons	1	2	3	4	5	6
Number of stars	8	10				

㉓

I like flowers.

Number of stalks	1	2	3	4	5	6
Number of petals	4	8				

㉔

I like monsters, but I don't know how to sew a duvet cover.

Number of eyes	2	3	4	5	6	7
Number of legs	2	4				

㉕

I am able to sew a very simple pattern only.

Number of squares	1	2	3	4	5	6
Number of triangles	3	4				

㉖

I use squares to make diamonds.

Number of diamonds	1	2	3	4	5	6
Number of squares						

Complete the number sentences so that the answers are the same on both sides of each balance. You may use a calculator.

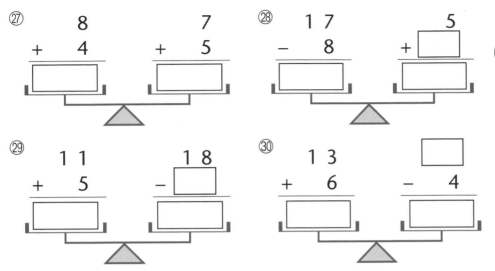

Quick Tip

To balance both sides means to make the number sentences on both sides have the same answers. You can determine the missing term in an equation by balancing both sides of the equation.

Determine the missing term in each equation. You can use the 'guess-and-test' method or a calculator.

③¹ $63 = 60 + \blacksquare$

$\blacksquare$ = _____

③² $37 = 42 - \blacktriangle$

$\blacktriangle$ = _____

③³ $2 + 3 + 5 = 16 - \heartsuit$

$\heartsuit$ = _____

③⁴ $12 - 8 = \clubsuit + 3$

$\clubsuit$ = _____

③⁵ $a + 7 = 12 + 18$

a = _____

③⁶ $b - 6 = 20 - 10$

b = _____

③⁷ $c - 10 = 16 + 9$

c = _____

③⁸ $d + 2 = 25 - 20$

d = _____

MIND BOGGLER

Fill in the missing numbers.

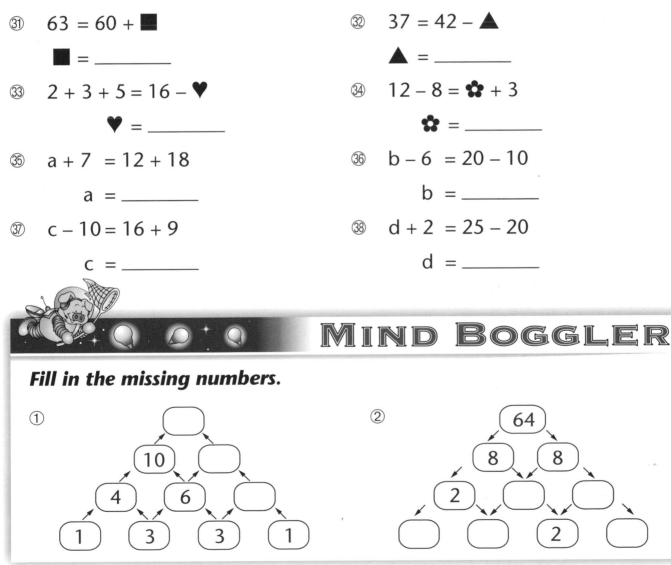

14 Graphs and Probability

Ms. Beatty's class is visiting Uncle Tim's farm. Uncle Tim uses a pictograph to show the children the type and number of animals on his farm. Read the graph to find the answers.

① Tally the number of animals.

Pig	Horse	Cow	Hen	Sheep	Duck

Quick Tip

Remember that each tally mark 卌 stands for 5 animals.

② There are _____ types of animals on Uncle Tim's farm.

③ The animal greatest in number is _____ . There are _____ on the farm.

④ The animal fewest in number is _____ . There are _____ on the farm.

⑤ There are equal numbers of _____ and _____ .

⑥ There are _____ more sheep than cows.

⑦ There are _____ fewer ducks than hens.

⑧ There are altogether _____ animals on Uncle Tim's farm.

The tally chart below shows what the children have for lunch. Answer the questions and complete the bar graph.

Hot dog	Hamburger	Pizza	Fried chicken wing	Others
卌 |||	卌		||||	||||	|||

⑨ How many children choose hot dog for lunch? _____ children

⑩ How many fewer children choose hamburger than hot dog? _____ fewer

⑪ How many more children choose hamburger than pizza? _____ more

⑫ Which 2 food items are chosen by the same number of children?

_____

⑬ How many children are there in Ms. Beatty's class? _____ children

⑭ What does the word 'Others' mean in the tally chart? Suggest an example that may be included in this column.

_____

_____

⑮

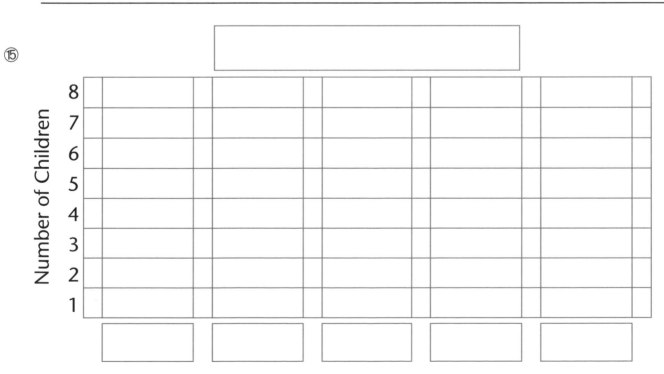

Number of Children

8
7
6
5
4
3
2
1

Food

The children use a spinner to determine what activity to go for after lunch. Look at the spinner below and compare the outcomes with the words given.

| More probable | Equally probable | Less probable |

⑯ Landing on A compared to B _____

⑰ Landing on C compared to A _____

⑱ Landing on B compared to C _____

⑲ Landing on B compared to A _____

⑳ Why is it more probable to land on A than B with this spinner?

_____

_____

Janice and Pete toss two coins to decide who gets an extra lollipop. Organize all the possible outcomes using a tree diagram and answer the questions.

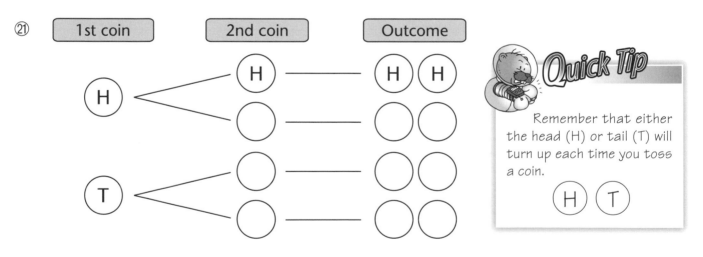

| 1st coin | 2nd coin | Outcome |

Quick Tip

Remember that either the head (H) or tail (T) will turn up each time you toss a coin.

⑫ How many possible outcomes are there in all? _____

㉓ Write the outcome that is more probable than the others. _____

㉔ What is the probability of getting H H compared to T T? _____

㉕ Which outcome should Pete get if he wants to get the extra treat? _____

Uncle Tim has two prizes for the children. Each child draws a 3-D shape on a card and the one with the shape that meets the criteria set will win. Write the children's names in the boxes to find out which two can take the prizes.

㉖

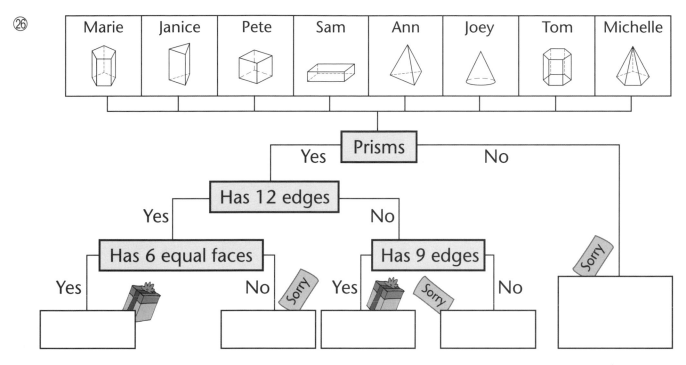

㉗ Which two shapes should the children draw to get the prizes?

_____

㉘ Are there any other shapes that meet the criteria for getting the prizes?

_____

The children used the spinner on the right to decide the drinks they would get. Read the results and label the spinner.

➵ Janice spun 6 times and got 'Coke' 3 times.

➵ Marie spun 8 times and got 'Hot chocolate' 2 times.

➵ Michelle spun 20 times; she got 'Milk' 5 times and 'Juice' 5 times.

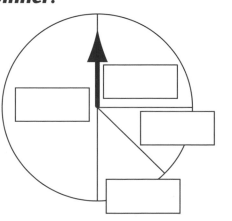

Circle the letter which represents the correct answer in each problem.

① Five thousand six hundred forty is _____ .

A. 5064   B. 5046   C. 5604   D. 5640

② Which number has 4 in the hundredths place?

A. 1403   B. 1.43   C. 1.34   D. 14.03

③ What is the greatest number that can be formed by 7, 2, 4, 6?

A. 7642   B. 6427   C. 4267   D. 2467

④ What is the product of 530 x 4?

A. 212   B. 2020   C. 2120   D. 202

⑤ What is the remainder of 71 ÷ 6?

A. 5   B. 11   C. 6   D. 1

⑥ _____ ÷ 5 = 121R3

A. 605   B. 368   C. 363   D. 608

⑦ The fraction $\frac{47}{100}$ expressed as a decimal is _____ .

A. 4.7   B. 0.47   C. 4.07   D. 47.0

⑧ Four and nine hundredths is _____ .

A. 4.9   B. 0.49   C. 4.09   D. 4.90

⑨ Which is a proper fraction?

A. $\frac{3}{5}$ B. $\frac{5}{5}$ C. $\frac{6}{5}$ D. $1\frac{3}{5}$

⑩ Which of the following are parallel lines?

A.   B.   C.   D.

⑪ Which is the reflection image of ?

A.   B.   C.   D.

⑫ Which is the image of after a quarter-turn?

A.   B.   C.   D.

⑬ The height of Janice is 105 _____ .

A. millimetres   B. centimetres   C. decimetres   D. metres

⑭ The mass of Baby Johnny is _____ .

A. 10.5 kg   B. 105 g   C. 10.5 g   D. 105 kg

⑮ The capacity of Marie's water bottle is _____ .

A. 45 mL   B. 4.5 L   C. 450 mL   D. 4.5 mL

⑯ The floor area of Pete's bedroom is _____ .

A. 64 m^2 B. 6400 cm^2 C. 6.4 m^2 D. 640 cm^2

⑰ How much change will Michelle get if she pays for a model that costs $28.76 with a $50 bill?

A. $22.34   B. $21.34   C. $31.24   D. $21.24

⑱ How many years are there in 3 centuries 5 decades?

A. 3500   B. 350   C. 305   D. 3050

Help Janice draw a similar figure and a congruent figure for the triangle. Use a protractor to measure angles A, B, and C.

⑲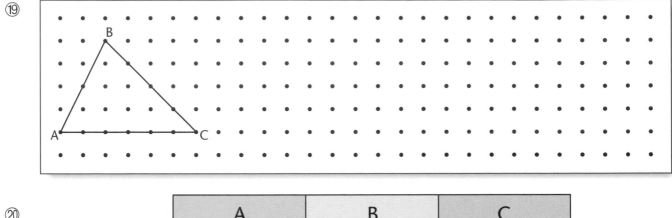

⑳

	A	B	C
Angle			

Pete wants to make skeletons of 3-D shapes with toothpicks and plasticine. Help him draw the shapes in the boxes and fill in the numbers or names of the shapes.

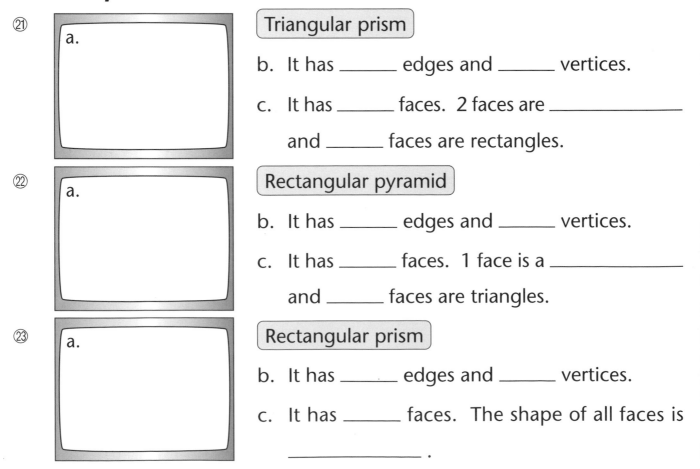

㉑ a.

Triangular prism

b. It has _____ edges and _____ vertices.

c. It has _____ faces. 2 faces are _____

and _____ faces are rectangles.

㉒ a.

Rectangular pyramid

b. It has _____ edges and _____ vertices.

c. It has _____ faces. 1 face is a _____

and _____ faces are triangles.

㉓ a.

Rectangular prism

b. It has _____ edges and _____ vertices.

c. It has _____ faces. The shape of all faces is

_____ .

Look at the shapes on the centimetre grid paper. Answer the questions and draw the diagrams.

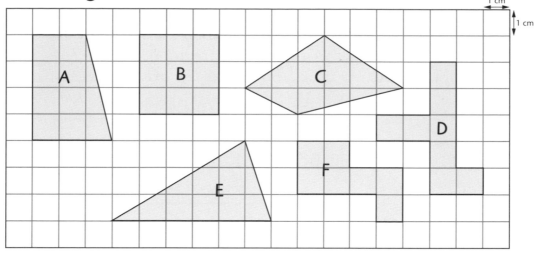

㉔ Which shapes are quadrilaterals? _____

㉕ What is the area of each shape?

A		B		C	
D		E		F	

㉖ What is the perimeter of each of the following shapes?

B		D		F	

㉗ Draw a rectangle G which has the same area as B but a different perimeter. Label the perimeter of G.

㉘ Draw a rectangle H which has the same perimeter as B but a different area. Label the area of H.

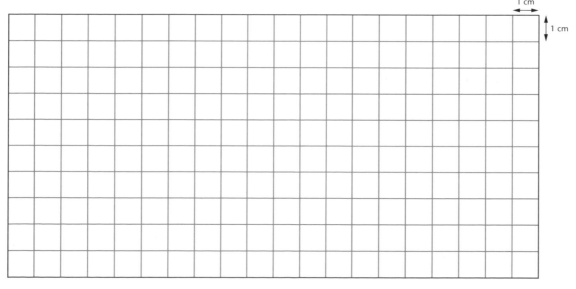

Final Test

Fill in the missing numbers and write the rule of each pattern.

㉙ 100   90   80   _____   _____   50   _____   _____

Rule _____

㉚ 80   78   74   68   _____   _____   _____

Rule _____

㉛ 60   58   61   59   62   _____   _____   _____

Rule _____

㉜ 25   26   28   31   _____   _____   _____   _____

Rule _____

Look at Michelle's saving pattern. Complete the table and answer the question.

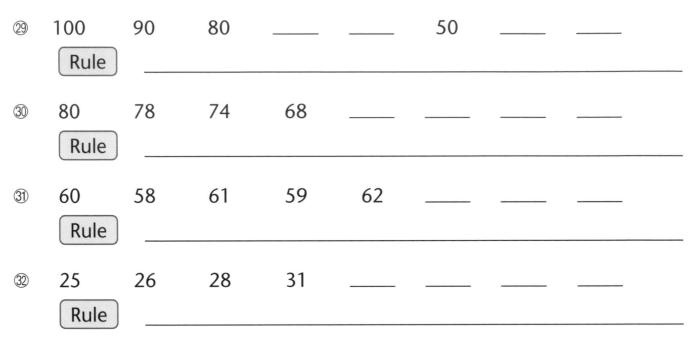

㉝

Day	1	2	3	4	5	6	7
Number of coins							

㉞ If the pattern continues, how much will Michelle save on Day 10? $ _____

Find the missing term in each equation.

㉟ $200 - 100 = a + 65$

a = _____

㊱ $b - 48 = 38 + 62$

b = _____

㊲ $56 + m = 10 \times 8$

m = _____

㊳ $163 - 43 = n - 50$

n = _____

Pete is designing a symmetrical shape. Help him complete the shape on the grid below.

③⑨ Write the coordinates of the following points.

A (____ , ____)   B (____ , ____)   C (____ , ____)

D (____ , ____)   E (____ , ____)   F (____ , ____)

④⓪ Locate the following points on the grid.

G (13 , 5)   H (13 , 3)   I (11 , 3)   J (8 , 1)

K (7 , 3)   L (5 , 3)   M (4 , 1)   N(1 , 3)

④① Complete the shape by joining the points in alphabetical order from A to N, and then from N to A.

④② Draw and label the line of symmetry of the shape completed in ④①.

④③ Which are their possible translation images? Give one example each.

a. line BC   _____   b. line CD   _____

④④ Which are their reflection images about the line of symmetry?

a. line ABC   _____   b. line DEF   _____

④⑤ Which are their possible rotation images? Give one example each.

a. line CD   _____   b. line AB   _____

④⑥ Pete wants to change the shape so that it will have 1 more line of symmetry. Help him shade the part that should be cut out from the shape in ④①. Draw and label the new line of symmetry of the shape.

The tally chart below shows the numbers of coloured marbles Janice has. Complete the bar graph and the sentences.

㊼

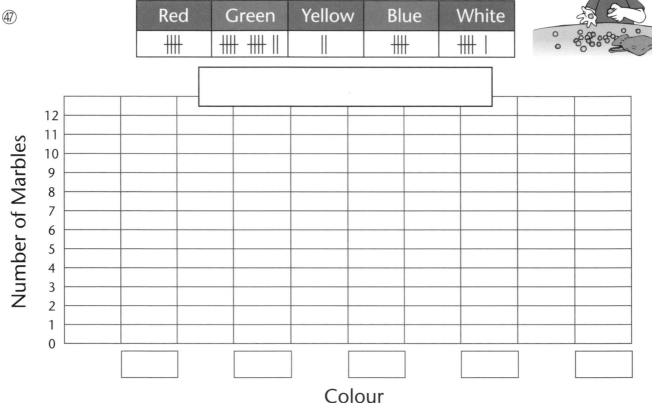

	Red	Green	Yellow	Blue	White
	卌	卌 卌 ||	||	卌	卌	

Number of Marbles

12
11
10
9
8
7
6
5
4
3
2
1
0

Colour

㊽ The marbles greatest in number are _____ .

㊾ The marbles fewest in number are _____ .

㊿ There are _____ more green marbles than yellow marbles.

51 There are the same number of _____ marbles and _____ marbles.

52 Janice has _____ marbles in all.

53 _____ of Janice's marbles are not white.

54 Compare the probabilities of picking a marble from Janice's collection using 'More probable', 'Equally probable', or 'Less probable'.

a. Picking a red marble compared to a blue one _____

b. Picking a green marble compared to a white one _____

c. Picking a yellow marble compared to a green one _____

Overview

In Section II, arithmetic skills were developed and practised.

In Section III, all four arithmetic operations and mixed operations are applied in the context of word problems using whole numbers and decimals.

Emphasis is placed on careful reading and translating into mathematical "language". Answers are written in full sentences using appropriate units and students are encouraged to check whether or not their answers are reasonable.

The relationship between fractions and decimals is explored in context.

Equations are introduced as a way to represent real-life situations mathematically. Solving a word problem often involves solving an equation.

Numeration

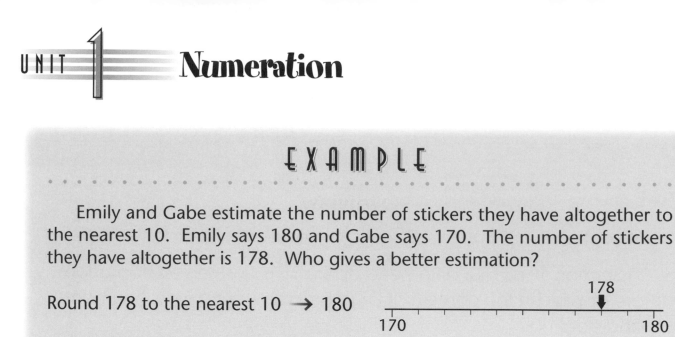

EXAMPLE

Emily and Gabe estimate the number of stickers they have altogether to the nearest 10. Emily says 180 and Gabe says 170. The number of stickers they have altogether is 178. Who gives a better estimation?

Round 178 to the nearest 10 → 180

178
170   180

Answer : Emily gives a better estimation.

Use the table below to solve the problems. Show your work.

Name	Emily	Gabe	Doug	Megan	Clare	Elaine
No. of Stickers	2000	1245	2650	1225	2700	945

① Who has the most stickers? How many? Write in words.

Answer : _____ has the most stickers. _____ stickers.

② Who has the fewest stickers? How many? Write in words.

Answer : _____

③ Who has 50 stickers more than Doug?

Answer : _____

④ Who has 700 stickers fewer than Clare?

Answer : _____

⑤ Doug buys one pack of stickers each week. In each pack there are 10 stickers. He starts with 2650 stickers. How many stickers will he have after 4 weeks?

Answer : _____

⑥ If Elaine gives 100 stickers to her friends each week, how many stickers will she have after 3 weeks?

Answer : _____

⑦ If each week Emily gives 100 stickers to Megan, how many stickers will each of them have after 3 weeks?

Answer : _____

⑧ If Gabe gives 5 stickers to Megan each week, how long will it take for them to have the same number of stickers?

Answer : _____

⑨ If Doug buys 60 stickers each week and gives 10 to Emily, how many stickers will each of them have after 4 weeks?

Answer : _____

⑩ How long will it take Emily to give away all her stickers if she gives 400 away each week?

Answer : _____

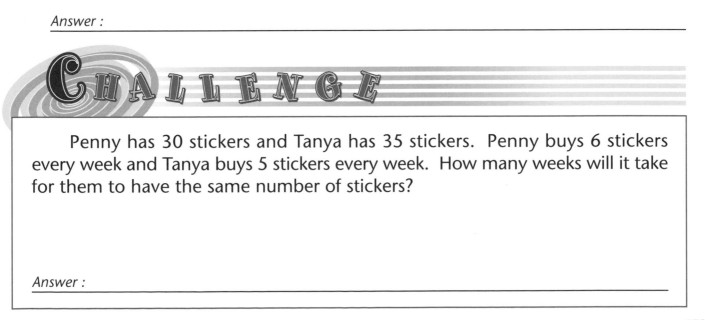

CHALLENGE

Penny has 30 stickers and Tanya has 35 stickers. Penny buys 6 stickers every week and Tanya buys 5 stickers every week. How many weeks will it take for them to have the same number of stickers?

Answer : _____

Addition and Subtraction of Whole Numbers

EXAMPLE

Emily ran 1462 m. Gabe ran 1287 m. How much farther did Emily run than Gabe?

Think : how much farther ... than ... ➡ Subtraction problem

Write : 1462 − 1287 = 175

Answer : Emily ran 175 m farther than Gabe.

Estimate the answer in each situation by rounding the number of marbles to the nearest 100. Show your work.

① Gabe has 428 marbles. He gives Emily 99 marbles. How many marbles has he left?

Answer : He has about ___ marbles left. ___

② Emily has 183 green marbles and 214 blue marbles. How many green and blue marbles does Emily have altogether?

Answer : ___

③ Jill has 507 marbles but gives 197 to her brother. How many marbles has she left?

Answer : ___

④ Mark buys a bag of 89 marbles. He adds it to his collection of 280 marbles. How many marbles does he have altogether?

Answer : ___

⑤ Joe has 317 marbles and buys a bag of 88 marbles. Wayne gives 95 marbles to Joe. How many marbles does Joe have?

Answer : ___

⑥ Which children have about 300 marbles in the end?

Answer : ___

The table shows how many metres Emily travelled on her bike last week. Use the table to solve the problems. Show your work.

	SUN	MON	TUE	WED	THU	FRI	SAT
Distance (m)	876	328	829	515	372	686	1425

⑦ How far did Emily travel altogether on the weekend?

Answer : _____

⑧ How far did Emily travel altogether on Monday and Tuesday?

Answer : _____

⑨ How far did Emily travel altogether on Wednesday, Thursday and Friday?

Answer : _____

⑩ How far did Emily travel altogether last week?

Answer : _____

⑪ How much farther did Emily travel on Saturday than on Thursday?

Answer : _____

⑫ How much farther did Emily travel on Friday than on Monday?

Answer : _____

⑬ If Emily wanted to travel 700 m on Monday, how much farther would she have to travel?

Answer : _____

⑭ If George travelled 288 m more than the distance Emily travelled on Tuesday, how far did he travel?

Answer : _____

• For question 10, you may make use of the answers from questions 7, 8 and 9. ← Read this first.

The table shows the number of cans collected by each group in the past two weeks. Use the table to answer the questions. Show your work.

Group	A	B	C	D	E
No. of cans collected in week 1	651	394	1823	973	574
No. of cans collected in week 2	479	503	795	885	931

⑮ How many more cans did Group A collect in week 1 than in week 2?

Answer : _____

⑯ How many more cans did Group E collect in week 2 than in week 1?

Answer : _____

⑰ How many cans did Group A collect in all?

Answer : _____

⑱ How many cans did Group B collect in all?

Answer : _____

⑲ How many cans did Group C collect in all?

Answer : _____

⑳ How many cans did Group D collect in all?

Answer : _____

㉑ How many cans did Group E collect in all?

Answer : _____

㉒ Put the groups in order from the one with the most cans to the one with the fewest.

Answer : _____

㉓ How many more cans did Group C collect than Group B?

Answer : _____

㉔ How many more cans did Group E collect than Group A?

Answer : _____

Solve the problems. Show your work.

A total of one thousand five hundred sixty-seven people attended the first day of a tennis tournament. The next day, one thousand eight hundred twelve people attended. The ticket sales were six thousand seven hunderd eight dollars for the first day and seven thousand eight hundred twelve dollars for the second day.

㉕ What was the difference in attendance between the two days?

Answer : _____

㉖ How many people attended the two-day tournament?

Answer : _____

㉗ If six hundred eighty men and one hundred seventy-five children attended the first day of the tournament, how many women were there?

Answer : _____

㉘ What was the difference in the ticket sales between the two days?

Answer : _____

CHALLENGE

①

No. of blocks	1	10	100	1000
Weight (g)	100	1000		

② If the weight of the blocks is 2000 g, how many blocks are there?

Answer : _____

Multiplication and Division of Whole Numbers

EXAMPLE

Emily buys 125 grams of candies each week. How many grams of candies will Emily have altogether after 5 weeks?

Think : 5 groups of 125

Write : 5 × 125 = 625

Answer : Emily will have 625 grams of candies after 5 weeks.

Emily and Gabe are helping out on Uncle Smith's farm. Solve the problems. Show your work.

① Emily picks 300 cobs of corn and splits them into 5 piles. How many cobs of corn are there in each pile?

Answer : There are _____ cobs of corn.

② Gabe picks 48 apples off each of 9 trees. How many apples does Gabe pick altogether?

Answer : _____

③ Emily has 3 baskets. Each basket holds 163 carrots. How many carrots does Emily have?

Answer : _____

④ Gabe picks 8 baskets of strawberries. Each basket holds 132 strawberries. How many strawberries are picked?

Answer : _____

⑤ There are 135 apple trees. Emily picks 6 apples from each tree. How many apples does Emily pick?

Answer : _____

⑥ There are 260 blueberries. If they were shared among 4 children, how many blueberries would each child get?

Answer : _____

⑦ Gabe picks 328 apples. The apples are packed in bags with 9 in each bag. How many apples will be left over?

Answer : _____

⑧ Emily pulls up carrots. Every time she has pulled 8, she ties them together. If she pulls up 230 carrots, how many carrots will not be tied up?

Answer : _____

⑨ Gabe picks 6 tomatoes from each plant. If he picked 163 tomatoes, how many tomatoes did he pick from the last plant?

Answer : _____

⑩ Emily and 4 of her friends are sharing 121 cherries equally among them. How many cherries will be left over?

Answer : _____

⑪ Gabe and 3 of his friends are sharing 207 peanuts equally among them. How many peanuts will be left over?

Answer : _____

⑫ Gabe has a bucket with 320 cherries in it. If he puts them into 6 boxes evenly, how many cherries will be left over?

Answer : _____

⑬ Emily puts 315 onions in 8 bags. How many onions are left over?

Answer : _____

⑭ Gabe puts 124 pears in boxes. Each box holds 9 pears. How many boxes does he need?

Answer : _____

⑮ Emily picks 156 strawberries and packs 8 in each basket. How many baskets does she need?

Answer : _____

⑯ Each box holds 6 potatoes. Gabe puts 215 potatoes into boxes. How many boxes does he need?

Answer : _____

• *For questions 14, 15 and 16, don't forget that the remainder needs a container too.*

Read this first.

Elaine and Winston have gone with their class to a fruit farm. See how their teacher, Mrs Winter, put them into groups. Solve the problems.

Group **A** :11 students   Group **B** :13 students   Group **C** :12 students

⑰ If each student in Group A was allowed to pick 14 apples, how many apples were picked?

Answer : _____

⑱ If each bag holds 7 apples, how many bags are needed to hold all the apples picked by Group A?

Answer : _____

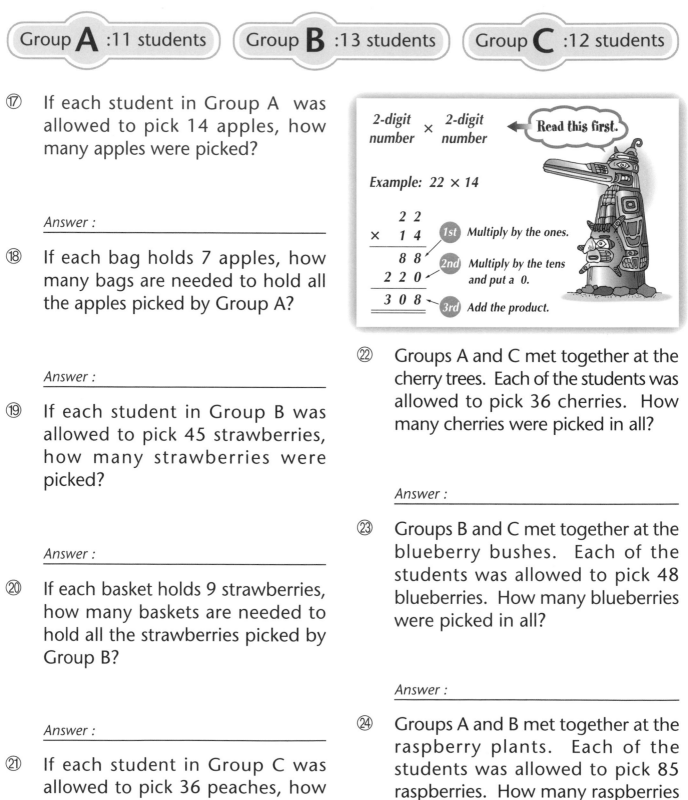

2-digit number × 2-digit number ← Read this first.

Example: 22 × 14

```
    2 2
 ×  1 4
    ————
    8 8     1st  Multiply by the ones.
  2 2 0     2nd  Multiply by the tens
    ————          and put a 0.
  3 0 8     3rd  Add the product.
```

⑲ If each student in Group B was allowed to pick 45 strawberries, how many strawberries were picked?

Answer : _____

⑳ If each basket holds 9 strawberries, how many baskets are needed to hold all the strawberries picked by Group B?

Answer : _____

㉑ If each student in Group C was allowed to pick 36 peaches, how many peaches were picked?

Answer : _____

㉒ Groups A and C met together at the cherry trees. Each of the students was allowed to pick 36 cherries. How many cherries were picked in all?

Answer : _____

㉓ Groups B and C met together at the blueberry bushes. Each of the students was allowed to pick 48 blueberries. How many blueberries were picked in all?

Answer : _____

㉔ Groups A and B met together at the raspberry plants. Each of the students was allowed to pick 85 raspberries. How many raspberries were picked in all?

Answer : _____

Help the farm owner, Mr Smith, solve the problems. Show your work.

㉕ An apple costs 34¢. What is the total cost of 25 apples?

Answer : _____

㉖ A bag of potatoes costs $4.00. How many bags of potatoes can be bought with $102.00?

Answer : _____

㉗ What is the cost of 98 baskets of strawberries if each basket costs $6.00?

Answer : _____

㉘ Each box of cherries costs $5.00. Is $173.00 enough to buy 34 boxes of cherries?

Answer : _____

㉙ A bag of corn weighs 826 grams. What is the mass of 6 bags of corn?

Answer : _____

㉚ Mr Stanley pays with a $100 bill for 9 big bags of onions and gets $37.00 back. How much does each bag of onions cost?

Answer : _____

㉛ Each bag of potatoes weighs 95 grams. What is the mass of 17 bags of potatoes?

Answer : _____

CHALLENGE

Emily and 3 of her friends earned $38.00 each for helping on the farm. If they were paid altogether in $5 bills, how much change would they have to give back?

Answer : _____

Mixed Operations of Whole Numbers

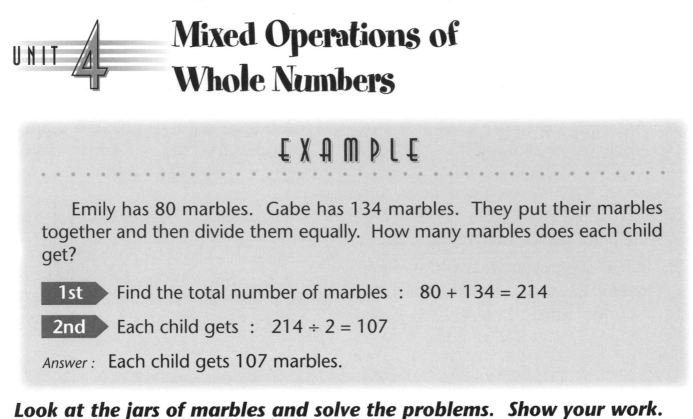

EXAMPLE

Emily has 80 marbles. Gabe has 134 marbles. They put their marbles together and then divide them equally. How many marbles does each child get?

1st ▶ Find the total number of marbles : 80 + 134 = 214

2nd ▶ Each child gets : 214 ÷ 2 = 107

Answer : Each child gets 107 marbles.

Look at the jars of marbles and solve the problems. Show your work.

Red 312   Blue 256   Black 193   Green 250   Yellow 446   Purple 224

① How many marbles are red or blue?

Answer : _____

② If the green marbles were shared among 5 people, how many would each person get?

Answer : _____

③ If Emily takes 113 marbles from each jar, how many marbles will she have?

Answer : _____

④ If Gabe takes 176 yellow marbles, how many yellow marbles will be left?

Answer : _____

⑤ If Gabe puts the purple marbles into 3 bags equally, how many purple marbles will there be in each bag? How many purple marbles will be left?

Answer : _____

⑥ Emily took a jar and split the marbles into 7 groups. Each group had 36 marbles and 4 marbles were left over. Which jar did Emily take?

Answer : _____

⑦ Gabe took 2 marbles from a jar and split the rest of the marbles into 4 equal shares of 62 marbles each. Which jar did Gabe take?

Answer : _____

⑧ Gabe made 6 piles of 65 yellow marbles. When he was done, how many yellow marbles were left in the jar?

Answer : _____

⑨ Emily took the purple marbles and divided them equally among 7 children. Then each child put 10 back into the jar. How many marbles did each child actually get?

Answer : _____

⑩ Emily had 236 marbles, and Gabe had 432 marbles. They put the marbles together and divided them into 4 equal shares. How many marbles were there in each share?

Answer : _____

⑪ Ray had 300 white marbles. He took 30 and divided the rest among 5 children. How many marbles did each child get?

Answer : _____

⑫ Emily had 8 bags of 56 marbles each. Gabe gave her 39 marbles. How many marbles did Emily have?

Answer : _____

⑬ Ray put his marbles equally into 6 bags and 4 marbles were left. If each bag had 72 marbles, how many marbles would Ray have?

Answer : _____

⑭ Gabe had 5 jars of 56 marbles each. If he split all his marbles equally into 4 jars, how many marbles would be in each jar?

Answer : _____

• *Questions 6 to 14 are two-step problems. First split each problem into 2 parts. Then solve the first part before working on the other.*

Read this first.

Emily and Gabe have been playing video games. Look at their scores and solve the problems. Show your work.

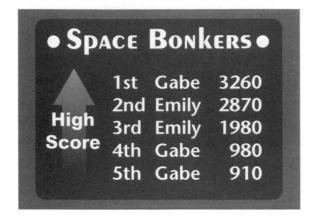

• SPACE BONKERS •

High Score

1st	Gabe	3260
2nd	Emily	2870
3rd	Emily	1980
4th	Gabe	980
5th	Gabe	910

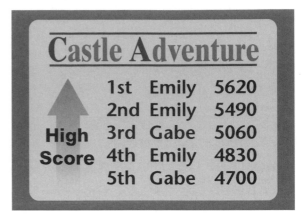

Castle Adventure

High Score

1st	Emily	5620
2nd	Emily	5490
3rd	Gabe	5060
4th	Emily	4830
5th	Gabe	4700

⑮ What is the difference between the first and last highest scores in Space Bonkers?

Answer : The difference is _____ .

⑯ What is the difference between the first and last highest scores in Castle Adventure?

Answer : _____

⑰ If Ray scored 470 in each of 6 rounds of Space Bonkers, what would his total score be?

Answer : _____

⑱ Can Ray beat the 1st highest score in Space Bonkers?

Answer : _____

⑲ If Jane scored 830 in each of 7 rounds of Castle Adventure, what would her total score be?

Answer : _____

⑳ Can Jane beat the 1st highest score in Castle Adventure?

Answer : _____

㉑ If Emily got 63 points every minute, what would her total score be in 15 minutes?

Answer : _____

㉒ If Emily got 972 points in 9 minutes, how many points would she get in 1 minute?

Answer : _____

Solve the problems. Show your work.

㉓ 234 cherries were eaten by 6 birds. If each bird ate the same number of cherries, how many cherries did each bird eat?

Answer : _____

㉔ There were 6 trees. Each tree had 32 birds in it. How many birds were there?

Answer : _____

㉕ 233 birds were in the tree and 69 more joined them. How many birds were there altogether?

Answer : _____

㉖ 8 crows ate 134 cherries each. How many cherries did they eat altogether?

Answer : _____

㉗ A crow ate 108 cherries from one tree and 156 cherries from another. How many cherries did the crow eat altogether?

Answer : _____

㉘ If a crow ate 333 cherries evenly from 9 trees, how many cherries did it eat from 1 tree?

Answer : _____

㉙ There were 763 cherries. If 319 cherries were eaten, how many cherries would be left over?

Answer : _____

㉚ There were 872 cherries, but 427 turned bad. How many good cherries were there?

Answer : _____

CHALLENGE

Emily buys 6 bags of milk for her 4 cats. Each bag holds 2 L of milk. Each cat drinks 1 L in a week. After feeding the cats for 1 week, Emily has 2 L of milk left. Is this story correct or not? Explain.

Answer : _____

EXAMPLE

Emily's Math test scores are 80, 70, 60 and 74. What is her average score?

Total score : 80 + 70 + 60 + 74 = 284   **Number of addends :** 4

Average : 284 ÷ 4 = 71

Answer : Her average score is 71.

Emily and her friends are playing video games. Use the table to solve the problems. Show your work.

Game	1st	2nd	3rd	4th
Emily	1230	758	1080	980
Joe	866	1008	982	520
Peter	790	562	1682	858

① What is Emily's average score?

Answer : Her average score is _____ .

② What is Joe's average score?

Answer : _____

③ What is Peter's average score?

Answer : _____

④ What is the difference in the average scores between Emily and Joe?

Answer : _____

⑤ What is the difference in the average scores between Emily and Peter?

Answer : _____

⑥ What is the difference in the average scores between Joe and Peter?

Answer : _____

Solve the problems. Show your work.

⑦ Gabe has an average of 200 marbles in 4 jars, which 4 of these jars are his?

 A 300   **B** 125   **C** 175   **D** 200   **E** 400

Answer : _____

⑧ If all the above jars belonged to Gabe, what would be the average number of marbles in each jar?

Answer : _____

⑨ Wayne has an average of 90¢ in 4 piggy banks, which 4 of these piggy banks are his?

 A 55¢   **B** 60¢   **C** 80¢   **D** 70¢   **E** 150¢

Answer : _____

⑩ If all the above piggy banks belonged to Wayne, what would be the average amount in each piggy bank?

Answer : _____

CHALLENGE

Emily got these scores on the English tests : 76, 92, 80 and 72.

① What is her average score?

Answer : _____

② If Emily got 0 on the next test, what would be her average score?

Answer : _____

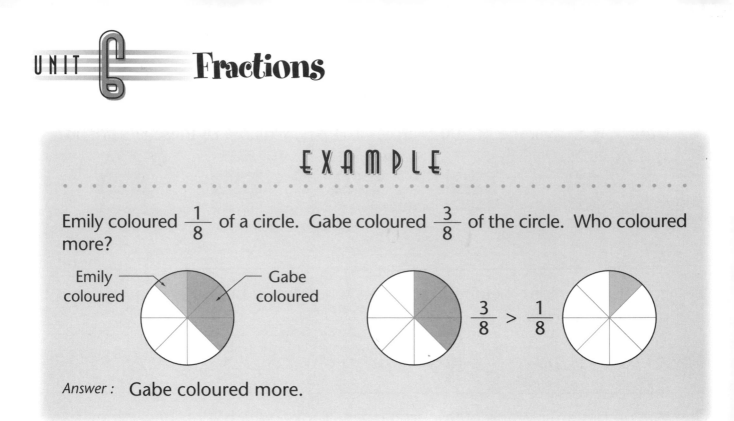

EXAMPLE

Emily coloured $\frac{1}{8}$ of a circle. Gabe coloured $\frac{3}{8}$ of the circle. Who coloured more?

Emily coloured — Gabe coloured

$\frac{3}{8} > \frac{1}{8}$

Answer : Gabe coloured more.

Emily asked some classmates about their favourite fruits. Use her table to solve the problems. Show your work.

Fruit	Apple	Orange	Banana	Grape	Peach
No. of classmates	4	2	1	3	2

① How many classmates did Emily ask?

Answer : Emily asked 12 classmates.

② What fraction of her classmates prefer apples?

$\frac{4}{12}$

Answer :

③ What fraction of her classmates prefer bananas?

$\frac{1}{12}$

Answer :

④ What fraction of her classmates prefer oranges or grapes?

Answer :

⑤ What fraction of her classmates do not like oranges?

$\frac{10}{12}$

Answer :

⑥ What fraction of her classmates do not like bananas or grapes?

$\frac{8}{12}$

Answer :

Colour the pictures and solve the problems.

⑦ Emily has 8 apples. $\frac{3}{8}$ are red and the rest green. What fraction of the apples are green?

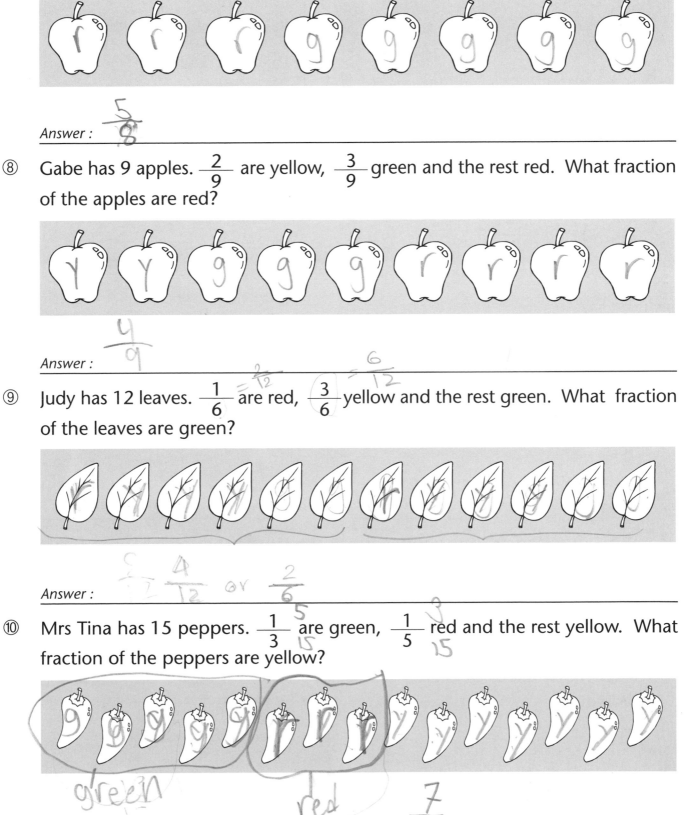

Answer : $\frac{5}{8}$

⑧ Gabe has 9 apples. $\frac{2}{9}$ are yellow, $\frac{3}{9}$ green and the rest red. What fraction of the apples are red?

Answer : $\frac{4}{9}$

⑨ Judy has 12 leaves. $\frac{1}{6} = \frac{2}{12}$ are red, $\frac{3}{6} = \frac{6}{12}$ yellow and the rest green. What fraction of the leaves are green?

Answer : $\frac{4}{12}$ or $\frac{2}{6}$

⑩ Mrs Tina has 15 peppers. $\frac{1}{3}$ $\frac{5}{15}$ are green, $\frac{1}{5}$ $\frac{3}{15}$ red and the rest yellow. What fraction of the peppers are yellow?

green   red $\frac{7}{15}$

Answer : $\frac{7}{15}$

Solve the problems. Show your work.

Mrs Winter ordered 2 party pizzas for her class. Each pizza had 24 slices.

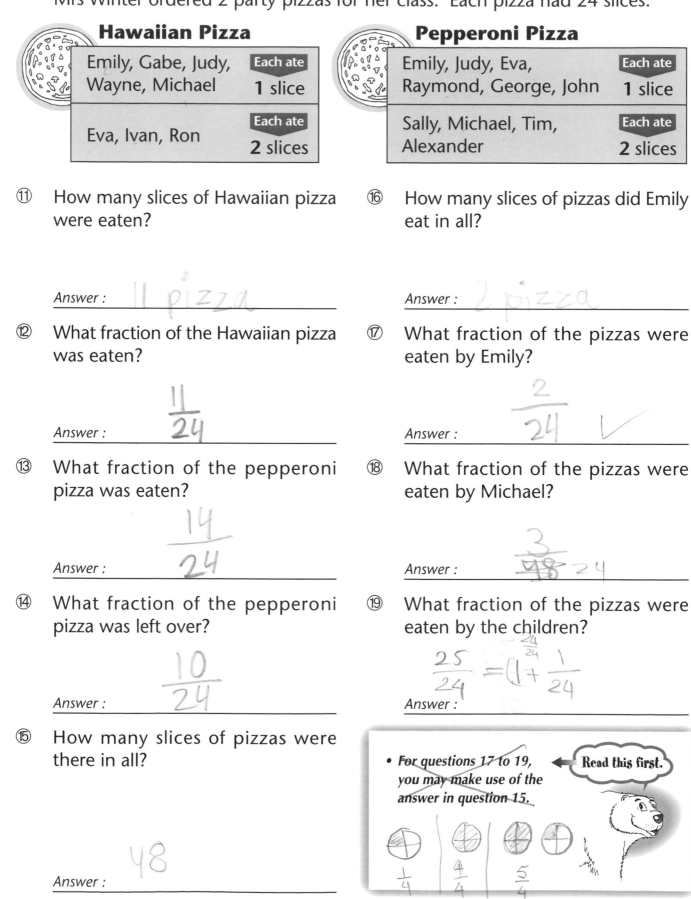

Hawaiian Pizza

| Emily, Gabe, Judy, Wayne, Michael | Each ate 1 slice |
| Eva, Ivan, Ron | Each ate 2 slices |

Pepperoni Pizza

| Emily, Judy, Eva, Raymond, George, John | Each ate 1 slice |
| Sally, Michael, Tim, Alexander | Each ate 2 slices |

⑪ How many slices of Hawaiian pizza were eaten?

Answer : ___11 pizza___

⑫ What fraction of the Hawaiian pizza was eaten?

Answer : $\dfrac{11}{24}$

⑬ What fraction of the pepperoni pizza was eaten?

Answer : $\dfrac{14}{24}$

⑭ What fraction of the pepperoni pizza was left over?

Answer : $\dfrac{10}{24}$

⑮ How many slices of pizzas were there in all?

Answer : ___48___

⑯ How many slices of pizzas did Emily eat in all?

Answer : ___2 pizza___

⑰ What fraction of the pizzas were eaten by Emily?

Answer : $\dfrac{2}{24}$ ✓

⑱ What fraction of the pizzas were eaten by Michael?

Answer : $\dfrac{3}{24}$

⑲ What fraction of the pizzas were eaten by the children?

$\dfrac{25}{24} = 1 + \dfrac{1}{24}$

Answer :

• For questions 17 to 19, you may make use of the answer in question 15.

← Read this first.

$\dfrac{1}{4}$ $\dfrac{4}{4}$ $\dfrac{5}{4}$

Write a mixed number to show how many pizzas each person has. Then solve the problems.

Aunt Betty	Aunt Sharon	Uncle Bob	Uncle Sam	Uncle Tim

20 Aunt Betty has $2\frac{2}{8}$ pizzas.

21 Aunt Sharon has $3\frac{2}{6}$ pizzas.

22 Uncle Bob has $2\frac{5}{8}$ pizzas.

23 Uncle Sam has $1\frac{3}{4}$ pizzas.

24 Uncle Tim has $3\frac{5}{6}$ pizzas.

Read this first.

There are 1 whole pizza and $\frac{2}{3}$ of a pizza.

There are $1\frac{2}{3}$ pizzas. $\frac{3}{3} + \frac{2}{3} = \frac{5}{3}$

There are one and two-third pizzas.

25 Who has more pizzas, Aunt Betty or Uncle Bob? Explain.

Answer : Betty $2\frac{2}{8} < 2\frac{5}{8}$ Bob

26 Who has more pizzas, Aunt Sharon or Uncle Tim? Explain.

Answer : $3\frac{2}{6} < 3\frac{5}{6}$

CHALLENGE

Mr Stanley ate $\frac{1}{2}$ of a pie. Yvon ate $\frac{2}{4}$ of a pie. George ate $\frac{4}{8}$ of a pie. They said that they had eaten the same amount of a pie. Are they correct? Colour the pies below to prove your answer.

Mr Stanley :   Yvon :   George :

Answer : yes they have same amount

$\frac{1}{2} = \frac{10}{20}$

Solve the problems. Show your work.

The children in Mrs Frek's class sold apples for charity. Mrs Frek divided the children into 3 groups and gave each group a box for collecting money.

① There were 24 boxes of apples. Each box had 36 apples. How many apples were there in all?

$$\begin{array}{r} 36 \\ \times\ 24 \\ \hline 144 \\ 720 \\ \hline 864 \end{array}$$

Answer : 850

② Mrs Frek divided the apples equally into 3 groups. How many apples were in each group?

$$288 \\ 3\overline{)864}$$

Answer : 288

③ Emily's group had 5 children. Each child sold 39 apples. How many apples did they sell in all?

$$\begin{array}{r} 39 \\ \times\ 5 \\ \hline 195 \end{array}$$

Answer : 195

④ Doug's group had 6 children. Each child sold 38 apples. How many apples did they sell in all?

$$228 \qquad \begin{array}{r} 38 \\ \times\ 6 \\ \hline 228 \end{array}$$

Answer : 228 ✓

⑤ Emily said if her group sold 30 more apples, they would beat Doug's group. Was she correct? Explain.

$$\begin{array}{r} 195 \\ +\ 30 \\ \hline 225 \end{array}$$

Answer : No

⑥ Gabe's group had 6 children. They sold 252 apples in all. How many apples did each child sell?

$$\begin{array}{r} 42 \\ 6\overline{)252} \\ 24 \\ \hline 12 \\ 12 \end{array}$$

Answer : 42

⑦ How many more apples did Gabe's group sell than Emily's group?

$$252 - 195 = 57$$

Answer : 57 ✓

⑧ How many apples did Emily's group and Gabe's group sell in all?

$$195 + 252 = 447$$

Answer : 447 ✓

⑨ Which group sold the most apples?

Answer : Gabe's

⑩ How many apples did the children sell in all?

Answer : 675

⑪ What is the average number of apples each group sold?

$$\begin{array}{r} 195+ \\ 228 \\ 252 \end{array} \qquad \begin{array}{r} 225 \\ 3\overline{)675} \\ 6 \\ \hline 7 \\ 6 \\ \hline 15 \\ 15 \end{array}$$

Answer : 675

Use the information on P.22 to complete the table.

⑫

	Emily's group	Doug's group	Gabe's group
No. of children in each group	5	6	6
No. of apples Mrs Frek gave each group	288	288	288
No. of apples sold	195	228	252
No. of apples left over	288 -195 93	288 -228 60	288 -252 36
No. of apples each child sold (on average)	39	38	42

⑬ How many apples were left over in all?

$$\begin{array}{r} 93 \\ 60 \\ + 36 \\ \hline \end{array}$$

Answer : _____

⑭ Emily sold 40 apples. 17 of them were green. What fraction of the apples that Emily sold were green?

$$\frac{17}{40}$$

Answer : _____

⑮ Doug sold 38 apples. 20 of them were green. What fraction of the apples that Doug sold were not green?

$$\begin{array}{r} 38 \\ - 20 \\ \hline 18 \end{array}$$ $$\frac{18}{38}$$

Answer : _____

⑯ Emily's group collected $54.00, Doug's group $63.00 and Gabe's group $81.00. How much more money did Gabe's group collect than Emily's group?

$$\begin{array}{r} 81 \\ - 54 \\ \hline \end{array}$$ 27

Answer : _____

⑰ How much money did the three groups collect in all?

$$\begin{array}{r} 54 \\ 63 \\ + 81 \\ \hline 198 \end{array}$$

⑱ How much did each group collect on average?

66

Answer : _____

Solve the problems. Show your work.

Gabe and his friends went to the store to buy lemonade mix.

⑲ Which container holds the greatest amount of lemonade mix? How much? Write in words.

Answer : Lemon lime

A Lemon Blast 384 g

B Lemonade 772 g

C Lemonade 312 g

D Lemon Lime 1264 g

E Lemon Fizz 460 g

F Cool Lemonade 632 g

⑳ What is the total amount of lemonade mix in A and F?

Answer :

㉑ How much more does D hold than B?

Answer :

㉒ Which container holds 952 g less than D?

Answer :

㉓ Which 2 containers hold the same amount as B?

Answer :

㉔ Which container holds half the amount in D?

Answer :

㉕ Gabe bought 936 g of lemonade in 3 identical containers. Which container was it?

Answer :

㉖ Emily bought 1648 g of lemonade mix in 2 different containers. Which 2 containers were they?

Answer :

㉗ Doug bought 8 cans of A. How many grams of lemonade mix were there altogether?

Anwer :

Circle the correct answer in each problem.

㉘ Gabe made 9 jugs of lemonade. There were 7650 mL of lemonade. How many millilitres of lemonade were there in each jug?

A. 850 mL   B. 950 mL   C. 1050 mL   D. 1150 mL

㉙ Gabe sold 3142 mL of lemonade in the morning and 4 L in the afternoon. How many millilitres of lemonade did he sell altogether?

A. 3146 mL   B. 3542 mL   C. 7142 mL   D. 3172 mL

㉚ How much more millilitres of lemonade did he sell in the afternoon than in the morning?

A. 1858 mL   B. 142 mL   C. 1142 mL   D. 858 mL

㉛ Emily sold 152 cups of lemonade in 4 hours. How many cups of lemonade did she sell in 1 hour on average?

A. 148 cups   B. 38 cups   C. 28 cups   D. 48 cups

㉜ A cup of lemonade costs 25¢. If the children sold 89 cups, how much money would they make?

A. $22.15   B. $22.25   C. $21.25   D. $21.15

㉝ Gabe had 65 cups of lemonade. Emily had 15 cups fewer than Gabe. How many cups of lemonade did Emily have?

A. 50 cups   B. 55 cups   C. 60 cups   D. 70 cups

㉞ Doug had 100 cups of lemonade more than Emily. How many cups of lemonade did Emily have?

A. 155 cups   B. 160 cups   C. 150 cups   D. 170 cups

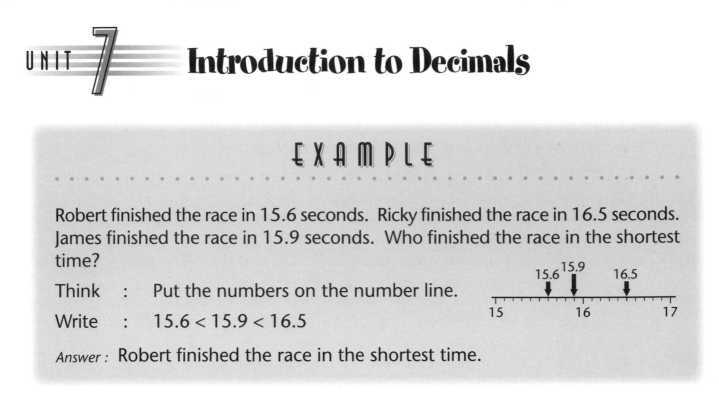

EXAMPLE

Robert finished the race in 15.6 seconds. Ricky finished the race in 16.5 seconds. James finished the race in 15.9 seconds. Who finished the race in the shortest time?

Think : Put the numbers on the number line.

Write : 15.6 < 15.9 < 16.5

Answer : Robert finished the race in the shortest time.

Emily recorded the results of the race. Look at the table and solve the problems. Show your work.

	Robert	Raymond	Ricky	Winston	George
Time (s)	15.6	19.5	18.7	15.9	17.8

① Who was the first to finish the race?

was the first to

Answer : finish the race. robert

② Who was the last to finish the race?

Answer : raymond

③ Write out the race results.

	Name
1st	robert
2nd	winston
3rd	George
4th	ricky
5th	raymond

④ If Doug joined the race and finished in 16.7 seconds, where would he be placed?

Answer : 3erd

⑤ If Gabe joined the race and finished in nineteen and two-tenths seconds, where would he be placed?

Answer : last

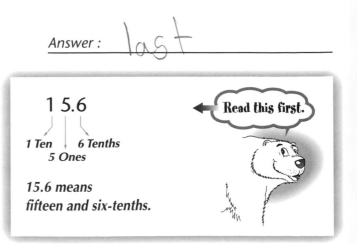

1 5.6

1 Ten | 6 Tenths
5 Ones

15.6 means
fifteen and six-tenths.

Read this first.

The table shows the height of the children. Use the table to solve the problems. Show your work.

	Jason	Judy	Emily	Nicky	Gabe	Sally
Height	1.25 m	1.18 m	1.05 m	1.20 m	1.28 m	1.08 m

(handwritten above headers: 2, 4, 6, 3, 1, 5)

⑥ Who is taller than Jason?

Answer : Gabe

⑦ Who is shorter than Sally?

Answer : emily

> • To compare the decimals with the same whole number parts:
> First compare the tenths digit. If they are the same, then compare the hundredths digit.

Read this first.

⑧ Who is shorter than Nicky, but taller than Sally?

Answer : Judy

⑨ Who is taller than Nicky, but shorter than Gabe?

Answer : Jason

⑩ Write the names in order of height from the tallest to the shortest.

Answer : Gabe, Jason, Nicky, Judy, Sally, emily

⑪ How many children are there with a height above 1.23 m?

Answer : 2 children

⑫ How many children are there with a height below 1.10 m?

Answer : 2 children

⑬ If Nicky says his height is 1.2 m instead of 1.20 m, is he correct? Explain.

Answer : Yes   1.2 = 1.20

⑭ If Sally says her height is 1.80 m instead of 1.08 m, is she correct? Explain.

Answer : NO   1.80 > 1.08

Uncle Sam has a lot of containers. Help him decide which container he should use to hold each type of juice. Write the letters in the boxes.

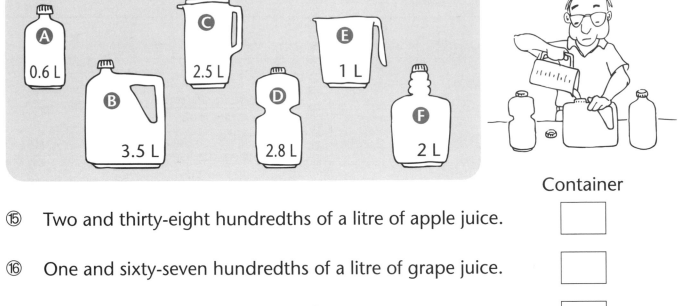

Container

⑮　Two and thirty-eight hundredths of a litre of apple juice.　☐

⑯　One and sixty-seven hundredths of a litre of grape juice.　☐

⑰　Seventy-nine hundredths of a litre of orange juice.　☐

⑱　Two and seven tenths of a litre of pineapple juice.　☐

⑲　Sixty hundredths of a litre of papaya juice.　☐

⑳　Three and two hundredths of a litre of lemon juice.　☐

Look at the containers again and solve the problems.

㉑　Which containers have a capacity greater than 1.5 L?

Answer : _____

㉒　How many containers have a capacity smaller than 2.15 L?

Answer : _____

㉓　Which containers have a capacity greater than 1.5 L but smaller than 3.15 L?

Answer : _____

Read the clues. Write the names and times of the children in the race.

- Albert came third.
- John had a time of 10.8 minutes.
- Sue came after Peter and took exactly 20.4 minutes.
- Peter had a time of 15.8 minutes.
- Jack took 1.2 minutes more than Larry who was sixth.
- Lisa came in 0.6 minute faster than Albert who took 11.2 minutes.
- Jack's time was 12 minutes longer than Lisa's.
- Lisa won the race.

㉔ _____ , _____ min.

㉕ _____ , _____ min.

㉖ _____ , _____ min.

㉗ _____ , _____ min.

㉘ _____ , _____ min.

㉙ _____ , _____ min.

㉚ _____ , _____ min.

FINISH

CHALLENGE

If Gabe entered the race and came in half way between John and Lisa, what would be his time? Draw a number line to show your answer.

Answer : _____

EXAMPLE

Judy swam one lap in 1.6 minutes and another lap in 1.8 minutes. How long did it take her altogether?

Think : altogether ⟶ addition

Write : 1.6 + 1.8 = 3.4

Answer : It took her 3.4 minutes altogether.

Solve the problems. Show you work.

① Judy swims the first lap in 1.5 minutes and the next two in 3.7 minutes. How long does it take her to swim 3 laps?

Answer : It takes her _____ minutes.

> • To add or subtract decimal numbers, first line up the decimal points and then place a decimal point in the answer.
> e.g.   2.5 + 4.7 = 7.2
>
>   2.5
>   + 4.7
>   ———
>   7.2
>
> **Read this first.**

② On Wednesday, Judy practised swimming for 1.3 hours. On Thursday she practised for 2.5 hours. How long did she practise altogether?

Answer : _____

③ How much longer did Judy practise swimming on Thursday than on Wednesday?

④ Judy swims 3 laps. Her times are 1.45 minutes, 1.37 minutes and 1.61 minutes. What is her total time?

Answer : _____

⑤ What is the time difference between Judy's best 2 laps?

Answer : _____

Answer : _____

⑥ Judy beat her best time by 0.4 minute. If her best time used to be 1.62 minutes, what is her new best time?

Answer : _____

⑦ Kate took 80.1 seconds to finish the race. Judy swam 6.3 seconds faster than Kate. What was Judy's time?

Answer : _____

⑧ Judy swam 1.68 km in the morning, and 1.07 km in the afternoon. How many kilometres did she swim in all?

Answer : _____

⑨ Judy can swim 3.8 km without stopping. Her friend can swim 2.95 km without stopping. How much farther can Judy swim than her friend?

Answer : _____

⑩ Judy raced against Emily. Judy's time was 74.2 seconds. Emily's time was 80.3 seconds. By how many seconds did Emily lose the race?

Answer : _____

⑪ Justin entered a race. He finished the 2-lap race in 89.7 seconds. If he swam the 1st lap in 42.9 seconds, how long did it take him to swim the 2nd lap?

Answer : _____

⑫ Sally entered a 3-lap race. She swam the 1st lap in 1.23 minutes, the 2nd in 1.45 minutes and finished the race in 4.05 minutes. How long did it take her to swim the 3rd lap?

Answer : _____

Solve the problems. Show your work.

Distance from St. Mount	
Littleton	1.25 km
Jonesville	1.88 km
Ashmorly	2.59 km
Peterston	4.45 km
Shelby	6.48 km
Jacob	8.67 km

* map not to scale

Littleton   Jonesville

St. Mount

Ashmorly

Shelby

Jacob   Peterston

⑬ What is the distance between Littleton and Jonesville?

Answer : _____

⑭ What is the distance between Peterston and Jacob?

Answer : _____

⑮ Which station, Ashmorly or Shelby, is closer to Peterston?

Answer : _____

⑯ Which station, Peterston or Jacob, is closer to Shelby?

Answer : _____

⑰ What is the distance from Ashmorly to the nearest station?

Answer : _____

⑱ Judy lives in Littleton and works in St. Mount. If she takes the subway to work and back, how far does she travel a day?

Answer : _____

⑲ Emily travelled 3.2 km. If she started at Littleton, which station did she arrive at?

Answer : _____

⑳ May travelled 2.57 km. If she started at Peterston, which station did she arrive at?

Answer : _____

㉑ Which two stations are closest to each other?

Answer : _____

Solve the problems. Show your work.

Railway Fares	
Adult	$1.86
Student (with student I.D.)	$1.28
Child (12 years or under)	$0.95
Senior (age 65 or over)	$0.95
Infant (in arms)	free
Party ticket (2 adults and 3 children)	$5.80

㉒ Amy is 12 years old. If Mr Von, Mrs Von and Amy took the railway, how much would be their fares?

Answer : _____

㉓ If Mr Von had $3.19, how much more would he need to pay for their fares?

Answer : _____

㉔ George forgot to bring his student I.D. How much more money does he need to pay for the adult ticket instead of the student ticket?

Answer : _____

㉕ If 2 adults and 3 children bought a party ticket instead of paying the exact fares, how much money would they save?

Answer : _____

㉖ Mr and Mrs Smith are seniors and they have two grandchildren who are 3 years old and 4 months old. If they took the train with their grandchildren, how much would their fares be?

Answer : _____

CHALLENGE

Look at the above railway fares again.

Uncle Sam is 35 years old. His father is 32 years older than he. His mother is 4 years younger than his father. Uncle Sam has a son and twin daughters who are 3 years old and 6 months old. Uncle Sam's wife, Susan, is 3 years younger than he. If Uncle Sam takes the train with his parents, wife and children, what tickets should he buy? How much should he pay?

Answer : _____

Relationship between Fractions and Decimals

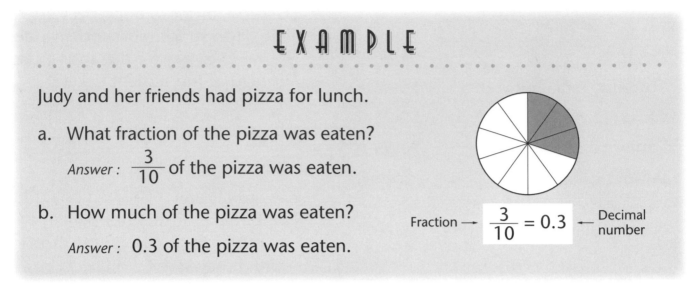

EXAMPLE

Judy and her friends had pizza for lunch.

a. What fraction of the pizza was eaten?

Answer: $\frac{3}{10}$ of the pizza was eaten.

b. How much of the pizza was eaten?

Answer: 0.3 of the pizza was eaten.

Fraction → $\frac{3}{10} = 0.3$ ← Decimal number

Look at the candies. Solve the problems.

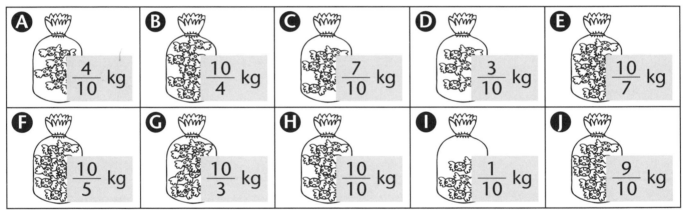

A $\frac{4}{10}$ kg

B $\frac{10}{4}$ kg

C $\frac{7}{10}$ kg

D $\frac{3}{10}$ kg

E $\frac{10}{7}$ kg

F $\frac{10}{5}$ kg

G $\frac{10}{3}$ kg

H $\frac{10}{10}$ kg

I $\frac{1}{10}$ kg

J $\frac{9}{10}$ kg

① Which bag of candies weighs 0.3 kg?

Answer: Bag D weighs 0.3 kg.

② Which bag of candies weighs 0.7 kg?

Answer: bag C   0.7

③ Which bag of candies weighs 0.1 kg?

Answer: bag I   0.1

④ Which bag of candies weighs ten tenths of a kilogram?

Answer: bag H   0.10

⑤ Which bag of candies weighs nine tenths of a kilogram?

Answer: bag J   0.9

⑥ Which bag of candies weighs four tenths of a kilogram?

Answer: bag A   0.4

The children sold cookies for charity. Read the announcement. Then colour the diagrams to show the cookies sold and solve the problems.

The cookie sale is over. The third winner is Emily Von who sold one and two-tenths boxes of cookies. The second winner, Wayne Smith, sold three and six-tenths boxes and the first winner is David Winter who sold four and nine-tenths boxes of cookies.

⑦ **Boxes of Cookies Sold by Each Child**

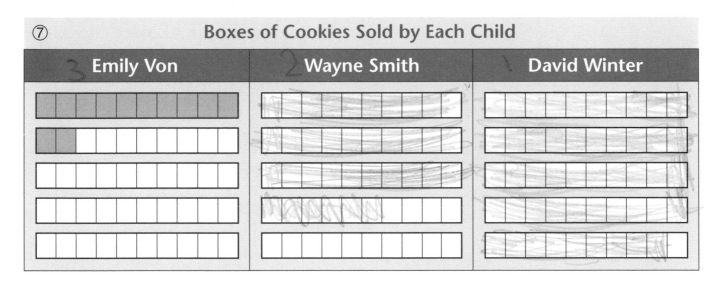

| Emily Von | Wayne Smith | David Winter |

⑧ Write the number of boxes of cookies Emily sold as a fraction.

Answer : _____

⑨ Write the number of boxes of cookies Wayne sold as a fraction.

Answer : _____

⑩ Write the number of boxes of cookies David sold as a fraction.

Answer : _____

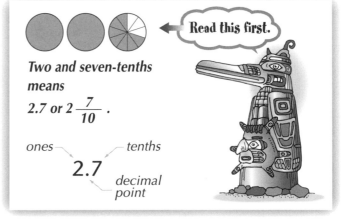

Two and seven-tenths means

2.7 or 2 $\frac{7}{10}$.

ones — tenths

2.7

decimal point

Read this first.

⑪ Three-tenths of a box of cookies is chocolate flavoured. What fraction is not chocolate flavoured?

Answer : _____

Use your calculator to put the answers in decimal numbers.

⑫ Emily saved $\frac{4}{5}$ of her allowance for charity. How much of her allowance was saved?

Answer : _____ 0.8 _____

Read this first.

- $\frac{4}{5}$ on a calculator is entered as 4 ÷ 5.
- You will get the answer by pressing these keys:

4 ÷ 5 =

⑬ Gabe ate $\frac{3}{4}$ of his pie. How much of his pie was eaten?

Answer : _____ 0.75 _____

⑭ George drank $\frac{12}{25}$ of a glass of water. How much of a glass of water did he drink?

Answer : _____ 0.48 _____

⑮ Elaine spent $\frac{13}{20}$ of a lesson doing classwork. How much of a lesson did she spend on classwork?

Answer : _____ 0.65 _____

⑯ How much of a box of eggs was eaten?

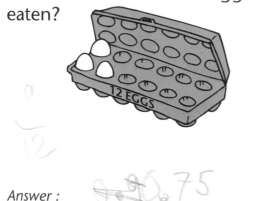

Answer : _____ 0.75 _____

⑰ How much of a box of chocolates is left over?

$\frac{32}{50}$

Answer : _____ 0.64 _____

⑱ How much of a bag of buns was eaten?

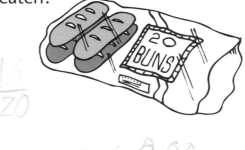

$\frac{16}{20}$

Answer : _____ 0.80 _____

⑲ 3 cupcakes are left over. How much of a box of cupcakes is left over?

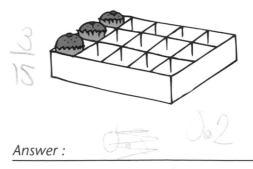

$\frac{3}{15}$

Answer : _____ 0.2 _____

Look at the recipe. Write each fraction or decimal in words to complete what Mrs Max says.

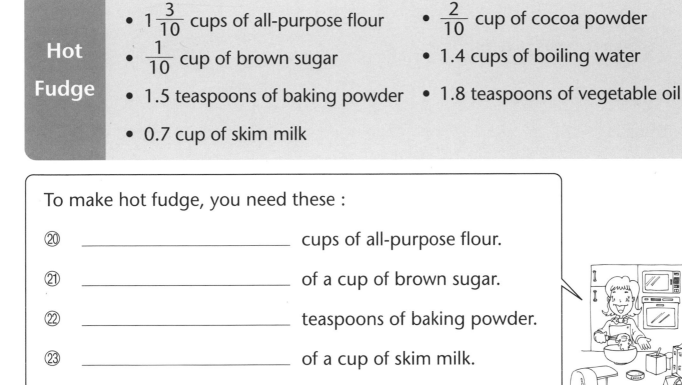

Hot Fudge

- $1\frac{3}{10}$ cups of all-purpose flour
- $\frac{1}{10}$ cup of brown sugar
- 1.5 teaspoons of baking powder
- 0.7 cup of skim milk
- $\frac{2}{10}$ cup of cocoa powder
- 1.4 cups of boiling water
- 1.8 teaspoons of vegetable oil

To make hot fudge, you need these :

20 _____ cups of all-purpose flour.

21 _____ of a cup of brown sugar.

22 _____ teaspoons of baking powder.

23 _____ of a cup of skim milk.

24 _____ of a cup of cocoa powder.

25 _____ cups of boiling water.

26 _____ teaspoons of vegetable oil.

CHALLENGE

① Emily has $\frac{17}{20}$ of a box of chocolates. George has 0.68 of a box of chocolates. Who has more chocolates?

$0.85 > 0.68$

$\frac{17}{20} = 0.85$

Answer : _____Emily_____

② Emily has $1\frac{1}{5}$ boxes of pencils. Elaine has 1.25 boxes of pencils. Who has more pencils?

$1\frac{1}{5} = 1.2 \Rightarrow 1.2 < 1.25 \Rightarrow$ Elaine has more

Answer : _____

Patterns

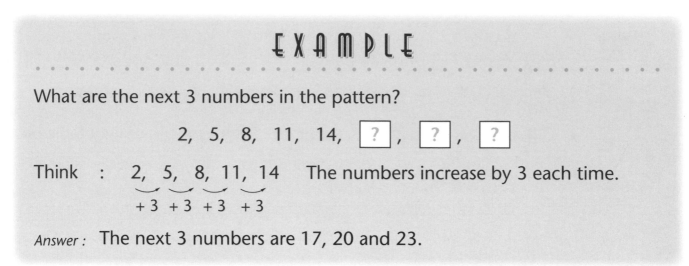

EXAMPLE

What are the next 3 numbers in the pattern?

2, 5, 8, 11, 14, [?], [?], [?]

Think : 2, 5, 8, 11, 14   The numbers increase by 3 each time.
+3 +3 +3 +3

Answer : The next 3 numbers are 17, 20 and 23.

Complete the tables and solve the problems.

① Judy put some money in her piggy bank each week. She saved 5¢ in the 1st week, 10¢ in the 2nd week, 15¢ in the 3rd week and so on. How much would she save in the 7th week?

Week	1	2	3	4	5	6
Amount (¢)	5					

Answer : She saved _____ ¢ in the 7th week.

② Nicky collected 2 stickers in the first week, 4 stickers in the 2nd week and 6 stickers in the 3rd week. How many stickers did he collect in the 7th week?

Week	1	2	3	4	5	6
No. of stickers	2					

Answer :

③ Gabe bought 5 marbles. Each week after that he bought 2 more marbles than the week before. How many marbles did he buy in the 8th week?

Week	1	2	3	4	5	6
No. of marbles	7					

Answer :

④ Emily saw 2 birds in her backyard on Sunday, 3 birds on Monday, 5 birds on Tuesday and 8 birds on Wednesday. How many birds would Emily see on Saturday?

Day	Sun	Mon	Tue	Wed	Thu	Fri	Sat
No. of birds	2						

Answer : _____

⑤ Mrs Winter had 100 pencils. Every week she gave 10 pencils to her students. How many pencils did she have after 7 weeks?

Week	1	2	3	4	5	6
No. of pencils left	90					

Answer : _____

⑥ A nickel weighs about 4 grams. How many nickels weigh 32 grams?

No. of Nickels	1	2	3	4	5	6
Weight (g)	4					

Answer : _____

⑦ Joe is building a tower with his blocks. Each layer has 1 more block than the one above it. How many blocks are needed for 7 layers?

Layer	1	2	3	4	5	6
No. of blocks in all	1	3	6			

Answer : _____

⑧ Joe ran a 6-lap race. He finished the first lap in 15 seconds. After that, for every lap, he took 5 seconds more than the time for the previous lap. How long did Joe take to complete the race?

Lap	1st	2nd	3rd	4th	5th	6th
Time for each lap (s)	15					

Answer : _____

Draw the missing figures. Then use 'pattern', 'size', 'shape' or 'orientation' to answer the questions.

⑨ a.

b. Which two attributes do these figures have in common?

Answer : All the figures have the same _____ and _____ .

⑩ a.

b. Which two attributes do these figures have in common?

Answer : _____

⑪ a.

b. Which two attributes do these figures have in common?

Answer : _____

⑫ a.

b. Which two attributes do these figures have in common?

Answer : _____

⑬ a.

b. Which two attributes do these figures have in common?

Answer : _____

Look at the calendar. Then complete the tables and solve the problems.

September						
SUN	MON	TUE	WED	THU	FRI	SAT
		1	2	3	4	5
6	7	8	9	10	11	12
13	14	15	16	17	18	19
20	21	22	23	24	25	26
27	28	29	30			

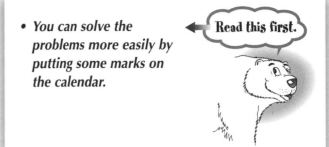

- *You can solve the problems more easily by putting some marks on the calendar.*

Read this first.

⑭ Emily walks her dog on September 1. After that, she will walk it every 3 days.

Day	1st	2nd	3rd	4th	5th
Date	Sept. 1	Sept. 4			

⑮ Which date is the 8th time that Emily walks her dog in September?

Answer : _____

⑯ Emily plays basketball every Wednesday.

Day	1st	2nd	3rd	4th	5th
Date	Sept. 2				

⑰ Which date is the 1st time that Emily plays basketball in October?

Answer : _____

CHALLENGE

On Monday, Judy bought 10 candies and ate 3. The next day, she bought 12 candies and ate 6. The following day she bought 14 candies and ate 9. If this pattern continued, how many candies would Judy buy and eat on Thursday?

Answer : _____

UNIT 11 Equations

Use the pictures to solve the problems. Show your work.

① Gabe started with 15 marbles. After Emily hid some of his marbles, there were 9 left. How many marbles did Emily hide?

15 – ? = 9

Answer : Emily hid 6 marbles.

② Emily started with 20 marbles. After Gabe hid some of her marbles, there were 12 left. How many marbles did Gabe hide?

20 – ? = 12

Answer : 8

③ Gabe had 9 marbles. Emily and Gabe had 12 marbles altogether. How many marbles did Emily have?

12 – ? = 9

Answer : 3

④ Emily had 12 marbles. Gabe and Emily had 18 marbles altogether. How many marbles did Gabe have?

12 + ? = 18

Answer : 6

Write an equation with a ? to solve each problem.

⑤ Gabe has 9 pencils. How many pencils does he need to bring his total up to 15 pencils?

___9___ + ? = ___15___

Answer : 6

⑥ Emily had 20 pencils. She gave some to Gabe and has 15 left. How many pencils did she give to Gabe?

20 - ? = 15

Answer : 5

⑦ Gabe ate 6 candies and has 8 left. How many candies did Gabe have to start with?

8 + 6 = ?

Answer : 14

⑧ Gabe gave 8 candies to David. Then David has 21 candies. How many candies did David have to start with?

21 - 8 = ?   ? + 8 = 21

Answer :

⑨ Emily started with 27 candies and ended up with 19 candies. How many candies did she eat?

19 + ? = 27

Answer : 8

⑩ The total cost of a candy and a pencil is 45¢. A candy costs 16¢. What is the cost of a pencil?

45 - 16 = ?

Answer : 29

⑪ The cost of a sticker is 5¢ more than a candy. If the cost of a sticker is 16¢, what is the cost of a candy?

candy + 5 = 16

Answer : 11

⑫ Emily bought a candy with 50¢ and got 21¢ back. How much does a candy cost?

50 - ? = 21

Answer : 29

⑬ Gabe bought some pencils and got 8¢ back. The pencils cost 67¢. How much did Gabe pay?

8 + 67 = ?

Answer : 75

⑭ Gabe ate 12 candies and had 29 left. How many candies did he have to start with?

12 + 29 = ?

Answer : 41

⑮ If Emily gives David 5 stickers, David will have 63 stickers. How many stickers does David have?

63 - 5 = ?

Answer : 58

⑯ If Gabe gives Emily 39¢, he will have 36¢ left. How much does Gabe have?

39 + 36 = ?

Answer : 75

Swap the shapes for numbers to solve the problems.

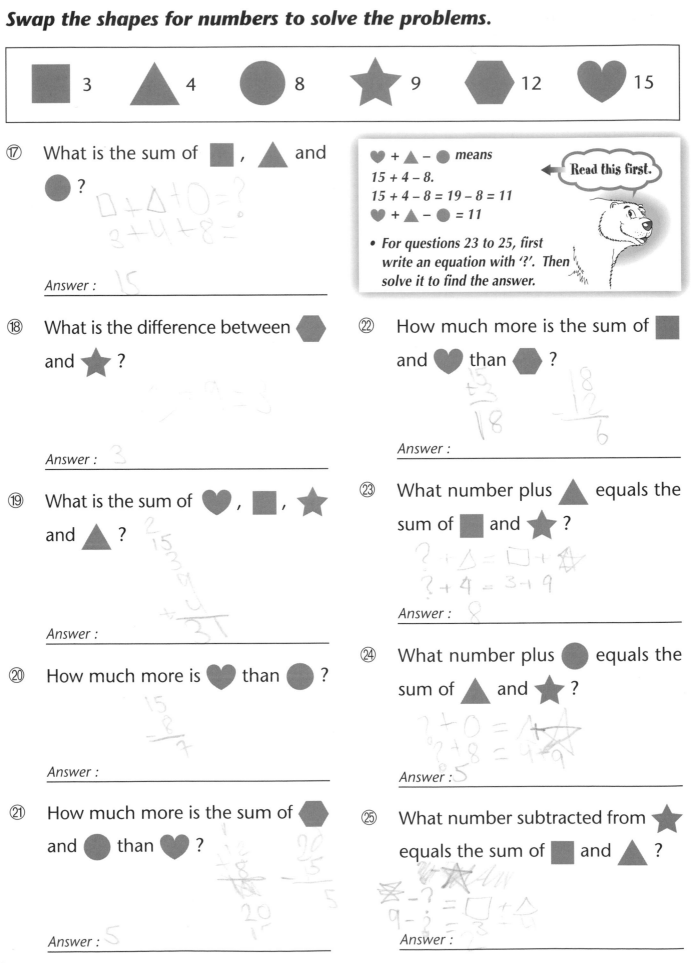

■ 3	▲ 4	● 8	★ 9	⬡ 12	♥ 15

⑰ What is the sum of ■ , ▲ and ● ?

□ + △ + ○ = ?
8 + 4 + 8 =

Answer : 15

⑱ What is the difference between ⬡ and ★ ?

Answer : 3

⑲ What is the sum of ♥ , ■ , ★ and ▲ ?

Answer :

⑳ How much more is ♥ than ● ?

15
8
7

Answer :

㉑ How much more is the sum of ⬡ and ● than ♥ ?

20

Answer : 5

> ♥ + ▲ − ● means
> 15 + 4 − 8.
> 15 + 4 − 8 = 19 − 8 = 11
> ♥ + ▲ − ● = 11
>
> • For questions 23 to 25, first write an equation with '?'. Then solve it to find the answer.

Read this first.

㉒ How much more is the sum of ■ and ♥ than ⬡ ?

15
18

18
12
6

Answer :

㉓ What number plus ▲ equals the sum of ■ and ★ ?

? + △ = □ + ☆
? + 4 = 3 + 9

Answer : 8

㉔ What number plus ● equals the sum of ▲ and ★ ?

? + ○ = ▲ + ☆
? + 8 = 4 + 9
5

Answer : 5

㉕ What number subtracted from ★ equals the sum of ■ and ▲ ?

☆ − ? = □ + △
9 − ? = 3 + 4

Answer :

194   COMPLETE MATHSMART (GRADE 4)

Read the clues. Write the height and weight of the children.

- Brixby is 5 cm shorter than Sandy, but 2 kg heavier than she.

- Guster is 3 cm taller than Sandy, but 1 kg lighter than she.

- Woodly is as heavy as Guster.

- Thorborn is shorter than Woodly. Their difference in height is 2.5 cm.

- The total weight of Sandy and Brixby is the same as the total weight of Boltrun and Thorborn. Boltrun is as heavy as Thorborn.

- The difference in height between Sandy and Woodly is the same as the difference in height between Boltrun and Guster. Boltrun is taller than Guster.

	Height (cm)	Weight (kg)
Sandy	130	30
㉖ Woodly	128	
㉗ Brixby		
㉘ Guster		
㉙ Boltrun		
㉚ Thorborn		

CHALLENGE

Reston had a box of chocolates. He shared it equally with 5 of his friends and each friend gave 1 chocolate back to him. Then he shared the chocolates with Jane and each of them got 4. How many chocolates did Reston have at the beginning?

Answer :

Emily and her cousins are building towers out of blocks. Each block is 1.5 cm high.

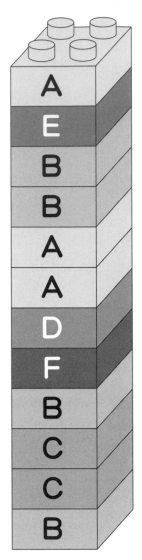

① What fraction of the blocks in the tower have a letter A on them?

Answer : _____

② Write the answer for question 1 as a decimal number in words.

Answer : _____

③ If Emily stacks up all the blocks with A on them, how tall will the tower be?

Answer : _____

④ Emily builds another tower by using the blocks with B and C on them. What fraction of the blocks from the first tower does she use?

Answer : _____

⑤ How tall is the tower that is built with blocks B and C?

Answer : _____

⑥ Emily's cousin, James, builds each tower with 7 blocks. Complete his table.

No. of towers	1	2	3	4	5	6	7
No. of blocks	7						

⑦ James wants to build 11 towers. How many blocks does he need?

Answer : _____

⑧ James tries to stack up all his 7-block towers. Each tower is 10.5 cm tall. Complete the table.

No. of stacked-up towers	1	2	3	4	5	6	7
Height of new tower (cm)	10.5						

⑨ James wants to have a new tower 94.5 cm tall, how many 7-block towers does he need?

Answer : _____

⑩ Would it be easy for James to make a tower 94.5 cm tall? Explain.

Answer : _____

⑪ If each block weighs about 65 grams, how heavy will 14 blocks be?

Answer : _____

⑫ If Emily shares 952 blocks with 3 cousins, how many blocks will each child get?

Answer : _____

⑬ If four-fifths of a bag of blocks are red, how much of a bag of blocks is red? Write in decimal number.

Answer : _____

⑭ Emily built her first tower in 2.45 minutes and the next one in 3.16 minutes. How long did she take to build the two towers?

Answer : _____

⑮ How much more time did Emily spend on building the second tower than the first one?

Answer : _____

Emily got a big box of building blocks. There were 1500 blocks in it.

⑯ Emily made a house with 623 blocks. How many blocks were left?

Answer : _____

⑰ Emily divided the remaining blocks into piles. She put 200 blocks in each pile. Complete the table.

No. of piles	1	2	3	4
No. of blocks	200	400		

⑱ What was the maximum number of piles that Emily got?

Answer : _____

⑲ How many blocks were left?

Answer : _____

⑳ James took Emily's blocks to build 3 cars. Each car was made up of 375 blocks. How many blocks did James need?

Answer : _____

㉑ Did he have enough blocks left over to make another car?

Answer : _____

㉒ Emily used $\frac{4}{15}$ of a box of blocks to build her tower. James used $\frac{7}{15}$ of the same box of blocks to build his tower. Who used more blocks? Explain.

Answer : _____

㉓ $\frac{3}{10}$ of a box of blocks is yellow, $\frac{1}{10}$ blue, $\frac{4}{10}$ green and $\frac{2}{10}$ red. Write the colours in order from the most to the fewest.

Answer : _____

㉔ James built a tower with 25 blocks. Then he took off 7 blocks. What fraction of the blocks were left?

Answer : _____

㉕ If a 16-block tower is 0.16 m tall, how tall will a 32-block tower be?

Answer : _____

㉖ How many 16-block towers are needed to make a new tower 0.64 m tall?

Answer : _____

Each block has 4 vertical faces. Emily put some stickers on each face.

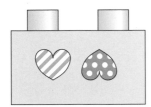

Face 1   Face 2   Face 3   Face 4

No. of blocks	1	2	3	4	5
㉗ No. of stickers on Face 1	2	4			
㉘ No. of stickers on Face 2	1	2			
㉙ No. of stickers on Face 3	5	10			
㉚ No. of stickers on Face 4	3	6			
㉛ Total no. of stickers	11				

㉜ If Emily used 88 stickers, how many blocks with stickers would there be?

Answer : _____

㉝ If Emily wanted to have 9 blocks with stickers, how many stickers would she need?

Answer : _____

㉞ If Emily wanted to have 7 stickers on face 2, how many more stickers would she need for each block?

Answer : _____

㉟ Look at Emily's stickers. Which two attributes do the stickers have in common?

Answer : _____

㊱ If each sticker costs 15¢, how much will Emily pay for the stickers on 1 block?

Answer : _____

㊲ How much will Emily pay for the stickers on 3 blocks?

Answer : _____

Circle the correct answer in each problem.

38 Which of these pizzas has had $\frac{1}{8}$ eaten?

A. B. C. D.

39 Which of these equations could be used to check whether $120 \div 5 = 24$?

A. $120 - 24 = 96$ B. $120 \times 5 = 600$ C. $24 \times 5 = 120$ D. $24 + 5 = 29$

40 Which shape is next in this pattern?

A. ♡   B. △   C. ⬤   D. ◐

41 Gabe had 200 stickers and Emily had 150. They put them together and then shared them equally. Which two operations should be used to find the number of stickers that each child had?

A. $-$, $\div$ B. $+$, $\div$ C. $+$, $\times$ D. $-$, $\times$

42 What is the answer for question 41?

A. 175   B. 125   C. 150   D. 700

43 Which number is next in this pattern?

| 80 | 75 | 70 | 65 | 60 | 55 | ? |

A. 65   B. 50   C. 40   D. 45

44 Which decimal number has the same value as $\frac{12}{16}$?

A. 1.33   B. 0.25   C. 0.75   D. 0.70

Section IV

Overview

Word problems in Section III were solved using the four basic arithmetic operations.

In Section IV, the problems involve measurement of area, length, perimeter, volume and time as well as money applications.

Spatial concepts are expanded to include measurement of angles using a protractor and applying transformations (rotation, reflection, translation) to shapes. Graphing applications include pictographs, bar graphs and coordinate plotting.

Tree diagrams are used to illustrate possible outcomes such as flipping a coin and tossing a die so that probabilities can be calculated.

Writing answers in full sentences with appropriate units is stressed throughout.

EXAMPLE

Mandy's school is 1 km from her home. Every day she walks to school and back. How far does she walk in metres?

Think :   1 km = 1000 m

Distance (in metres) : 1000 × 2 = 2000

Answer : She walks 2000 m.

Check ✓ the correct units. Then solve the problems. Show your work.

Irene goes painting in the countryside. She brings along some brushes, pencils, 3 sheets of drawing paper, a box of water colours, a stool and a drawing board.

		mm	cm	dm	m	km
①	Irene is 11 years old. She is about 110 _____ tall.		✓			
②	She has a brush which is about 3 _____ long.			✓		
③	The countryside is about 10 _____ from her home.					✓
④	She has to take a bus which is about 12 _____ long.				✓	
⑤	She reads a book on the bus. It is about 5 _____ thick.	✓	✓			

⑥ One of Irene's brushes is 15 cm long. How many mm long is it?

Answer : It is ⎸50 ₥ long.

⑦ The drawing paper is 3 dm wide. How many cm wide is it?

Answer : 30 cm

⑧ Her stool is 80 cm high. How many dm high is it?

Answer : 8 dm

⑨ A tube of water colour is 70 mm long. How many cm long is it?

Answer : 7 cm

• *Remember :* ← Read this first.
  1 cm = 10 mm
  1 dm = 10 cm
  1 m   = 10 dm
  1 m   = 100 cm
  1 km = 1000 m

⑩ Irene sees a lake in the countryside. It is about 1 km across. How many m across is it?

Answer : _____1000 m_____

⑪ A boy is fishing in the lake. He is about 135 cm tall. How many mm tall is he?

Answer : _____1350 mm_____

⑫ There is a tree. It is about 12 m away from Irene. How many dm is it away from her?

Answer : _____120 dm_____

⑬ The tree in Irene's picture is 200 mm tall. How many dm tall is it?

Answer : _____2 dm_____

⑭ Irene can see 2 houses, one red and one yellow. The red house is 8 m tall and the yellow house is 750 cm. Which house is taller? How many dm taller?

Answer : _____8 m > 750 cm , 5 dm_____

⑮ A kite is flying 120 m above ground. Another kite is flying 300 dm higher. How many m is it above ground?

Answer : _____150 m_____

⑯ 2 dogs, one white and one black, are running in the field. The white dog can run 120 m and the black dog 1300 dm in 10 seconds. Which dog runs farther? How many cm farther?

Answer : _____130 m_____

⑰ There are 2 trails in the countryside. One is shorter than the other by 3000 m. The longer trail is 15 km. How many km is the shorter trail?

Answer : _____12 km_____

⑱ Irene uses 2 pencils to draw a picture. One of her pencils is 15 cm long. The other is 20 mm longer. How many cm long is the other pencil?

Answer : _____17 cm_____

CHALLENGE

Irene has 75 sheets of paper. She lays them end to end on the floor. If 4 sheets of paper are 112 cm long, how long will her line of paper be in cm, dm and m?

Answer : _____2100 cm   210 dm 21 m_____

EXAMPLE

Jane flew from Sydney, Australia to Tokyo, Japan. She took off at 2:00 p.m. and landed at noon the next day. How long was the flight?

No. of hours from 2:00 p.m. to midnight : 12 – 2 = 10

No. of hours from midnight to noon : 12

Total no. of hours : 10 + 12 = 22

Answer : The flight was 22 hours.

Solve the problems. Show your work.

Irene's grandparents live in Vancouver. They come to visit Irene and her parents in Toronto every year.

① This year, Irene's grandparents arrived at noon on August 28 and left on September 22 at noon. How many days did they stay in Toronto?

Answer : They stayed for 25 days.

② They took off at 2:10 p.m. Toronto time and arrived at 7:28 p.m. How long was the flight?

Answer : 5:18

③ Every morning they took 20 minutes to walk to a park from home. They stayed there for one and a quarter hours. How many minutes did they stay in the park? 60
+15
75

Answer : 75 minut

- **Remember :**   ◄ Read this first.
  1 minute is 60 seconds.
  1 hour is 60 minutes.
  1 day is 24 hours.
  1 week is 7 days.
  1 year is 52 weeks.
  1 year is 365 days (366 days in a leap year).

④ They left home for the park at quarter to eight. When did they return home?

7:45 + 20 7:5 + 20min
min + min

Answer : 9:40

⑤ Grandma needed three quarters of an hour to take a bath. How many minutes did she need in a week?

45x7 = 315 min

Answer :

Irene does similar things every morning on weekdays. This is a time line of her morning.

Wake up 7:00	Brush teeth 7:20	Catch bus 8:00	Get to school 8:35	Class starts 9:00		Recess 10:00
7:10 Get dressed	7:30 Eat breakfast		8:30	8:50 Bell rings	9:30	

⑥ How long after she wakes up does Irene get dressed?

Answer : 10 min

⑦ If Irene gets out of bed 6 minutes after she wakes up, what time does she get out of bed?

Answer : 7:06 Am

⑧ How long does Irene spend on the school bus every morning?

Answer : 35 min

⑨ Will she be late for school if the bus comes at 8:30?

Answer : Yes

⑩ If Irene has French at 9:35 and it goes on until recess, how long is her French class?

Answer : 25 min

⑪ If Irene leaves home 8 minutes before her bus comes, what time does she leave home?

Answer : 7:52

CHALLENGE

Look at Irene's time line again. If lunch is 1 hour and 45 minutes after recess starts, how much time does Irene have between breakfast and lunch?

11:45
7:30
4:15

Answer : 255 min

COMPLETE MATHSMART (GRADE 4)   205

Operations with Money

EXAMPLE

Mrs Collins paid for some groceries with 3 ten-dollar bills, 4 toonies, 1 loonie, 3 quarters, 2 dimes, 1 nickel and 4 pennies. How much did the groceries cost?

No. of dollars : $10 \times 3 + 2 \times 4 + 1 \times 1 = 39$

No. of cents : $25 \times 3 + 10 \times 2 + 5 \times 1 + 1 \times 4 = 104$

Total cost : $39 + 1.04 = 40.04$

Answer : The groceries cost $40.04.

Solve the problems. Show your work.

Irene and Alan were helping their teacher count the money for the class book orders.

① Janice's order had 1 loonie, 1 quarter and 2 dimes. Which book did she order?

② Paul's order had 2 five-dollar bills, 1 quarter and 2 dimes. Which book did he order?

Answer : She ordered Jumping in and out .

Answer : Bugs Bees and Beetles

③ Gary paid with 1 five-dollar bill, 1 toonie and 5 dimes. Which book did he order?

Answer: 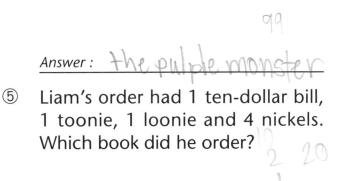 it's raining fish

④ Jessie paid with 2 toonies, 3 quarters, 2 dimes and 4 pennies. Which book did she order?

Answer: the pulple monster

⑤ Liam's order had 1 ten-dollar bill, 1 toonie, 1 loonie and 4 nickels. Which book did he order?

Answer: how to Hair pins

⑥ Joan's order had 2 toonies, 1 loonie and 1 quarter. Which book did she order?

Answer:  Soxn not again

⑦ Leslie paid with 1 ten-dollar bill, 3 loonies, 3 quarters, 1 dime and 2 pennies. What was his order?

Answer: Stamp colect manual

⑧ Brian paid with 2 five-dollar bills, 1 toonie, 3 dimes, 1 nickel and 1 penny. What was his order?

Answer: how fast is fast

Fill in the blanks.

The following students ordered several books each. Show how they paid with the smallest number of bills and coins.

	Name	Order	Bill			Coin					
			$20	$10	$5	$2	$1	25¢	10¢	5¢	1¢
⑨	Barry	$20.34	1						3		4
⑩	Wendy	$18.17		1		4			1	1	2
⑪	Ash	$12.73		1		1			7		3
⑫	Rica	$8.48			1	1	1		4	1	3
⑬	Tara	$11.36		1			1		3	1	8
⑭	Kaitlin	$32.40	1	1		1		1	1	1	
⑮	Justin	$41.70	2				1		7		

Solve the problems. Show your work.

Irene and Alan helped their teacher give change to their classmates. Calculate how much change each person received and write the smallest number of bills and coins for the change.

⑯ Peter's books cost $5.73 and he gave a ten-dollar bill.

Answer : _____

⑰ Jackie's books cost $11.35 and she gave $15.00.

Answer : _____

⑱ Lillian's books cost $18.43 and she gave a $20 bill.

Answer : _____

⑲ Ryan's books cost $22.14 and he gave $23.00.

Answer : _____

⑳ James gave $30.00 for his books that cost $21.15.

Answer : _____

㉑ Lisa gave a $20 bill for her books that cost $12.88.

Answer : _____

㉒ Randy gave $10.00 for his books that cost $4.71.

Answer : _____

㉓ Tony gave $15.00 for his books that cost $13.82.

Answer : _____

Another book fair was held in Birchway Public School. The students could buy books, posters and stationery there.

㉔ Steven bought 2 comic books. Each book cost $1.47. How much did he pay?

Answer : _____

㉕ Mimi bought a book for $3.99 and a poster for $1.25. How much did she pay?

Answer : _____

㉖ Delia bought 3 books. They cost $2.75, $3.99 and $4.16. How much did she pay?

Answer : _____

㉗ Mandy bought 3 posters that were $2.60 each. How much did she pay?

Answer : _____

㉘ Jasmine bought 2 books that cost $3.74 and $4.19. She also bought a bookmark for $0.81. How much did she pay?

Answer : _____

㉙ John bought a big dictionary for $21.32 and a poster for $2.60. How much did he pay?

Answer : _____

㉚ Mike bought 3 books. They cost $5.72, $3.69 and $2.15. He also bought a rollerball pen for $4.30. He received $0.14 change. How much did he give the cashier?

Answer : _____

CHALLENGE

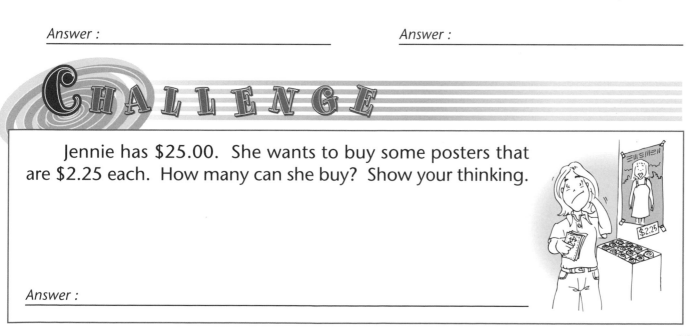

Jennie has $25.00. She wants to buy some posters that are $2.25 each. How many can she buy? Show your thinking.

Answer : _____

**Area and Perimeter**

EXAMPLE

Dave drew a rectangle and an irregular shape.

a. Find the perimeter and the area of the rectangle.

Perimeter : 4 + 2 + 4 + 2 = 12

Area : 2 rows of 4 squares

2 × 4 = 8

Answer : The perimeter is 12 cm and the area is 8 cm².

b. Find the area of the irregular shape.

Count : 3 squares are completely inside the shape, and 6 squares are mostly inside the shape.

Area : 3 + 6 = 9

Answer: The area is about 9 cm².

Measure and answer.

Irene has some magnets of different shapes. Help her measure the perimeter of each magnet with a ruler with millimetres.

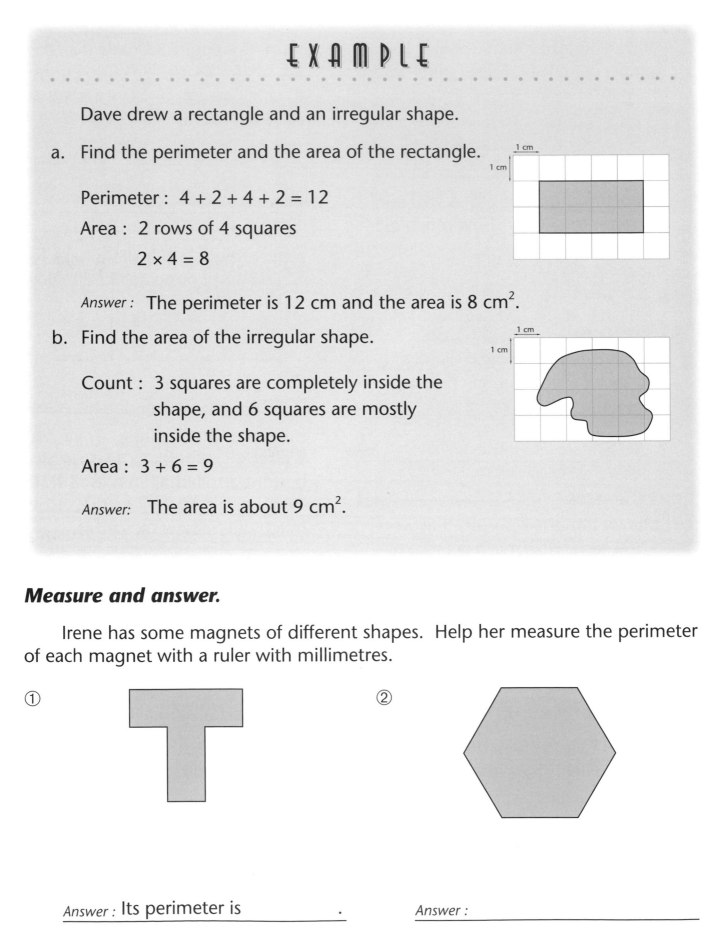

①

②

Answer : Its perimeter is _____ .

Answer : _____

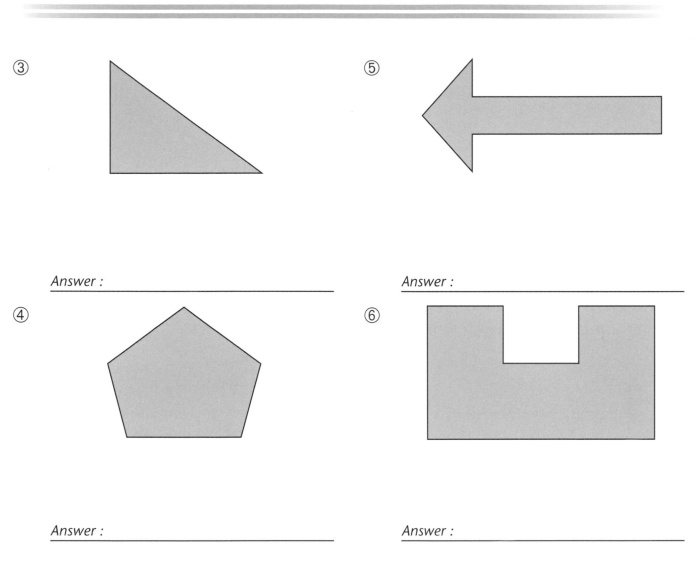

③

Answer : _____

⑤

Answer : _____

④

Answer : _____

⑥

Answer : _____

Solve the problems. Show your work.

Irene is measuring the furniture and some of the things in her bedroom with a tape.

⑦ There is a rectangular photograph on the wall. The length and width of the photograph are 30 cm and 20 cm. What is its perimeter?

Answer : _____

⑧ There is a square-shaped noticeboard. One of its sides is 60 cm. What is its perimeter?

Answer : _____

⑨ There is a triangular pennant on the noticeboard. Two of its sides are 36 cm long and the other is 24 cm. What is its perimeter?

Answer : _____

⑩ Irene's bedroom is a big rectangle. Two of the walls are 8 m long and the other two are 6 m long. What is the perimeter of her bedroom?

Answer : _____

⑪ Irene's bed is 3 m long and 1.2 m wide. What is the perimeter of her bed?

Answer : _____

⑫ There is a window with a height of 9 dm and a width of 16 dm. What is the perimeter of the window in metres?

Answer : _____

⑬ Irene has a rug with 5 sides of equal lengths. The perimeter of the rug is 350 cm. What is the length of each side of the rug?

Answer : _____

Draw the shapes and solve the problems.

Irene wants to find out the areas of the magnets she has collected. Help her draw the magnets on the grids and write their areas.

⑭ Magnet A is a rectangle with a length of 4 cm and a width of 3 cm.

⑮ Magnet B is a square with a perimeter of 12 cm.

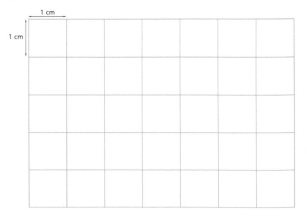

Answer : _____   *Answer :* _____

⑯ Magnet C looks like a letter T. The width of the magnet is 5 cm and the height is 6 cm. The strokes are 1 cm wide.

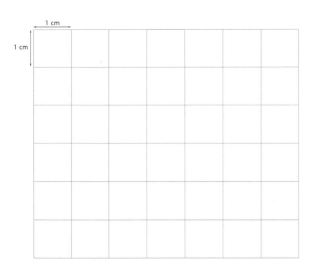

Answer : _____

⑰ Magnet D looks like a letter L with a width of 5 cm and a height of 6 cm. The strokes are 2 cm wide.

Answer : _____

⑱ Compare the area and perimeter of magnets C and D.

Answer : _____

⑲ Magnet E looks like a cross ✠. The width is 5 cm and the height is 6 cm. The strokes are 1 cm wide.

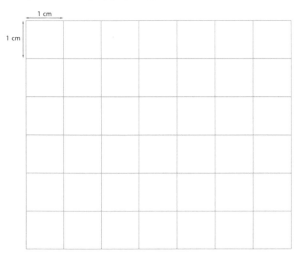

Answer : _____

⑳ Magnet F looks like a letter ☐ with a width of 3 cm and a height of 4 cm. The strokes are 1 cm wide.

Answer : _____

㉑ Compare the area and perimeter of magnets E and F.

Answer : _____

Irene's mother has baked some cookies of irregular shapes.

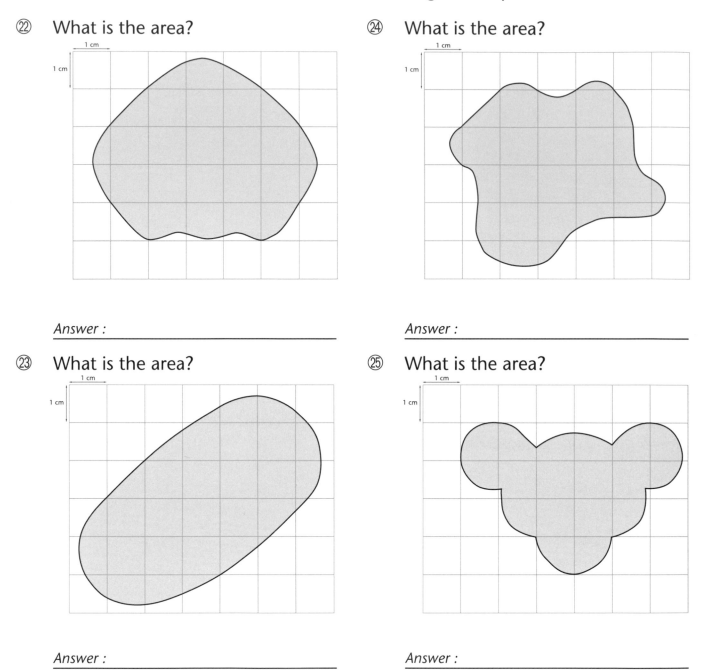

㉒ What is the area?

1 cm

1 cm

Answer : _____

㉔ What is the area?

1 cm

1 cm

Answer : _____

㉓ What is the area?

1 cm

1 cm

Answer : _____

㉕ What is the area?

1 cm

1 cm

Answer : _____

Solve the problems. Show your work.

Irene is helping her dad build a new run for their dog. They have to decide how much fence to put around the run and how much space to give the dog.

㉖ The pen has an area of 12 m^2, and there is a rectangular kennel which is 2 m long and 1 m wide.

a. What is the area of the kennel?

Answer : _____

b. How much space is left in the pen for the dog to run in?

Answer : _____

㉗ The pen has 2 sides of 4 m and 2 sides of 3 m. If there is 12 m of fencing, how much more fencing is needed?

Answer : _____

㉘ The pen has 2 sides of 4 m and 2 sides of 3 m. If the longer side is lengthened by 1 m and the shorter side shortened by 1 m, what will be the difference in area between these 2 pens?

Answer : _____

㉙ Irene wants to enclose a rectangular pen with 12 m of fencing.

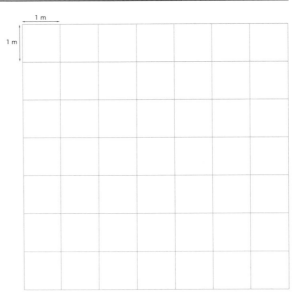

a. Draw as many different rectangles or squares as you can on the grid with the above measurement.

b. Colour the pen with the biggest area.

c. How did Irene get the biggest area with a 12-m fence?

Answer : _____

CHALLENGE

The backyard of Tom's house is rectangular in shape with a perimeter of 42 m. If the length is twice as long as the width, how long is each side?

Answer : _____

Capacity, Volume and Mass

EXAMPLE

a. Irene has built a straight tower of blocks. The volume of each block is 1 cm³.

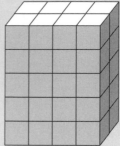

    i.   What is the volume of the tower?

          Think : There are 5 layers of 8 blocks.
          Volume of the tower : $1 \times 8 \times 5 = 40$

        Answer : The volume of the tower is 40 cm³.

    ii.   Each block has a mass of 10 g. What is the mass of the tower?

          Mass : $10 \times 40 = 400$

        Answer : The mass of the tower is 400 g.

b. Irene has a small bucket which can hold 6 bottles of water. If the capacity of each bottle is 500 mL, what is the capacity of the bucket in L?

    Capacity in mL : $500 \times 6 = 3000$

    Write : 1000 mL = 1 L → 3000 mL = 3 L

    Answer : The capacity of the bucket is 3 L.

Irene cannot decide what units to use for the following. Help her check ✓ the correct units.

	Event	Unit					
		g	kg	cm³	m³	mL	L
①	Pouring some cough syrup into a spoon						
②	Measuring how much water a bath tub can hold						
③	Finding how heavy a watermelon is						
④	Calculating the space occupied by a fridge						
⑤	Finding how heavy a pencil is						
⑥	Measuring how much space a recorder occupies						
⑦	Recording the amount of water in a glass						

Solve the problems. Show your work.

Irene has some small blocks that are 1 cm³ in volume. She and her friends are building some towers with the blocks at home.

⑧ Irene has built a straight tower. What is the volume of her tower?

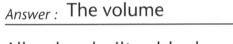

Answer : The volume _____ .

⑩ Look at Peter's tower. What is its volume?

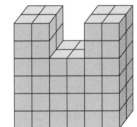

Answer : _____

⑨ Allan has built a block pyramid. What is its volume?

Answer : _____

⑪ Look at Gigi's tower. What is its volume?

Answer : _____

The children found some containers and a 1-L jug in the basement. They are trying to find the capacity of each container with the jug.

⑫ Irene can fill the 1-L jug with 4 glasses of water. What is the capacity of each glass?

Answer : _____

⑭ Irene fills a glass using 5 egg cups of water. What is the capacity of each egg cup?

Answer : _____

⑬ 20 glasses of water can fill a bucket. What is the capacity of the bucket in L?

• **Remember:**   ← **Read this first.**

   1 L = 1000 mL
   1 mL = 0.001 L

Answer : _____

⑮ What is the capacity of 1 bucket and 10 glasses in L?

Answer : _____

⑯ There is a big mug which can hold half a jug of water. What is the capacity of the mug?

Answer : _____

⑰ Irene can fill 5 bottles with 1 jug of water. What is the capacity of each bottle?

Answer : _____

⑱ How many glasses of water can fill a tub with a capacity of 250 L?

Answer : _____

Irene and Alan are hungry. They go to the supermarket to buy some snacks.

⑲ Irene has enough money to buy 4 bags of cookies that weigh 21 g each or 1 big bag that weighs 80 g. Which would give her more cookies?

Answer : _____

⑳ Alan's favourite candies come in small bags of 43 g each and big bags of 150 g each. Which would give him more candies, 3 small bags or 1 big bag?

Answer : _____

㉑ Sixteen 50-g packets of potato chips cost the same as five 165-g packets of potato chips. Which have more potato chips?

Answer : _____

Mr Smith has made a big scale to weigh the animals on his farm. He only knows that the mass of a rabbit is 1 kg and every animal of the same kind weighs the same. Look how he weighs his animals and solve the problems.

㉒ What is the mass of a cat?

Answer : _____

㉓ What is the mass of a dog?

Answer : _____

㉔ What is the mass of a pig?

Answer : _____

㉕ What is the mass of a calf?

Answer : _____

㉖ How many rabbits would be needed to balance a calf?

Answer : _____

㉗ How many rabbits would be needed to balance 2 cats and 1 dog?

Answer : _____

㉘ How many dogs would be needed to balance a calf?

Answer : _____

㉙ How many cats would be needed to balance a calf?

Answer : _____

㉚ How many cats must be added to 6 dogs in order to balance a calf?

Answer : _____

㉛ If Mr Smith puts 6 cats on one side of the scale and a pig on the other side, which side will weigh more?

Answer : _____

㉜ Is it possible to balance a calf with 6 dogs and 4 cats together? Explain.

Answer : _____

CHALLENGE

John, Ben and Tim are playing on a teeter-totter. John has a mass of 50 kg. Ben is 6 kg heavier than Tim. If John can balance Ben and Tim together, what is the mass of Tim?

Answer : _____

Two- and Three-Dimensional Figures

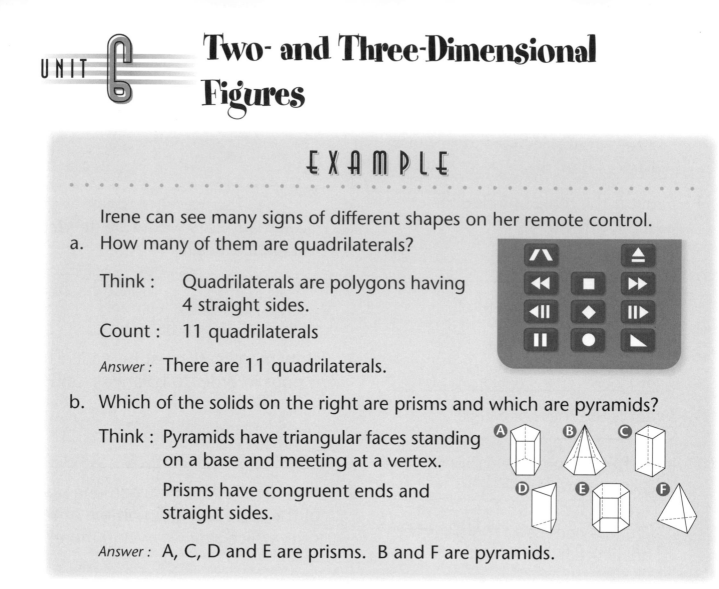

EXAMPLE

Irene can see many signs of different shapes on her remote control.

a. How many of them are quadrilaterals?

Think :   Quadrilaterals are polygons having 4 straight sides.

Count :   11 quadrilaterals

Answer : There are 11 quadrilaterals.

b. Which of the solids on the right are prisms and which are pyramids?

Think : Pyramids have triangular faces standing on a base and meeting at a vertex.

Prisms have congruent ends and straight sides.

Answer : A, C, D and E are prisms. B and F are pyramids.

Count and colour. Show your thinking and answer the questions.

Irene's teacher has several boxes of shapes. She wants Irene to sort and colour them. Help Irene finish her work.

① Irene has to sort out all the rectangles and colour them red.

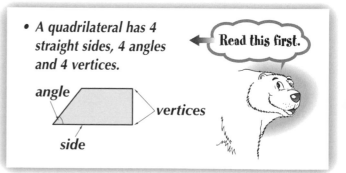

- A quadrilateral has 4 straight sides, 4 angles and 4 vertices.

Read this first.

angle

vertices

side

a. How do you know they are rectangles?

Answer : _____

b. How many shapes in the box are not quadrilaterals? Explain.

Answer : _____

② Irene has to sort out all the pentagons from a box of polygons. Colour them green. Is the shape marked A a pentagon? Explain.

Answer : _____

③ Irene has to sort out all the hexagons from a box of polygons. Colour them yellow. How do you know they are hexagons?

Answer : _____

④ Irene has to colour the rhombuses brown and the parallelograms blue. What are the similarities and differences between a rhombus and a parallelogram?

Answer : _____

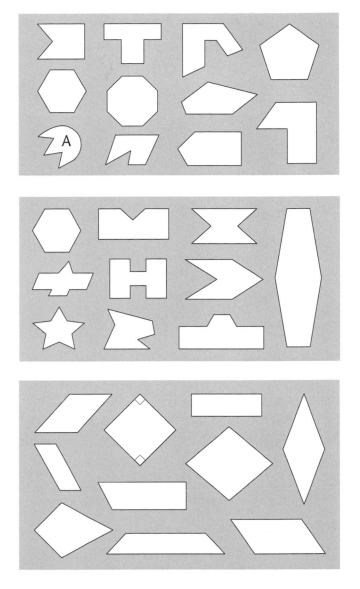

Write the names of the polygons.

Irene is making some shapes for her teacher. Read what she says and write the shape she is making.

⑤ 'This shape has 4 right angles. Two of its sides are longer than the others.'

Answer : _____

⑥ 'This quadrilateral has 4 equal sides but the angles are not right angles.'

Answer : _____

⑦ 'This shape has 5 straight sides and 5 angles.'

Answer : _____

⑧ 'This shape has 6 angles and 6 vertices. The sides are equal in length.'

Answer : _____

⑨ 'I can get these 2 congruent shapes by cutting a rectangle into halves from corner to corner.'

Answer : _____

⑩ 'This quadrilateral has all the sides equal in length and all the angles equal in size.'

Answer : _____

⑪ 'This shape has 2 pairs of parallel lines. The opposite sides and angles are equal.'

Answer : _____

⑫ 'This shape has 8 angles and 8 vertices. All its sides are equal in length.'

Answer : _____

Write the names of the solids.

⑬ There is a box which has congruent ends and straight sides. What kind of solid is it?

Answer : _____

⑭ In the box there is a container which has a square base and 4 edges meeting at a vertex. What kind of solid is it?

Answer : _____

- A prism has congruent ends and straight sides. e.g.

  Read this first.

  side   end

- A pyramid has a base and the edges meet at a vertex. e.g.

  vertex
  edge
  base

- A cone has a round base and a curved surface. e.g.

  curved surface

  base

⑮ In the box there is a big dice with 6 faces. The edges are equal in length and they meet at right angles. What kind of solid is it?

Answer : _____

⑯ Irene finds a hat for the snowman. The base of the hat is round and it has a curved surface which comes to a point. What does the hat look like?

Answer : _____

⑰ Irene finds a rod for the snowman, too. The rod has two circular ends and it is straight and long. What kind of solid is it?

Answer : _____

⑲ Irene's mother gives her a chocolate bar. The side view of the bar is a rectangle. The ends are triangles. What kind of solid is it?

Answer : _____

⑱ Irene makes a big snow ball for the head of the snowman. What kind of solid is it?

Answer : _____

⑳ Irene's mother also gives her a candy. The candy has 4 faces. Each face looks like a triangle. What kind of solid is it?

Answer : _____

Complete the table.

㉑ Irene wants to make a summary of the prisms and pyramids she saw today. Help her complete the table.

Solid	Number of faces	Number of straight edges	Number of vertices
Cube			
Rectangular prism			
Rectangular pyramid			
Triangular prism			
Tetrahedron			

CHALLENGE

Irene has 2 nets for making 2 solids. What solids is she going to make?

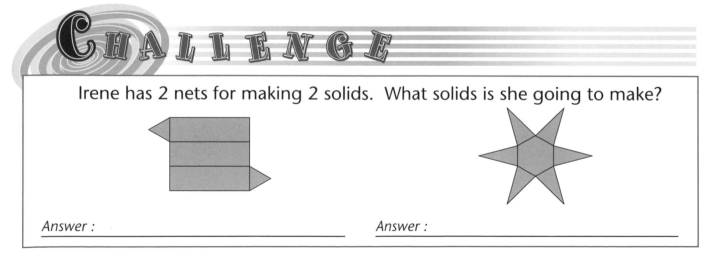

Answer : _____

Answer : _____

Solve the problems. Show your work.

Irene is helping her father build a rectangular flower bed. The width of the flower bed is 3 m and the perimeter is 16 m.

① Draw a sketch to show the shape and sides of the flower bed.

[grid diagram with 1 m scale markings]

② Irene's dad wants to build a brick edging around the outside of the flower bed. If the edging costs $80.00 for 5 m, how much does it cost for 1 m?

Answer : _____

③ What is the total cost for the edging?

Answer : _____

④ Special soil in 15-kg bags costs 40¢ per kg. How much does Irene's dad pay for 1 bag of special soil?

Answer : _____

⑤ How much does he pay for 35 bags of special soil?

Answer : _____

⑥ Irene's dad started digging at 9:45 in the morning. He worked for 4 hours with two 25-minute breaks. When did he finish working?

Answer : _____

⑦ What is the area of the flower bed?

Answer : _____

⑧ Is the flower bed bigger or smaller if it is a 4-m square?

Answer : _____

⑨ Irene will grow 12 flowers on 1 m^2 of land. How many flowers will there be on the flower bed?

Answer : _____

⑩ Rose food costs $8.89 a box plus a tax of $1.33. How much will Irene's dad pay for 1 box of rose food?

Answer : _____

⑪ If Irene's dad paid for the rose food with a $10 bill and a quarter, what was the change?

Answer : _____

Mr Smith is going to build a path leading to the front door of his house with either bricks or slabs. He is now browsing in a shop selling construction materials.

⑫ There are 3 piles of bricks in the shop. The volume of each brick is 1000 cm³. What is the volume of each pile of bricks?

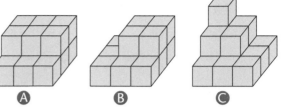

Ⓐ   Ⓑ   Ⓒ

Answer :

⑬ If the 3 piles of bricks are to be stacked in a straight tower with 4 bricks in each layer, how many layers will there be? How many bricks will be left over?

Answer :

⑭ If each brick is 10 cm high, what will be the height of the brick tower in metres?

Answer :

⑮ What will be the volume of the brick tower in cm³?

Answer :

⑯ The bricks cost 50¢ each in this shop. They cost 10 for $4.50 in AA shop. Which offers a better deal? Explain your thinking.

Answer :

⑰ 9 slabs can cover an area of 1 m². If the path is 10 m², how many slabs should Mr Smith buy?

Answer :

⑱ Each slab costs $3.00 and the shop charges $25.50 for delivery. How much will Mr Smith pay for the slabs including delivery?

Answer :

⑲ Mr Smith is paying for some tools which cost $37.28 including tax with a $50 bill. What is the fewest number of bills and coins he receives as change?

Answer :

Jenny and Mike are playing in the backyard. Their mother brings them some cold drinks and snacks.

⑳ Look at the containers of the cold drinks and snacks. Write what 3-dimensional shapes you can see.

Answer : _____

㉑ The diagrams below are the labels found on the containers of TT biscuits and BB chocolates. What are their areas?

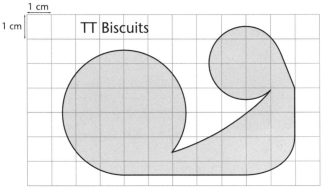

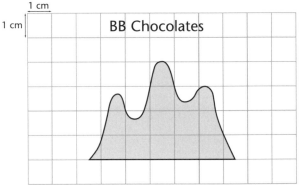

Answer : _____

㉒ Jenny has a jug which can hold 5 boxes of apple juice. If each box of apple juice is 400 mL, how many litres of juice can the jug hold?

Answer : _____

㉓ Jenny's mother has made 80 ice cubes each weighing 25 g. What is the total weight of the ice cubes in kg?

Answer : _____

㉔ The ice cubes took 25 minutes to melt in a jug of juice. Jenny's mother made the juice at 1:38 p.m. When would all the ice cubes melt?

Answer : _____

Circle the correct answer in each problem.

㉕ Irene walks her dog around a regular pentagonal field with each side 230 m long. What is the perimeter of the field?

A. 1380 m   B. 1150 m   C. 1610 m   D. 920 m

㉖ Irene gets paid $4.00 an hour to walk her neighbour's dog. She walks for 30 minutes on each weekday and 1 hour on Saturdays and on Sundays. How much does she earn each week?

A. $21.00   B. $28.00   C. $24.00   D. $18.00

㉗ Irene wanted to weigh her dog. She and her dog both stepped onto a scale. The scale reading was 55 kg. If Irene weighed 41.5 kg, how much did her dog weigh?

A. 96.5 kg   B. 9.65 kg   C. 13.5 kg   D. 1.35 kg

㉘ Emily uses a glass which is a cylinder to cut cookies out of dough. What shape are the cookies?

A. square   B. round   C. hexagonal   D. pentagonal

㉙ If Emily spent $5.00 to make 100 cookies, how much would she spend to make 1000 cookies?

A. $50.00   B. $0.50   C. $500.00   D. $100.00

㉚ What shape can be made with the net?

A. a hexagonal pyramid
B. a pentagonal prism
C. a cylinder
D. a hexagonal prism

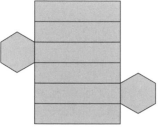

㉛ Peter has 3 $5 bills, 2 twoonies, 1 loonie, 3 quarters, 4 nickels and 13 pennies. How much money does he have?

A. $20.13   B. $21.08   C. $20.08   D. $21.13

㉜ It is 10:35 a.m. and Jenny has been out of bed for 2 hours 40 minutes. When did Jenny get out of bed?

A. 7:55 a.m.   B. 8:55 a.m.   C. 7:00 a.m.   D. 8:00 a.m.

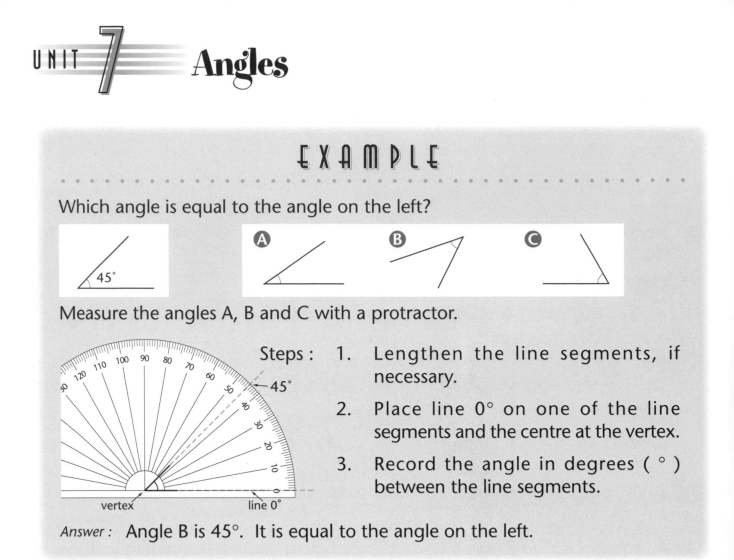

EXAMPLE

Which angle is equal to the angle on the left?

45°

Ⓐ   Ⓑ   Ⓒ

Measure the angles A, B and C with a protractor.

Steps : 1. Lengthen the line segments, if necessary.

2. Place line 0° on one of the line segments and the centre at the vertex.

3. Record the angle in degrees (°) between the line segments.

Answer : Angle B is 45°. It is equal to the angle on the left.

Solve the problems.

① Measure and mark the angles which show how the rocket flies.

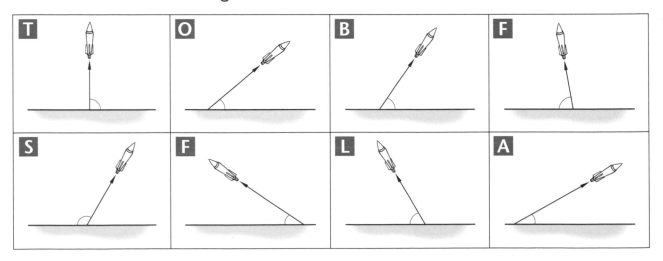

T   O   B   F

S   F   L   A

② Which angle above is greater than a right angle?

③ The sum of which 3 angles above equals the angle of a straight line?

Answer : _____ is greater than a right angle.

Answer :

④ Write the letters represented by the angles to see what Alan is saying.

| 55° | 60° | 30° | 120° | 90° | 40° | 80° | 35° |

Draw the clock hands. Measure and mark the angles on the clock.

Irene is playing with a toy clock.

⑤ If it is 3 o'clock, what angle is made by the clock hands?

⑦ It is 9:00. What angle is made by the clock hands?

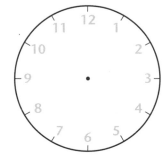

⑥ The hour hand is at 6. Where is the minute hand if the angle between the clock hands is 180°?

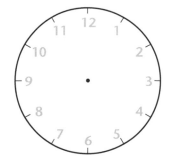

⑧ Irene turns the clock to 7:00 and then to 8:00. What is the difference in the angles between the hands?

CHALLENGE

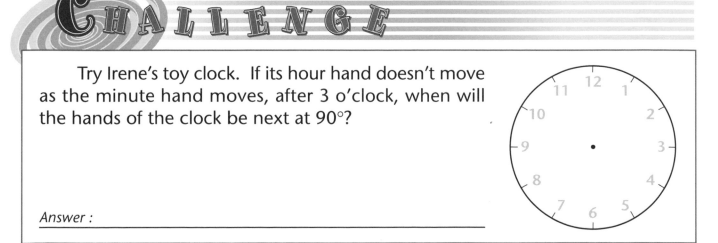

Try Irene's toy clock. If its hour hand doesn't move as the minute hand moves, after 3 o'clock, when will the hands of the clock be next at 90°?

Answer : _____

Transformations

Irene and Alan are playing with a set of plastic letters. They wonder how the letter E looks like if they slide it, turn it and flip it.

a. Sliding the letter (translation)

b. Making $\frac{1}{4}$ turn of the letter (rotation)

c. Flipping the letter (reflection)

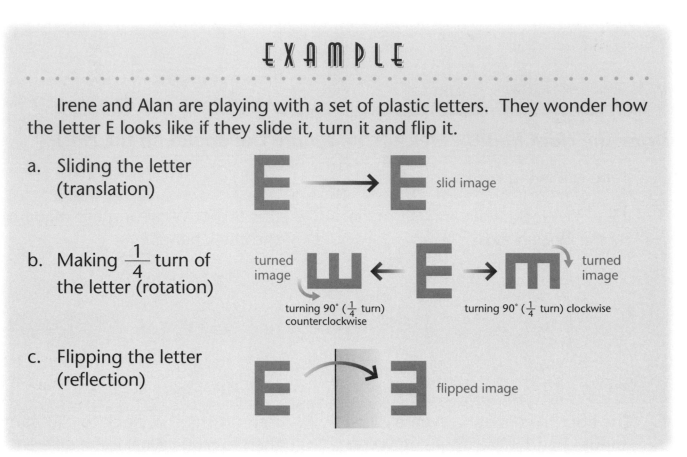

Write the transformations.

Irene and Alan have slid, turned and flipped some of their letters. Write what transformations they used.

① B → B → B → B

Answer : They used _____ .

② p → q → p → q → p

Answer : _____

③ Q → Q → Q → Q

Answer : _____

④ F → ⌐ → ⌐ → ⊤

Answer : _____

⑤ G → ⊃ → G → ⊃

Answer : _____

⑥ T → ⊢ → ⊥ → ⊢

Answer : _____

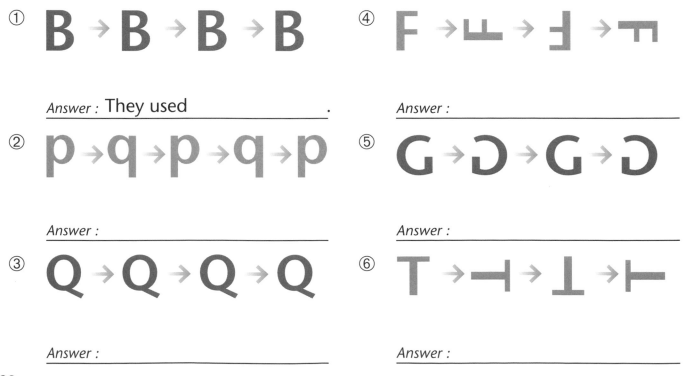

Draw the images and solve the problems.

Alan has made some shapes on a geoboard with elastic bands. He asks Irene to transform the shapes.

⑦ Irene has to flip the shape over the line l.

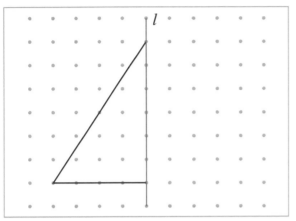

⑧ Irene has to flip the shape over the line l.

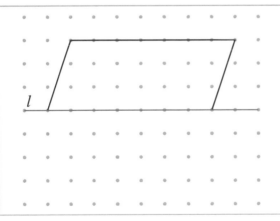

⑨ Irene has to slide the shape horizontally so that the image of point E is at E_1.

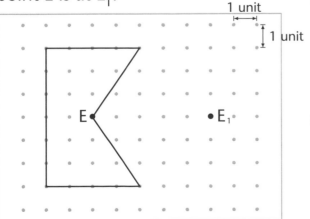

⑩ Irene has to slide the shape vertically so that the image of point X is at X_1.

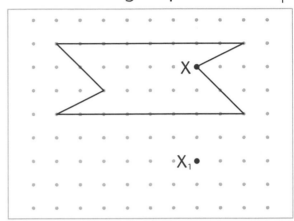

⑪ What transformation did Irene use to make the image of the shape?

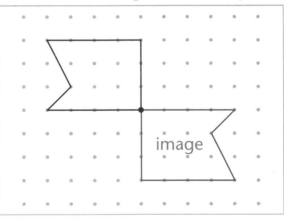

Answer : _____

⑫ How many units is the shape slid horizontally in question 9?

Answer : _____

⑬ Are the shapes and their images congruent?

Answer : _____

Look at the cards that Irene placed and solve the problems.

| 1 | 2 | 3 | 4 | 5 | 6 | 7 | 8 | 9 |

⑭ What transformation is used to form the pattern?

Answer : _____

⑮ How would you describe this pattern?

Answer : _____

⑯ What is the next card in the pattern?

Answer : _____

⑰ If there were 20 cards, how many would look like ♠ ?

Answer : _____

⑱ What would the 13th card in the pattern look like?

Answer : _____

⑲ How many cards would you need to repeat the pattern 6 times?

Answer : _____

⑳ If you only used every 2nd card, which cards would be in the pattern?

Answer : _____

㉑ If you only used every 2nd card, would the transformation be the same? Explain.

Answer : _____

㉒ If this pattern only used $\frac{1}{2}$ turned cards, how many cards would be in the pattern?

Answer : _____

㉓ What would cards 1 to 4 look like in a mirror if you stand a mirror on the bottom side of them? Draw the hearts in the boxes.

| | | | |

㉔ If this pattern started at 2 and turned $\frac{1}{4}$ clockwise, how would it look? Draw the hearts in the boxes.

| | | | |

Help Alan find the lines of symmetry that each shape has.

㉕ Which of the following shapes has the most lines of symmetry?

Ⓐ ♥ Ⓑ ♠ Ⓒ ♦ Ⓓ ♣

Answer : _____

㉖ How many lines of symmetry does a diamond ♦ have?

Answer : _____

㉗ How many lines of symmetry does a heart ♥ have?

Answer : _____

㉘ Which has more lines of symmetry, a diamond or a square? Explain.

Answer : _____

㉙ If Irene cut a square in half down the middle, how many lines of symmetry could Alan draw on each half?

Answer : _____

㉚ If Irene cut a square in half from corner to corner, how many lines of symmetry could Alan draw on each half?

Answer : _____

㉛ Irene has drawn a flower. Draw all the lines of symmetry on the flower.

CHALLENGE

Count the number of lines of symmetry on these 2 shapes. Predict the number of lines of symmetry that a decagon (10 sides) would have.

Hexagon

Octagon

Answer : _____

EXAMPLE

Look at the mail boxes in Parkway Building. Mr Brown lives in A3 and Mr Green lives in E5. Write what each of them receives today.

Think : Mr. Brown's mail box is in column A row 3. There is a tax return in box A3. Mr Green's mail box is in column E row 5. There are some coupons in box E5.

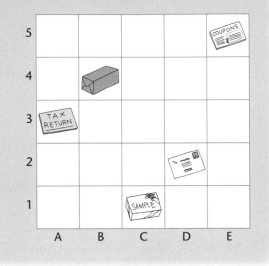

Answer : Mr Brown receives a tax return and Mr Green receives some coupons.

Draw the shapes and solve the problems.

Irene is drawing some shapes on a grid. Help her finish the drawing.

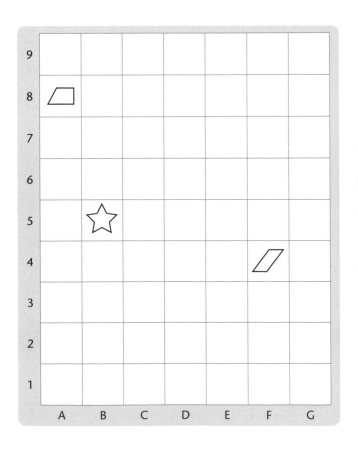

① Draw a circle in D4, a square in A1, a triangle in B2, a rhombus in C7, a rectangle in G7, and a black square in E5.

② What are the locations of ▱ and ☆ ?

Answer : _____

③ How many rows and columns are there on the grid?

Answer : _____

Solve the problems. Show your work.

Irene and Alan are playing a fishing game. They take turns to catch the fish. The one with the highest score wins the game.

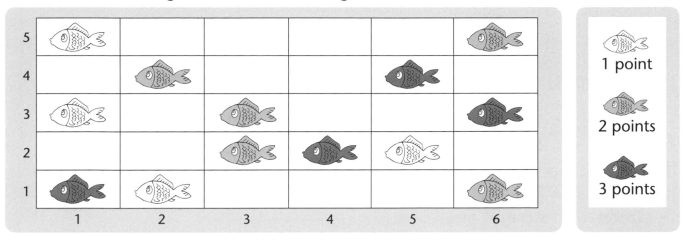

④ What are the ordered pairs of all the 🐟 ?

Answer : _____

⑤ What are the ordered pairs of all the 🐟 ?

Answer : _____

⑥ What are the ordered pairs of all the 🐟 ?

Answer : _____

⑦ Irene catches 3 fish. They are at (2, 1), (5, 4) and (6, 5). What is her score?

Answer : _____

⑧ Alan catches 2 fish. One is 2 units down from (1, 3) and the other is 2 units right from (3, 2). What is his score?

Answer : _____

⑨ Who is the winner?

Answer : _____

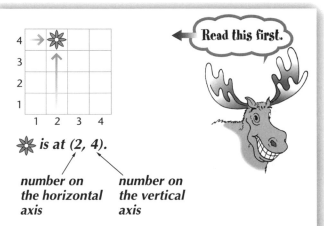

Read this first.

✾ is at (2, 4).

number on the horizontal axis

number on the vertical axis

Irene is helping Alan draw a picture. She has made a grid with the horizontal and vertical lines numbered. Then she gives Alan these instructions. Read what she says and finish the picture for Alan.

⑩ Plot the ordered pairs on the grid.

(3, 1), (3, 5), (1, 5), (3, 7), (9, 7), (9, 9), (10, 9), (10, 7), (12, 7), (14, 5), (12, 5), (12, 1), (8, 1), (8, 4), (6, 4), (6, 1)

⑪ Join the ordered pairs (3, 1), (3, 5) ... (6, 1) in order with straight lines.

⑫ What have you drawn?

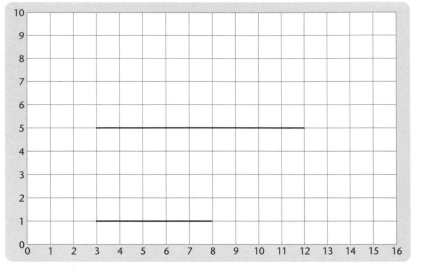

Answer : _____

⑬ If each of the squares on the grid is 1 cm², what is the area of the picture?

Answer : _____

⑭ If Alan wants to add a big square window on the right of the door, what are the ordered pairs of the window?

Answer : _____

Look at the triangle that Alan drew on the grid. Solve the problems.

⑮ What are the ordered pairs of the vertices?

Answer : _____

⑯ Which are the 2 ordered pairs for the line of symmetry of the triangle – (0, 4) and (5, 0), (6, 4) and (2, 0) or (3, 5) and (3, 0) ?

Answer : _____

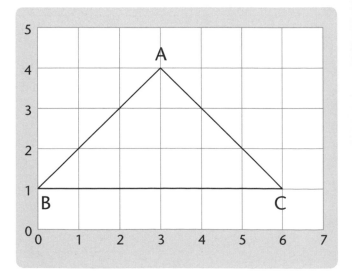

Look at Alan's picture on the grid. Solve the problems.

⑰ Label the horizontal and vertical axes.

⑱ Alan is going to describe his picture to Irene so she can copy it.

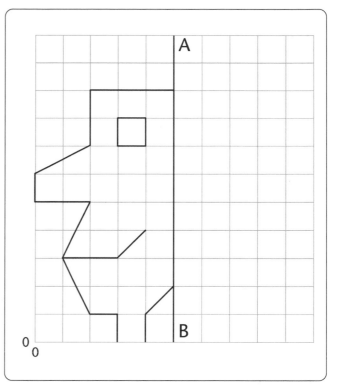

a. Which 4 ordered pairs will Alan give to describe the eye?

Answer : _____

b. Which 2 ordered pairs show the top of the head?

Answer : _____

c. Which 3 ordered pairs show the mouth?

Answer : _____

d. Which 4 ordered pairs are used to make the nose?

Answer : _____

CHALLENGE

① Look at Alan's picture again. If his picture was slid 4 units right and 1 unit up, which 4 ordered pairs would make the nose?

Answer : _____

② If the picture was flipped over the line AB, which 4 ordered pairs would make the eye?

Answer : _____

UNIT 10 Probability

EXAMPLE

a. Peter is tossing a loonie. What is the probability that he will get a head?

Think : There are 2 possible outcomes : head or tail.

Answer : The probability that he will get a head is 1 out of 2.

b. Jenny is tossing 2 loonies at a time. What is the probability that she will get 2 heads? Draw a tree diagram to explain your thinking.

Think : There are 4 possible outcomes : HH, HT, TH, TT.

Answer : The probability that she will get 2 heads is 1 out of 4.

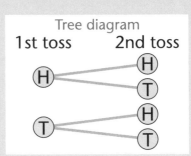

Check ✓ the right boxes.

Read each of these events and decide, following the probability rules, if the outcomes are likely or unlikely.

	Event	Outcomes	
		Likely	Unlikely
①	Irene rolls a die and gets a 6 twice in 12 rolls.		
②	Alan rolls a 6 three times in a row.		
③	Irene flips a coin 10 times and gets heads 3 times.		
④	Alan rolls a die 10 times and does not get a 1.		
⑤	Irene flips a coin 10 times and gets heads 5 times.		

Solve the problems. Show your thinking.

⑥ Alan has a die. If he rolls the die, how many possible outcomes will there be?

Answer : There will be _____ .

> • The number of possible outcomes stays the same but the number of desired outcomes changes.
>
> Read this first.

⑦ What is the probability that he will roll a 2?

Answer : _____

⑧ What is the probability that he will roll a 6?

Answer : _____

⑨ What is the probability that he will get a number less than 4?

Answer : _____

⑩ What is the probability that he will roll a 1 or a 2?

Answer : _____

⑪ What is the probability that he will get an even number?

Answer : _____

⑫ What is the probability that he will not roll a 3?

Answer : _____

⑬ Write 'equally probable', 'less probable', 'more probable' or 'not probable' for the following.

a. Rolling a 2 or rolling a 6.

Answer : _____

b. Rolling a number less than 4 or a 4.

Answer : _____

c. Rolling a number less than 4 or a number larger than 4.

Answer : _____

d. Rolling a number larger than 6.

Answer : _____

e. Never rolling a 1.

Answer : _____

Irene has made 2 spinners. Spinner A is divided into 4 equal sectors while spinner B is divided into 4 sectors of different sizes.

Spinner A

Spinner B

⑭ For spinner A, what is the probability of spinning a 🐶 ?

Answer : _____

⑮ For spinner A, what is the probability of spinning a 🐰 ?

Answer : _____

⑯ For spinner B, what is the probability of spinning a 🐶 ?

Answer : _____

⑰ For spinner B, what is the probability of spinning a 🐰 ?

Answer : _____

⑱ What is the probability of spinning a 🐍 on spinner B?

Answer : _____

⑲ If you want to spin a 🐰 , which spinner should you use? Explain.

Answer : _____

⑳ If you do not want to spin a 🐍 , which spinner should you use? Explain.

Answer : _____

㉑ If you want to spin a 🐵 , which spinner should you use?

Answer : _____

Irene's cousin, Jenny, has 4 balls – 1 red, 1 yellow and 2 blue. She puts the red ball and a blue ball in a bag and the rest in another bag. Then she asks Alan to pick a ball from each bag.

㉒ Draw a tree diagram to show the possible outcomes.

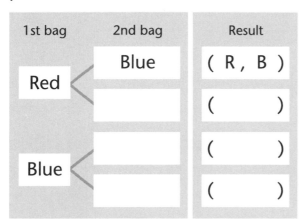

1st bag	2nd bag	Result
Red	Blue	(R , B)
		( )
Blue		( )
		( )

㉕ Alan says that he has a better chance of picking 2 blue balls. Is he correct? Explain.

Answer : _____

㉓ How many possible outcomes are there?

㉖ What is the probability of picking 2 red balls?

Answer : _____

Answer : _____

㉔ What is the probability of picking a red ball and a blue ball?

㉗ If Jenny put all the balls in a bag, would picking a red ball or a blue ball be equally likely?

Answer : _____

Answer : _____

CHALLENGE

Help the children decide where to put each letter on this spinner.

- Irene spun it 8 times and got 4 As.

- Alan only got 2 Cs when he spun it 8 times.

- Steve got 2 Bs and 2 Ds when he spun it 16 times.

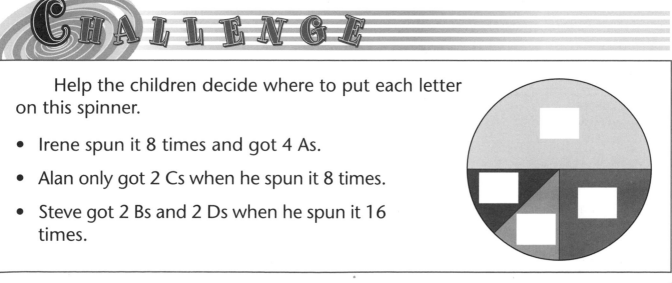

Pictographs and Bar Graphs

EXAMPLE

Irene did a survey to find the favourite drinks of the Grade 4 students.

Drink	Coke	Apple juice	Orange juice	Milkshake	Lemonade
No. of students	10	8	12	15	7

a. Make a tally chart to show her record.

Drink	No. of Students
Coke	⌗⌗ ⌗⌗
Apple juice	⌗⌗ ///
Orange juice	⌗⌗ ⌗⌗ //
Milkshake	⌗⌗ ⌗⌗ ⌗⌗
Lemonade	⌗⌗ //

* To make a tally chart, the numbers are counted in 5s (⌗⌗).

b. Draw a vertical bar graph to show the information.

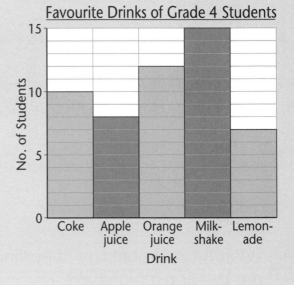

Solve the problems. Show your work.

Irene and Alan did a survey to find out in which months their friends had their birthdays.

Month	Jan	Feb	Mar	Apr	May	Jun	Jul	Aug	Sep	Oct	Nov	Dec
No. of people surveyed by Alan	3	4	4	6	3	6	6	4	4	2	2	8
No. of people surveyed by Irene	7	6	5	6	5	4	8	6	7	5	0	0

① How many people were surveyed?

② Who surveyed more people? How many more?

Answer :   people were surveyed.

Answer :

③ Make a tally chart for their findings and draw a bar graph to show the information.

Month	No. of People
Jan	
Feb	
Mar	
Apr	
May	
Jun	
Jul	
Aug	
Sep	
Oct	
Nov	
Dec	

④ What is the title of this graph?

Answer : _____

⑤ What is the label of the horizontal axis?

Answer : _____

⑥ What is the label of the vertical axis?

Answer : _____

⑦ Which month had the fewest birthdays?

Answer : _____

⑧ Which month had the most birthdays?

Answer : _____

⑨ What is the difference between the most and the fewest birthdays?

Answer : _____

⑩ How many months had 10 or more birthdays?

Answer : _____

⑪ Can you tell the age of the people surveyed from the graph?

Answer : _____

⑫ Does the graph show in which year the people were born?

Answer : _____

For their next survey, Irene and Alan asked 6 local businesses how many birthday parties they had in 1999. Burger Palace had 60 brithday parties. Taco Place 45, Swimming Pool 80, Game Room 55, Party Pizza 70 and Movie Masters 90.

⑬ Use their information to make a tally chart.

Venue	No. of Birthday Parties
Burger Palace	
Taco Place	
Swimming Pool	
Game Room	
Party Pizza	
Movie Masters	

⑭ Draw a horizontal bar graph to show their information. Label the horizontal and vertical axes and give a title to the graph.

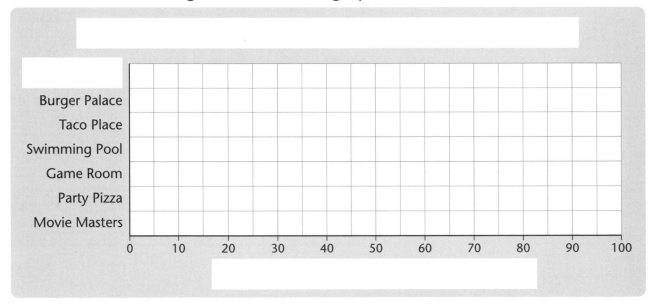

⑮ Which place held the fewest birthday parties?

Answer :

⑯ Which place held the most birthday parties?

Answer :

⑰ How many more birthday parties were held in Game Room than in Taco Place?

Answer :

⑱ How many birthday parties were there altogether?

Answer :

⑲ Make a pictograph to show the same information.

Venues for Birthday Parties	☺ = 10 parties
Burger Palace	
Taco Place	
Swimming Pool	
Game Room	
Party Pizza	
Movie Masters	

⑳ What is the best way to show 5 parties on the pictograph?

Answer :

㉒ How many people preferred to have their party at an activity centre?

Answer :

㉑ How many people chose to have their party at a restaurant?

Answer :

㉓ What fraction of the parties took place at the Swimming Pool?

Answer :

CHALLENGE

Irene drew a horizontal bar graph to show the weekly income of 4 people, A, B, C and D. Alan drew a circle graph to show the same information.

① Do these two graphs match? Explain.

Answer :

② What does the whole circle represent?

Answer :

Solve the problems. Show your work.

Irene is showing Peter how to draw a shape on a grid. Read her instructions and help Peter draw the shape and answer the questions.

① Mark these points on the grid:

A (1, 0),   B (1, 6),

C (4, 6),   D (4, 0)

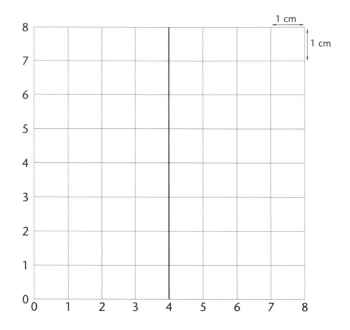

② Join the points A, B, C and D in order with straight lines.

③ What shape have you drawn?

Answer : _____

④ Reflect the shape over the black line and mark A', B', C' and D' for the images of A, B, C and D.

⑤ Which ordered pairs are now used to describe the location of the image A', B', C' and D'?

Answer : _____

⑥ What is the area of the shape ?

Answer : _____

⑦ What is the perimeter of the shape?

Answer : _____

⑧ Can you tell whether the image is a flipped image or a slid image by looking at the labelled vertices? Explain your thinking.

Answer : _____

⑨ Which is larger in area, the shape itself or the triangle bounded by the straight lines AB, BB' and B'A?

Answer : _____

Irene has made these shapes out of cardboard of different thickness.

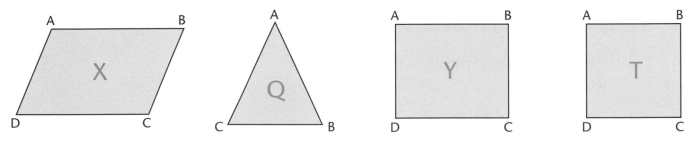

⑩ Write the names of each shape.

Answer : _____

⑪ Put the shapes in order from the one with the greatest perimeter to the one with the smallest perimeter.

Answer : _____

⑫ Each of the shapes weighs about 2 g. How many sets of these shapes would be needed to weigh 1 kg?

Answer : _____

⑬ If Irene wanted to make a rectangular prism, which shapes would she use? How many of each shape would she use?

Answer : _____

⑭ If Irene wanted to make a pyramid, which shapes would she use? How many of each shape would she use?

Answer : _____

⑮ Draw the $\frac{1}{4}$ turn clockwise rotation of shapes X and Q in the spaces below.

X	Q

Irene and Alan played a game of dice and recorded their rolls on a tally chart.

⑯ Complete the tally chart.

    a. Irene and Alan rolled twenty-four 1s.

    b. They rolled eighteen 2s.

    c. They rolled twenty-one 3s.

    d. They rolled sixteen 4s.

    e. They rolled twenty-two 5s and twenty-two 6s.

Roll	Tally
1	
2	
3	
4	
5	
6	

⑰ How many die rolls were made?

Answer : _____

⑱ Which number was rolled most often?

Answer : _____

⑲ Which number was rolled least often?

Answer : _____

⑳ How many more 1s were rolled than 3s in the game?

Answer : _____

㉑ The volume of the die is 8cm³. What is the volume of 500 dice?

Answer : _____

㉒ A container can hold 500 dice. What is its capacity in L?

Answer : _____

㉓ If each die roll and the recording of it took 10 seconds, how long did Irene and Alan take to create the tally chart?

Answer : _____

㉔ If they started at 11:04 a.m., when would they finish? (correct to the nearest minute)

Answer : _____

㉕ Use the tally chart to create a vertical bar graph.

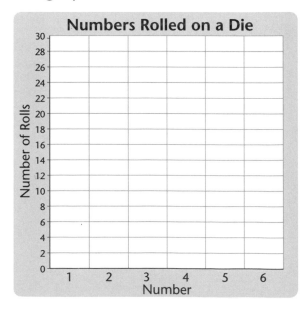

㉖ If the game followed probability rules, what results would they expect to see?

Answer : _____

㉗ After playing the game, Irene and Alan made a spinner. Look at their spinner. How would the spin results compare to the dice results? Explain your thinking.

Answer : _____

㉘ What is the probability of landing on a 4?

Answer : _____

㉙ What is the probability of landing on a number greater than 4?

Answer : _____

㉚ What is the probability of landing on a number less than 4?

Answer : _____

㉛ You are going to make another spinner. The probability of landing on each number on your spinner is 1 out of 8. Draw your spinner with a protractor in the space below.

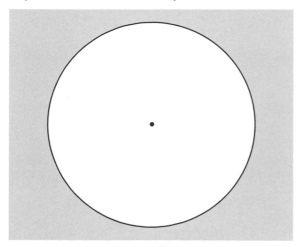

㉜ What is the size of each angle at the centre of Irene and Alan's spinner?

Answer : _____

㉝ What is the size of each angle at the centre of your spinner?

Answer : _____

㉞ If your spinner is the base of a solid, what can that solid be?

Answer : _____

Circle the correct answer in each problem.

㉟ It is 6 a.m. Which of these angles show the angle between the two hands on a clock?

A. 90°   B. 120°

C. 45°   D. 180°

㊱ Irene is sewing a seam that is 31 cm long. How many mm is that?

A. 3.1 mm   B. 310 mm

C. 0.31 mm   D. 3100 mm

㊲ There are 52 cards in a deck of playing cards. What is the probability of pulling a ◆ out of a deck?

A. 1 out of 4   B. 1 out of 13

C. 1 out of 26   D. 1 out of 56

㊳ In a pictograph, 65 cars are shown like this: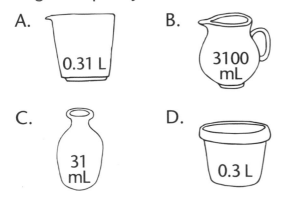
Which of these is true?

A. represents 5 cars.

B. represents 2 cars.

C. represents 10 cars.

D. represents 3 cars.

㊴ Which of these containers has the largest capacity?

A. 0.31 L   B. 3100 mL

C. 31 mL   D. 0.3 L

㊵ Alan spends about 2 hours and 20 minutes reading newspapers each week. How long does he take to read the newspapers each day?

A. 15 minutes   B. 30 minutes

C. 25 minutes   D. 20 minutes

㊶ A man can dig a hole in 45 minutes. If he finished digging at 12:08 p.m., when did he start digging the hole?

A. 12:53 p.m.   B. 11:23 a.m.

C. 11:08 a.m.   D. 11:37 p.m.

㊷ Irene made 4 shapes on a geoboard with elastic bands. Which of these is a trapezoid?

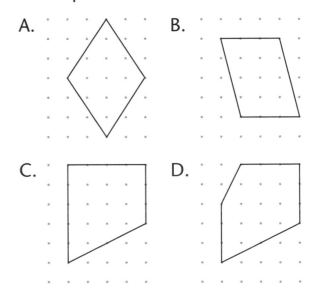

A.   B.

C.   D.

㊸ Which of these solid shapes has 4 vertices, 4 faces and 6 edges?

A. a tetrahedron

B. a square-based pyramid

C. a rectangular prism

D. a cone

1. Multiplication of Whole Numbers

* When multiplying 2-digit numbers by 2-digit numbers, remind children to put a zero under the ones column when multiplying by the tens digit.

* Encourage children to check if their answers are reasonable by rounding the numbers to the nearest ten or hundred, and estimating the products.

  Example   57 x 12 = ?

  Round up to 60   Round down to 10

  Estimated product
  = 60 x 10
  = 600
  The answer of 57 x 12 should be close to 600.

* To calculate the product of a number and multiples of 10, just multiply the number by the digits in front of the zeros in the multiples, and then add the same number of zeros in the factors at the end of the product.

  Example   25 x 300 = 7500

  25 x 3 = 75   add 2 zeros

* Even if the order of multiplication changes, the product remains the same.

  Example   5 x 9 x 6 = 9 x 6 x 5 = 9 x 5 x 6 = 6 x 5 x 9 = 6 x 9 x 5 = 5 x 6 x 9 = 270

2. Division of Whole Numbers

* Remind children to write a "0" in the quotient before they continue to divide if the dividend is smaller than the divisor.

  Example   325 ÷ 3 = ?

  $$\begin{array}{r} 1 \\ 3\overline{)325} \\ 3 \end{array}$$
  →
  $$\begin{array}{r} 10 \\ 3\overline{)325} \\ 3 \\ \hline 2 \end{array}$$
  Write a "0" in the quotient directly above 2, as 2 is smaller than 3; bring down 5 and continue to divide.
  →
  $$\begin{array}{r} 108\,R1 \\ 3\overline{)325} \\ 3 \\ \hline 25 \\ 24 \\ \hline 1 \end{array}$$

  108 x 3 + 1 = 325, so   325 ÷ 3 = 108R1 is correct.

* Encourage children to check the answers by using multiplication and addition.

* In solving story problems using division, give the appropriate answer according to the requirement of the question.

  Example   A box can hold 6 cakes. How many boxes are needed to hold 15 cakes?
  15 ÷ 6 = 2R3
  3 boxes are needed. ⟵ The answer is not 2 but 3, since the 3 cakes left over also need 1 box.

3. Multiples and Factors

* Multiples of a number can be formed by using repeated addition or multiplication. Using a number chart or a number line may be helpful.

* Children learn how to use multiplication and division to find the factors of a number, identify the common factors of two numbers, and determine their greatest common factor. When using multiplication to find the factors, children should write the multiplication sentences in order, starting with the smallest fac and stop when reaching a number they have already used for multipl

4. Mixed Operations and Brackets

↔ Remind children to perform the operations one at a time in the correct order :
- Do all operations in the brackets first.
- Then do multiplication and division in the order they occur from left to right.
- Lastly, do addition and subtraction in the order they occur.

5. Fractions

↔ Children learn how to identify proper and improper fractions and mixed numbers. Make sure children understand that the numerical value of a fraction equals 1 if its numerator and denominator are equal, and that any whole number can be written as an improper fraction with the denominator equals to 1.

↔ Practising how to find the equivalent fractions using multiplication/division first help children grasp the skills of simplifying fractions easily. Make sure they understand that equivalent fractions have the same value.

↔ When adding/subtracting mixed numbers, either add/subtract the whole numbers and fractions separately, or change the mixed numbers to improper fractions before calculating. Remind children to reduce the sums/differences to lowest terms (simplest form) and change improper fractions back to mixed numbers.

↔ When adding/subtracting fractions of unlike denominators, first write equivalent fractions with a common denominator. Then add/subtract the numerators and leave the denominator the same.

6. Addition and Subtraction of Decimals

↔ To do addition or subtraction, align the decimal points. Remember to put the decimal point in the answer.

↔ Remind children that only the zero(s) at the end of the decimals can be deleted without affecting the numerical value of the decimal numbers.

<u>Example</u>　　$2.50 = 2.5$　　　　　　　$2.00 = 2$　　　　　but　$2.05 \neq 2.5$

7. Multiplication and Division of Decimals

↔ Multiply or divide the decimals as with whole numbers. Remind children that :

a. The number of decimal places in the product is the same as that in the question. The zero(s) at the end of the product can be deleted after locating the decimal point.

<u>Example</u>

$$\begin{array}{r} 2.4\,8 \\ \times\qquad 5 \\ \hline 1\,2.4\,0 \end{array}$$

← 2 decimal places

← 2 decimal places

So $2.48 \times 5 = 12.40 = 12.4$

...e decimal point in the quotient is directly above the one in the dividend. ...n't forget to add a zero before the decimal point if necessary. If there is ...ainder, add zero(s) to the right of the dividend and continue to divide ...e remainder is zero or you have enough decimal places.

251

...RT (GRADE 4)

Example

$$5 \overline{)4.2} \quad \longrightarrow \quad \begin{array}{r} 8 \\ 5 \overline{)4.2} \\ \underline{40} \end{array} \quad \longrightarrow \quad \begin{array}{r} 84 \\ 5 \overline{)4.20} \\ \underline{40} \\ 20 \\ \underline{20} \end{array} \quad \longrightarrow \quad \begin{array}{r} 0.84 \\ 5 \overline{)4.20} \\ \underline{40} \\ 20 \\ \underline{20} \end{array}$$

Add a "0" and bring down to continue the division. Add a "0" to locate the decimal point.

8. Length, Perimeter and Area

↝ Children should remember the relationship between millimetre (mm), centimetre (cm), decimetre (dm), metre (m), and kilometre (km).

↝ Help children select the most appropriate standard unit to measure length and perimeter, and learn to measure with precision.

↝ In using grid paper with 1 cm² squares to find the area of an irregular shape, remind children that we can only find the approximate value of the area by counting the number of squares covered by the shape. To simplify our counting, a square that is more than half covered is counted as a whole, and a square that is less than half covered is not counted.

9. Capacity, Volume and Mass

↝ Children should remember the relationship between millilitre (mL), litre (L), cubic centimetre (cm³), cubic metre (m³), and also the relationship between gram (g) and kilogram (kg).

↝ Parents should help children visualize and select the most appropriate standard unit to measure different volumes through everyday examples.

10. 2- and 3- Dimensional Figures

↝ Children should be familiar with the properties of different quadrilaterals, pyramids and prisms to help them identify, sort and classify 2-D shapes and 3-D solids. They should also practise how to sketch the solids and their nets, and make skeletons for 3-D solids.

11. Angles

↝ To measure an angle, put the 0° line of the protractor on one of the arms of the angle with the centre of the protractor at the vertex of the angle; then record the angle in degrees by taking the reading on the other arm of the angle. Remind children that lengthening the line segments forming the two arms of the angle doesn't alter the measurement of the angle.

12. Transformations

↝ Encourage children to describe transformations using reflections, rotations or translations, and identify the transformation undergone from the image produced. Practising drawing images helps children understand the characteristics of different transformations.

↝ Remind children that a 2-D shape may have more than one line of symmetry.

13. Coordinate Systems

- Remind children that when describing the location of an object on a grid, its ordered pair should be given by writing the number on the horizontal axis first, followed by the number on the vertical axis.

14. Patterns

- Using a calculator may help children explore and recognize mathematical relationships in some number patterns.

- Advise children to make observations carefully, as some patterns are created by changing two or more attributes (e.g. size, orientation, shape) of the figures.

15. Algebraic Symbols and Equations

- Children should know that a letter or a symbol in a mathematical sentence or an equation represents an unknown number.

- At this stage, children find the unknown number by systematic trial only.

16. Pictographs and Bar Graphs

- Children learn that data collected in a survey are recorded using a tally chart or displayed using an appropriate graph.

- Make sure children know the quantity each picture represents in drawing a pictograph, and are able to recognize what is represented by each bar in a bar graph.

- Parents should try to discuss with children the important features of the graph and help them read and interpret the data it represents.

17. Probability

- Children practise drawing tree diagrams to show all the possible outcomes of a simple probability problem.

- Children compare the probability of different events using expressions such as more probable, equally probable, and less probable, or describe the probability of an event happening using words such as likely or unlikely.

- Do not ask children to express the probability of an event mathematically using a fraction at this stage. Encourage them to describe the probability as number of favourable outcomes out of the total number of possible outcomes.

    <u>Example</u>   The probability of getting a 2 by rolling a dice is 1 out of 6.